At the end of seven days the word of the Lord came to me: "Son of man, I have made you a watchman for the people of Israel; so hear the word I speak and give them warning from me. When I say to a wicked person, 'You will surely die,' and you do not warn them or speak out to dissuade them from their evil ways in order to save their life, that wicked person will die for their sin, and I will hold you accountable for their blood. But if you do warn the wicked person and they do not turn from their wickedness or from their evil ways, they will die for their sin; but you will have saved yourself."

Ezekiel 3:16–19, NIV

One Sip of This

One Sip of This

A Collection of Inspired Columns and Other Writings

2016–2019

by

Daniel Oliver

Pax in Bello Group
Washington, DC

Inquiries should be addressed to:
Daniel Oliver
3105 Woodley Road, NW
Washington, DC 20008 USA

DanielOliver@PAXQB.com

Hardcover   ISBN   978-1-7357811-4-3
Paperback   ISBN   978-1-7357811-5-0

1 2 3 4 5 6 7 8 9 10

For

William F. Buckley, Jr.,

mentor,

colleague,

friend,

for so many years

—in grateful memory

Acknowledgments

My thanks to the proprietors of the following where this material originally appeared: *American Greatness, American Action News, First Things, Fox News, Media Alert News, Newsmax, Ricochet, The American Spectator, The American Conservative, Daily Caller, The Federalist, The Washington Times, The Washington Examiner, The Western Journal,* and *Townhall.*

My thanks also, and again, but again belatedly, to the late Linda Bridges, who died on March 26, 2017. Linda worked at *National Review* for over four decades, serving as managing editor, senior editor, and editor-at-large, and personal assistant to William F. Buckley Jr. She was a copyeditor to the stars, and to me. Linda got all the jokes, and remembered others long forgotten. As I reread some of the pieces gathered in this volume, I could hear her laughing at jokes we shared over the decades. The last piece she edited for me was "Donald Trump, Congress, and the American Tradition," which ran on June 22, 2016.

My thanks also, again, to Dara Ekanger, who for the last few years has copyedited my pieces and has supervised the production of this book, as well as others. And my thanks to Charles King who designed the book's interior layout and the cover. And thanks also to Thomas Cheplick, research assistant (with Philip Marlowe's skills) and computer wizard.

Contents

Acknowledgments . . . . *viii*

Preface . . . . *xv*

"Hillary, It's Barack. We Need to Talk."
    (*January 7, 2016*) 1

Trump and the Restoration of Constitutional Government
    (*January 20, 2016*) 3

The Fat Lady, the Episcopal Church, and the Anglican
    Communion (*January 26, 2016*) 5

Donald Trump and Venereal Disease
    (*January 27, 2016*) 8

Homosaurus Rex
    (*February 16, 2016*) 11

Wm. F. Buckley Jr. on Justice Scalia's Death
    (*February 23, 2016*) 14

Harvard Law School Chases the Seal of Good Identity
    Politics (*April 4, 2016*) 17

The Progressive Media's Crocodile Fears over Donald
    Trump (*April 13, 2016*) 21

Drew Barrymore, Donald Trump, Scrooge, and the Pope, or
    Dearly Beloved (*April 27, 2016*) 24

Voting and the Fire Next Time
    (*May 1, 2016*) 28

Bathroom Bills Stall amid Shower of Criticism
    (*May 17, 2016*) 30

Monkey Time—and Monkey Business—at Harvard
    (*May 18, 2016*) 33

Donald Trump, Congress, and the American Tradition
    (*June 22, 2016*) 36

Let's Play "Pin the Mustache on the Donkey"
    (*July 14, 2016*) 40

Schadenfreude and the *New York Times*
    (*November 22, 2016*) 43

Donald Trump Brings Season of New Hope
(*January 2, 2017*). 45
Donald Trump and the Art of the Possible
(*January 5, 2017*). 47
Hillary Clinton and the Rule of Law
(*February 2, 2017*) 50
Draining the Independent Regulatory Agency Swamp
(*February 21, 2017*). 52
Drain the Research Swamp
(*March 13, 2017*) 55
Billionaires for Deregulation
(*April 4, 2017*) 58
Advice and Consent in the Time of Obstruction
(*April 25, 2017*). 60
Oilman Rex Tillerson and Ukraine
(*April 26, 2017*) 62
Trump's 100 Days vs. Democrats' 100 Days of Resistance:
A Progress Report (*April 29, 2017*) 64
John Jimenez Built That
(*May 4, 2017*). 67
Saying Goodbye to Grandma
(*May 10, 2017*) 69
Boarding School Daze
(*May 12, 2017*) 71
Piling On: The Desperation of the Left
(*May 17, 2017*) 74
Flied Lice and Golden Visas
(*May 23, 2017*) 76
Comey, Flynn, Trump, Brutish, and Short
(*May 25, 2017*) 78
Fear of Flying
(*May 26, 2017*) 81
Health Care Reform: Not in God's Lifetime
(*May 31, 2017*) 83
Closing Time for the Episcopal Church?
(*June 13, 2017*) 85
Solving the Mueller Problem
(*July 4, 2017*) 87

Obamacare Forces Policyholders to Pay for Health Risks
They Don't Have (*July 19, 2017*) 90

Prep Schools Like Milton Not Teaching Political Diversity
(*August 2, 2017*) 92

Who Promoted Emma Lazarus?
(*August 7, 2017*) 94

Summer Games for the Resistance
(*August 16, 2017*) 97

President Trump and the Navy's Welfare
(*August 23, 2017*) 99

Sex, College Sex—and Harvey Weinstein
(*October 12, 2017*) 101

Roy Moore and Jeff Sessions: Two Problems—and a
Solution (*November 12, 2017*) 104

A Tale of Two Cultures—and Two Bracelets
(*November 21, 2017*) 107

Merry Christmas, Bill Burke
(*December 22, 2017*) 109

Attorney General Sessions: Call Your Office
(*December 26, 2017*) 112

June 30: Pumpkin Time for Robert Mueller
(*January 7, 2018*) 114

DACA for Dummies: Nightmare for Dreamers
(*January 16, 2018*) 116

Snow White Didn't Come from Burkina Faso
(*January 25, 2018*) 118

Racism: The First and Final Insult of Losers
(*January 31, 2018*) 121

Russia Collusion Saga—Chapter 27
(*February 20, 2018*) 123

Should the Pentagon Bend Over Backwards to Support
Trans Military Personnel? (*March 15, 2018*) 125

Let the Word Go Forth: Chappaquiddick Invented the
Cover-up (*April 8, 2018*) 128

Kids, Gun Control, and *Lord of the Flies*
(*April 25, 2018*) 131

Why President Trump Should Veto the Bill Prohibiting
Him from Firing Robert Mueller (*April 27, 2018*) 133

Make Congress Work Again
(*April 30, 2018*) 136
What's Next for Conservatism?
(*June 2, 2018*). 138
D-Day 2018
(*June 5, 2018*). 142
Donald Trump Is No Franklin Roosevelt—Thank Heavens
(*July 26, 2018*) 144
History *Is* Bunk—If It's Not Taught Properly
(*August 6, 2018*) 147
Martin Luther King, History, and Donald Trump
(*August 28, 2018*). 149
But Who Will Investigate the Mueller Investigation?
(*September 4, 2018*). 151
Next Case: The Judge vs. The Vigilante
(*October 1, 2018*) 153
Brett Kavanaugh Should Sue Ford and *The WaPo* for
Defamation (*October 6, 2018*) 156
Banging the Diversity Drum
(*October 28, 2018*) 158
Explosive Politics? You Ain't Seen Nothing Yet
(*November 10, 2018*) 161
How Reagan Defeated Gorbachev: The Story Public Schools
Never Taught (*November 14, 2018*) 163
Whose Side Are You On, Anyway: Alexandria Ocasio-Cortez's
or Amazon's? (*November 23, 2018*) 165
Would the Democrats Really Pack the Supreme Court?
(*November 26, 2018*) 168
December 7, Pearl Harbor, and Franklin Delano Infamy
(*December 7, 2018*) 170
China, Trade, Donald Trump—and the Long Game
(*December 13, 2018*) 173
The Diabolically Clever Mr. Trump: An Alternative View
(*January 16, 2019*) 175
The PC Enforcers Ride Again
(*January 18, 2019*) 177
BuzzFeed's Flub Reveals Mueller May Not Have a Lot on the
President—and Never Will (*January 21, 2019*). 180

Is It Un-American to be Super-Super Rich?
(*January 29, 2019*) 181
Where Has All the Culture Gone?
(*February 8, 2019*) 184
A Quiz: How Should Neomi Rao Have Answered
Cory Booker? (*February 21, 2019*) 187
Max Boot, Bye-Bye
(*March 8, 2019*) 189
Rand Paul's Republicans Should Really Restrict Executive Power
Instead of Playing Democratic Games (*March 11, 2019*) . 191
Sex, Sin, and the Infield Fly Rule
(*March 23, 2019*) 193
China Disconnect: What's Wrong with a Great Trade War?
(*April 22, 2019*) 196
Free the Students. Sink the Colleges.
(*May 7, 2019*) 198
The Contest between Diversity and Merit
(*May 8, 2019*) 200
The China Problem—Or Is It the Joe Biden Problem?
(*May 19, 2019*) 202
D-Day, 2019
(*June 9, 2019*) 205
D-Day Soldiers Died to Save Western Values; That's a Legacy
Worth Preserving (*July 3, 2019*) 208
America Isn't Quebec, Mexico, or Brazil—And That's Worth
Celebrating (*July 4, 2019*) 210
Are the Four "Housewomen" of the Apocalypse better for
Democrats or for Trump? (*July 28, 2019*) 213
What Did We Really Learn from the Mueller Investigation?
(*July 29, 2019*) 215
Fifteen Questions to Peel the Skin Off the Democrats
(*July 29, 2019*) 218
Smearing at the Rhodes Scholar Level
(*August 5, 2019*) 221
What Happens If America Goes Bilingual?
(*August 14, 2019*) 223
Suicide Watch at the NRA
(*August 26, 2019*) 225

Counting Your Blessings—In the Age of Mass Shootings
(*August 28, 2019*) 227
Why Kirsten Gillibrand Dropped Out
(*August 31, 2019*) 230
David Brooks, Change, and White Tie and Tails
(*September 4, 2019*) 232
More Hypocrisy at the *New York Times*
(*September 6, 2019*) 235
Another Day, Another Shooting. Boring!
(*September 18, 2019*) 237
Laws, Guns, and Freedom
(*October 30, 2019*) 239
Colleges Are Suffering from a Sexual Assault Epidemic—And
Elites Want Us to Send More Kids (*November 1, 2019*) . . 242
Controversy's Name Is the Department of State's Commission
on Unalienable Rights (*November 5, 2019*) 244
Generalissimo Francisco Franco Is Still Dead. Or Is He?
(*November 9, 2019*) 248
Big Tech On Trial
(*November 10, 2019*) 250
Today Is Bill Buckley's Birthday: Tease a Liberal
(*November 24, 2019*) 252
Fascism Lives!
(*December 3, 2019*) 255
Antitrust and the Candlestick Makers
(*January 11, 2020*) 257

Introductions and Speeches

Introduction of Mark Steyn: Pacific Research Institute for Public
Policy Annual Dinner, Ritz Hotel
(*November 10, 2018*) 263
Introduction of Tucker Carlson: Pacific Research Institute for
Public Policy's 40th Anniversary Dinner, Ritz Hotel
(*March 23, 2019*) 265

Index 267
About the Author 279

Preface

This is my second collection of columns and other writings. The first, *Everyday Epiphanies*, covered the period from 1999 to 2015; this one, from 2016 to 2019. They were written for the edification of the public; they are collected for my grandchildren.

Writing these kinds of pieces, or preserving them, is risky: Will they hold up with time? And not just "hold up," but will they be seen as wise, whacky, or . . . a waste of time? My sense is that they have held up, so far—though the reader may disagree.

But how long do they have to hold up? Five years? Ten? If my youngest grandchild, Daniel Oliver III, reads these pieces when he is a sophomore in college (would he really read these before then?), he will be reading the most recent one about eighteen years after it was written. Will it still be in tune?

My favorite, or certainly one of them, is "Homosaurus Rex." One reader wrote: "As usual, hysterically funny and skewering at the same time. Impulse control disorder? Wonderful. Squeezing Hillary in— wonderful. Perhaps the most pleasure is in imagining our ideological adversaries swirling into apoplexy upon reading this. Wonderful." Comments like that tend to encourage the writer to misbehave.

"Wm. F. Buckley Jr. on Justice Scalia's Death" is useful because it reminds us of what Bill said, at least to me, many times: "Despair is a mortal sin." One correspondent wrote: "Didn't realize Buckley possessed the ability to define a mortal sin! Can't find a corroborative bit of scripture for this!" Please: See John 3:15 and Matthew 12:31; and see Angelo Stagnaro's comments in the *National Catholic Register*[*].

The pieces on Harvard will almost certainly be pertinent in eighteen years, either because they will reflect Harvard's weirder days . . . or its saner ones.

"Let's Play 'Pin the Mustache on the Donkey'" will remind people of the horrors of communism and totalitarianism, which in eighteen years may be a fading memory, at best. How do you tell when you're entering a totalitarian age?

[*] https://www.ncregister.com/blog/what-is-the-unforgivable-sin-that-our-lord-warned-us-about

xvi ———— Daniel Oliver

"Voting and the Fire Next Time" may remind readers about the dangers democracy faces, even in the land of the free. Who can tell how healthy our democracy will be in eighteen years? And "Bathroom Bills Stall Amid Shower of Criticism" will, we must hope, show how crazed we had become way back in 2016, and continuing up to and perhaps through 2034.

Aspiring writers may be interested in the construction of a column, in this case of "Donald Trump, Congress, and the American Tradition." On the other hand, they may not be.

"Draining the Independent Regulatory Agency Swamp" and "Drain the Research Swamp" limn how intrusive government has become and how it saps our freedom. Will that have changed in eighteen years? Even a tiny bit?

"Boarding School Daze" hit a nerve. One correspondent asked, "My god is this true?" Well, yes, it was. Some of the paragraphs were verbatim quotes from one of the boarding schools. One of them (see "Prep Schools Like Milton Not Teaching Political Diversity") had scheduled a panel discussion during its upcoming reunion weekend, with four left-wingers on it. So much for diversity! One reader wrote, "Very funny, except I used to date Imabita Confusio and am offended on her behalf." Chivalry lives. Mom: What's "chivalry"?

In response to "Who Promoted Emma Lazarus?" one correspondent (a national treasure, but now, alas, deceased) wrote: "Hear, hear!!! My mother and I arrived with two suitcases, $20 and zero English. We could hardly believe our good fortune. I still pinch myself. To say that we worked hard is an understatement. But "wretched"? "Tired"? You gotta be kidding! "Delighted" is more like it. It was my privilege, on August 8, 1955, to stand on the port side of the SS *Constitution*, along with a crowd of immigrants, as it slipped past the Statue of Liberty. There were tears of joy all around. The eagerness to get to work on a new life was palpable. All had been selected on a merit system. The Americans wanted to see my report card from school. I even got questions about my attitudes toward communism. Hell, we were supercharged!" A dream response for a writer.

"President Trump and the Navy's Welfare" remains an important piece, today. In eighteen years will it be seen as a last chance to have done something to revivify the navy? Or will the navy have been revivified?

"Sex, College Sex—and Harvey Weinstein" is about mores. What will they be like in eighteen years? Could they get worse than they are today?

"Merry Christmas, Bill Burke" was turned down by one publication because the editor thought it was just a fundraising piece for St. Sebastian's School. No really, that's true! At the request of a friend, I had met with Burke, the headmaster, and found writing about his school simply irresistible. It's a good bet that St. Sebastian's will still be a fine school in eighteen years.

The cultural statistics in "Snow White Didn't Come from Burkina Faso" reveal what people think today about race and family. Will they change much in eighteen years?

"Racism: The First and Final Insult of Losers" accurately describes the Democrat party as concerned solely with race, having nothing else to justify its existence. How long will *this* Democrat party survive—a party that elevated to superhero status a man who let a girl drown after driving his car off a bridge?

"Kids, Gun Control, and *Lord of the Flies*" received an unusual amount of fan mail, but seriously annoyed one reader who wrote: "You do know that *Lord of the Flies* is a work of fiction? You should not use a work of fiction to justify your argument. Didn't you learn that in school? . . . Really a very poorly written article. I give you a failing grade. Maybe you should contact a high school student for advise [sic] on how to prove an argument." Ah, that makes it all worthwhile.

In the published version of "What's Next for Conservatism?" I had written "What is the authority of the state—other than the Glock 22 with its 15 rounds of 9mm shells carried by most police officers—to command us to be nice to our fellow man?" Two people wrote to correct me. One said: "You were right about everything in your article except a 'Glock 22 with its 15 rounds of 9mm shells.' That gun is a .40 S&W." The other wrote: "Might I be so bold as to make one small criticism . . . ? The Glock 22 is indeed a very popular weapon with police, BUT it is a .40 cal. Another very popular police sidearm is the Glock 17, which has been around through 5 iterations since the Devil was a boy, and is a 9mm. You had a brief moment of ballistic-dyslexia." Fun. And reminds us that America is armed, and we must hope, dangerous to her enemies—foreign *and domestic*!

"Free the Students. Sink the Colleges." is one of many pieces I have written about college education and student debt. For some absolutely inexplicable reason, my advice (essentially, to forgive all student debt *and at the same time* cancel all aid to higher education) has not been taken. Yet. Sometimes the burden of genius weighs heavily.

Happy reading.

D.O.
Washington, DC
April 27, 2022

"Hillary, It's Barack. We Need to Talk."

January 7, 2016

Barack Obama has a problem. He wants to go down in history as a transformational president. Like Ronald Reagan. But that requires being succeeded by a Democrat. A Republican president could undo much of what Obama has done, and in large part because of the way he has done it: by executive order. It may be that not all of those who live by the sword die by the sword. But it is certain that those who transform by executive order, especially by unpopular executive orders, can expect to have that transformation reversed by the executive orders of their successors.*

At the moment, there *appears* to be only one Democrat with a serious chance of winning the presidential election next year: Ms. Hillary Clinton. But that's because she's the only Democrat running. She has sucked the air—the cash and the campaigning competence—out of the Democratic race. She is the "in" candidate—and there's no room for anyone else in the in.

But how good is her chance? At best, Ms. Clinton is only just likable enough. But a summer poll found that 60 percent of the public doesn't trust her. And she has serious problems with the law. That may be why a *Fox News* poll a few weeks ago had Donald Trump beating her by five points. *Donald Trump!* Sic transit Obama's legacy.

Barack Obama must know, and know better than any of the rest of us, how serious Ms. Clinton's legal problems are. We know that by having a non-governmental email account she didn't follow government policy, and that she is sneaky and secretive is not in doubt. Whether she sent or received classified documents is still unclear. So far, it appears she sent four such documents. It seems unlikely that among the 55,000 emails in question more classified documents won't be found.

What Ms. Clinton did that is not widely known may put her in even greater danger. It is true that for that danger to materialize, the FBI has to go public with the facts. The current head of the FBI,

---

* For a discussion of the magnitude of the problem Obama faces, see
http://bitly.com/obama-legacy-easily-erased.

James Comey, appears to be a straight shooter, even though he was picked by President Obama. Even so, the temptation to be improperly loyal to the man who appointed him will be great.

However, there must be at least a hundred people in the FBI who have seen the Clinton file and who know enough about Ms. Clinton's problems to send her back home to the arms of her loving husband—always assuming she isn't sent to the quarters occupied a few decades ago by Attorney General John Mitchell. What are the odds that not a single one of those FBI people in the know will spill the beans? Not good.

And even if they don't spill, think of the ads the Republicans will run, showing a secretive Hillary Clinton frantically deleting emails from her laptop to scary background music and a low-bass voice-over.

Ms. Clinton is in serious trouble. She knows it. We know it.

And Barack Obama knows it.

What to do? There's only one solution: get Ms. Clinton out of the race, and in time (i.e., *now*!) for a new candidate to make a credible run against the Republican candidate. But how?

Make a deal—make a deal that Donald Trump would be proud of.

"Hillary: listen up. You're in trouble. I've seen the FBI file. I know what's in it. And so do you. It's bound to leak. Which means you're poised to screw up my legacy by losing the election big-time. I don't want that. You've got to get out of the race and let someone else run. And you've got to get out now.

"Here's my deal: if you get out now, I will pardon you if the Republicans win. Then you'll be safe. If you don't get out now, I will not pardon you if the Republicans win. Then you will go to jail.

"You may be wondering how can you trust me? The answer is that there are some things in life we can never be sure of. It is true that the story of the pardon will not be buried back with the classifieds and the corset ads, in Nixon's memorable phrase. But you probably won't be the only person I'll have to pardon. The secretary of defense, that Ash Carter, will probably need a pardon too. And for doing just what you did, and doing it after all the publicity about you. How dumb can people be? And who knows how many others have done stupid things? But the more people I pardon, the more credibly I can say I am doing it to prevent a wholesale witchhunt by vindictive Republicans. Will it smell good? Of course not. But it will be better than having my secretary of state sent to jail. That's Nixon territory. Hillary, you can trust me on this because I'm not doing it for you. I'm doing it for me.

"I need an answer by next week, because another candidate needs to get going.

"And one more thing, Hillary: Happy New Year. To you and Bill."

Trump and the Restoration of Constitutional Government
January 20, 2016

A Trump nomination is the current nightmare of Republicans, both conservative and establishment. A noted conservative has written that "a Trump nomination would not just mean another Democratic presidency. It would also mean the loss of . . . a conservative party as a constant presence in US politics."* Another critic writes gloomily: "If Trump were the nominee, the GOP would cease to be."† Establishment Republicans probably agree. Both groups would wake up the day after election day and say, "DONALD WHO *#!@?"

Perhaps. But it doesn't have to be that way. Republicans should be brave and see a Trump nomination as an opportunity, not a disaster; as a crisis that should be managed, not wasted. It is true that that contortion would require thinking that Ms. Clinton would be a worse president than Trump. For a variety of reasons, having to do with government structure, personnel, and legacies—as well as Hllry Clntn's chractr (sorry, someone stole some of the letters)—that is surely true.

Trump has said he would not run as a third-party candidate. That promise might require the Republicans to support him if he gets the nomination, even though it is entirely likely—almost assured?—that Trump would renege on his promise if he didn't get the nomination. That's the kind of man he is.

What the Republicans need to do is make a deal with Trump. Will he deal? Of course he'll deal, because he fancies himself the world's leading dealmaker.

---

* http://bitly.com/trump-wins-conservative-gop-party-dies
† http://bitly.com/gerson-trump-oped-end-of-gop

Trump is not stupid. He knows he can't win without the support of Republicans, including Republicans running for office. But Republicans running for local, state, or national offices, or at least some of them, can win their races without Trump, especially given that the alternative at the top of the ticket will almost surely be Hillary Clinton (the missing letters were found, in the basement of a house located in Chappaqua, New York), who is currently distrusted by 60 percent of the American people (and must be unknown to the other 40 percent). That gives the Republicans the upper hand.

What's the deal? The deal is that a President Trump would return to governing in the way the Founders envisioned: Congress controls taxes, spending, and borrowing; Congress passes individual appropriation bills—no more continuing resolutions, which, by their nature, are difficult to reject without shutting down the government; and Congress takes back the lawmaking power it has relinquished to the regulatory agencies. No more governing by executive orders—except to repeal President Obama's executive orders.

If Trump wants to build a wall on our border with Mexico, he has to propose it and get Congress's permission. No permission, no wall. Deals with foreign powers, which we used to call treaties, must get Senate approval.

President Trump must promise to be the anti-Obama. And oddly enough—because it surely would be odd—if Trump ended the imperial presidency, *he* would truly be a transformational president.

How can Trump be trusted in any deal—the man who contracts to pay people who work for him but then welches on the deal when it comes time to pay up, so that they have to sue? He can't be trusted. But he doesn't have to be. If Congress were to hold firm and behave the way Congress is supposed to behave, there would be nothing Trump could do.

Trump could (that's the conditional tense, indicating a hypothetical case) be a better president, for conservatives, than either of the two previous Republican nominees for the office. A useful rule of thumb is, never vote for a man whose name is on the McCain–Feingold Act. That act, which limited campaign contributions, was the worst piece of legislation since the Kansas–Nebraska Act. If Senator John McCain had been elected president, who knows what manner of disasters he might have proposed and gotten enacted by a compliant Republican Congress? Likewise, Mitt Romney, the grandfather of ObamaCare, might well have proposed *legislationes horribiles* that, also, a compliant Republican Congress might have been unwilling not to enact.

Admittedly, this Congress, controlled by Republicans, has shown itself to be supine in the face of a president who cares not a whit for constitutional government. But in dealing with Trump, the Republicans might decide to be firm in controlling his excesses, and they could be expected to have the wholehearted support of the Democrats. Properly managed, a Trump presidency could be a watershed period for Republicans, the Congress, and the country, ushering in a Great Restoration.

There's one other reason Trump would have to behave. The Republicans could wield, and presumably with enthusiastic Democratic support, a much underused lightsaber: impeachment. Just the prospect makes the constitutionalist tingle.

If a Republican majority in Congress were not willing to confront Trump, then the country's problems go well beyond a Donald Trump nomination, and we should stop caterwauling about him.

Almost no one in Switzerland knows the name of the country's president, so inconsequential is he. Our dream should be—did you ever see a dream walking?—to have the American people, when told at the end of the second Trump administration who their president is, say, "Donald who?"

The Fat Lady, the Episcopal Church, and the Anglican Communion

January 26, 2016

She sang.

So it's over. The Anglican Communion has finally had it with the Episcopal Church.

At a meeting in Canterbury, England, the Anglican primates, the senior bishops of the thirty-eight Anglican provinces, decided that "for a period of three years The Episcopal Church will no longer represent us on ecumenical and interfaith bodies, should not be appointed or elected to an internal standing committee and that while participating in the internal bodies of the Anglican Communion, they will not take part in decision making on any issues pertaining to doctrine or polity." That's ecclesiastispeak for "You're suspended."

However, the Archbishop of Canterbury, the Right Reverend Justin Welby, who is the titular leader of Anglicans worldwide, made a clarification: This was not, in fact, a "suspension," he said—by which he seems to have meant that it was not something imposed by the primates. Rather, it was that the Episcopalians had done it to themselves, by their formal approval of homosexual marriage at their triennial General Convention last summer. In three years, the Episcopalians will have an opportunity at their next General Convention to undo their action, which is why their suspension-that-was-not-a-suspension was for only three years. But the presiding bishop of the Episcopal Church, Michael Curry, has already stated that there would be no going back: "I was clear with the primates that that's not going to happen."

There may be no going back, but it's not clear yet how far back "back" is. The Episcopal Church's Prayer Book hasn't been changed to endorse homosexual marriage, and the Prayer Book has a place of constitutional authority in the Episcopal Church. When it says holy matrimony is a union of a man and a woman, then the Episcopal Church, in some confused sense, still says that. In that sense, it is a bridge that has not yet been burned.

One objection to the Episcopal Church's approval of homosexual marriage seems to have been the manner in which it was accomplished: "They went ahead of the rest of the Church without consultation," said Archbishop Welby. Perhaps. But the wider Anglican Communion is not likely *ever* to approve homosexual marriage (which is contrary to the doctrine, discipline, and worship of the Communion—indeed, to the whole history of Anglicanism, which is closer than many may realize to Roman Catholicism*) in which case the Episcopalians would have to wait for . . . *ever*. That seems unlikely too.

There are some Episcopalians who see the action of the primates as holding the Episcopal Church accountable, and who also think, or

* See http://bitly.com/extra-henry-viii-denied-late-checkout-the-amer-conservative

hope, that the rift can, somehow, be . . . healed. Again, that seems unlikely.

The Anglican Communion consists of approximately 80 million people, only 1.8 million of whom are Episcopalians (down from 3.6 million in the sixties). There are many Anglicans in the Anglophone countries, of course, but most Anglicans live in far-off lands. There are, obviously, homosexual communicants in those lands: homosexuals may constitute about 2 percent of any population. But those lands don't do homosexual marriage. And they aren't going to change their ways any time soon. We'll have peace in the Middle East first.

The Archbishop of Canterbury said about homosexuals, more or less, that he felt their pain: "For me it's a constant source of deep sadness, the number of people who are persecuted for their sexuality," he said after encountering gay and lesbian protesters at the meeting of the primates. "I wanted to take this opportunity to say how sorry I am for the hurt and pain, in the past and present, the church has caused."

Maybe. But as they say on the debating circuit, "Name three"—name three people in the United States who have been persecuted for their sexuality. Perhaps Jack Phillips, who was fined $135,000 because he refused to bake a wedding cake for a queer couple. No. Wait a minute. He was persecuted because he was normal and wouldn't kowtow to the zeitgeist, which said he had to serve homosexuals.

And we can only hope the presiding bishop wasn't feeling any pain for Susan Russell, 'scuse me, "The Rev." Susan Russell, a senior associate rector at All Saints Church in Pasadena. She said sanctions would not change her position: "As a lifelong Episcopalian and a married lesbian priest, I think [the Episcopal Church's suspension is] not only an acceptable cost, it's a badge of honor in some ways." It wasn't reported whether she told the Anglican bishops where they could stuff their mitres.

This moment, these moments, have been long in coming. In 1960, James Pike, the Episcopal bishop of California, said the doctrine of the Trinity was "outdated, incomprehensible and nonessential." In 1961, he said the Virgin Birth of Christ was a "primitive myth." The Episcopal Church decided, unwisely, not to try Pike for heresy and defrock him. That was the beginning of the end. It meant that, doctrinally, anything goes. And since that time, a lot has.

The Archbishop of Canterbury may see homosexuals as persecuted individuals. But it is more accurate to see them as marauding vandals, come to destroy the icons and the tablets. The doctrine, discipline, and worship of the Episcopal Church and the Anglican Communion have been well established for centuries. People who want homosexual marriage to be considered normal (or don't believe in the Virgin Birth or the Trinity) should join—should have joined—a different church. The James Pikes of the '60s and the homosexuals of today set out to destroy the Episcopal Church. They are part of the Left's long march through the institutions. There is no reason whatsoever to feel sorry for them. And every reason to resist them.

It is not reasonable, probably, to expect much improvement in the fortunes of the Episcopal Church in the next three years, or probably the next thirty years. But after the vandals have done their work, what then? When they've won all the lawsuits and taken all the property, there are no monuments left to topple, and their preaching doesn't draw the people? And Social Security beckons. Perhaps they'll get bored and move on.

There are, apparently, young people who keep the faith, and the tablets. In years to come, they may discover, in a trunk in a dusty attic, the well-worn Prayer Book of their great-grandparents. And also in that dusty attic the rustle of God moving in a mysterious way.

So what did the Fat Lady sing? Perhaps hymn number 42: "Now the day is over." But more likely hymn 379: "God is working his purpose out as year succeeds to year."

Donald Trump and Venereal Disease
January 27, 2016

Catching a venereal disease may give you the opportunity to review the Seventh Commandment and the church's teaching on chastity and fidelity—as well as the sheer priapic unattractiveness of Bill Clinton. That opportunity, however, hardly seems a reason to go out and get a VD.

In a recent column on Donald Trump ("Trump and the Restoration of Constitutional Government," see page 3), I described how a Trump presidency, as distinguished from Trump himself, *could* bring back constitutional government. I wrote, and then took out, a disclaimer paragraph that said: "This column should not be understood as an endorsement of Donald Trump. Why vote for someone whose behavior might be so bad that it would goad a hitherto ungoadable Congress into performing its constitutional duty to control the president—and if necessary to impeach him—when there were other candidates in the race who seem, at least, to revere the Constitution and the limitation it places on executive branch authority. Exhibit A: Senator Ted Cruz."

Why did I take out the disclaimer? Because I concluded that no one reading what I had written about Trump would take it as an endorsement of him. Big mistake.

In that column I wrote that if Trump won the nomination, Republicans should be brave and see it as a crisis that should be managed, not wasted.

I said it was almost assured that Trump would renege on his promise not to run as a third-party candidate if he didn't get the nomination, and I added, "That's the kind of man he is."

I asked: "How can Trump be trusted in any deal—the man who contracts to pay people who work for him but then welches on the deal when it comes time to pay up, so that they have to sue? He can't be trusted."

Those are hardly descriptions of a man anyone would endorse for president. Nevertheless, some people thought I was endorsing—or perhaps just mini-endorsing—Donald Trump. I was not.

Why endorse a candidate who would have to be spanked by Congress, when there are several candidates (or at least one) who are genuine conservatives—"conservative" being understood as supporting constitutional *governance* and limited government, in addition to particular conservative policies (like cancelling the federal sugar program or the federal ethanol mandate).

There is no indication that Trump is a conservative, as the term is currently understood, although we must admit that either the term has become a bit ambiguous or that its ambiguities have become a bit more apparent. There is no indication that Trump has any understanding of constitutional governance.

It is true that Trump appeals to what Angelo Codevilla has described as the "Country Party," whose members are fed up with "America's ruling class." But that in itself makes him neither a conservative nor a good candidate for president, although it may explain his popularity: a popularity troubling to the traditional keepers of the conservative flame, though it is fair to ask if the conservatives of the current conservative movement have become pointy-head college professors who can't even park a bicycle straight—in George Wallace's memorable phrase. Some of the members of America's ruling class are the media consultants who—you know it's true—advise Republican candidates.

On the issues, Donald Trump lurches and rambles. Over the years he has been inconsistent to the point of incoherence, either because he has no governing principles whatsoever, or because he is opportunistically dishonest. He is certainly neither a conservative nor a man who will return us to constitutional governance. But conservatives need to ask at least themselves if that is what Americans really want.

Trump used to support abortion. He used to support the Democratic Party. He used to support the Clintons. In 1999, he proposed a one-time 14.25 percent tax on wealth. He has praised a single-payer health-care system. He has called himself a Republican, a Democrat, an Independent, and a Republican. In 1999, he said: "I just believe the Republicans are too crazy right." In 2001, he said: "It just seems that the economy does better under Democrats than Republicans." He supports private-sector unions, and was a big fan of Jimmy Hoffa, who even today may be still be supporting Trump—from the concrete foundations of the Trump Tower.

Those may be positions from the past. And a man is allowed to change his mind, as Ronald Reagan did on abortion. But a man who has changed a basketful of positions in the past few years, or months, is a man who probably has no positions.

He says, currently, that he would defund Planned Parenthood; that police are the most mistreated people in America; that he would eliminate the Department of Education and that he opposes Common Core; that climate change is a hoax; that we should eliminate the EPA; that we should get rid of the regulations that are destroying us; that there should be no limits on guns—they save lives; that we should replace Obamacare with Health Savings Accounts; etc., etc., etc.

Zounds! What's not to like? That should be conservative enough for any conservative. Raise and double.

But why should anyone believe that Trump will try to effect those policies if he gets elected? A case can be made for Trump, and has been by a number of people who call themselves conservatives and who have demonstrated over the years that they are conservatives (as we understand the term), on the basis of what Trump has said. The problem is his track record. The problem is that his positions are as ephemeral as a one-night stand.

I heard once that people suffering from seriously advanced chlamydia (a kind of infection—and any kind of infection can lead to death) tend, in the end stage, to lose their bearings, to lurch and ramble, and to say things that are inconsistent and incoherent. I'm not saying Donald Trump has chlamydia. I'm just raising issues.

And this column should not be taken as an endorsement of catching a venereal disease.

Homosaurus Rex
February 16, 2016

> *Is it good or bad that man has*
> *a burning desire for knowledge?*

On the same day that we read about "the mad science behind vegetable grafting"* we also learned about Chinese scientists who claim to have altered the genome of a human embryo.

The two pieces seem unrelated, perhaps, except as a demonstration of man's endless longing to tinker: long ago he learned how to make fire; slightly less than that long ago he learned how to burn people at the stake.

Apparently, you can now obtain, and online, a plant that will produce tomatoes on top and potatoes on the bottom. But you cannot, yet, produce on demand (not even in China) someone with Hillary Clinton's maniacal ambition but without the shameless corruption.

---

* http://bitly.com/some-scientists-claim-edited-embyros-human

Back in 1996, the year that President Bill Clinton signed the Defense of Marriage Act, some scientists at the University of Edinburgh cloned a sheep, named Dolly, from an adult somatic cell. That was a front-page news event: the sheep was greeted with the predictable headlines of "Hello, Dolly."

Of course, the promise of all this, or at least the tantalizing possibility, is that man will now be able, not just to cure diseases, but to prevent them from developing in the first place by tinkering with the human embryo.

But what's a disease? Hillary Clinton's erasermania? Her sticky fingeritis? Please, we're trying to be serious.

Well, then, let's be serious. The Diagnostic and Statistical Manual of Mental Disorders says, more or less, that kleptomania is an impulse control disorder characterized by the inability to resist the impulse to steal. We don't want to get lost in the weeds, even if we can make them produce truffles on the bottom and strawberries on the top, but we should ask, for the sake of Ms. Clinton's potential constituents (willing and unwilling), and the children, if there's any way to cure kleptomania? Whether there is or isn't, however, surely we can agree that kleptomania is a disease. Well, slow down.

First we have to decide what a disease is. Here's one definition: "A disordered or incorrectly functioning organ, part, structure, or system of the body resulting from the effect of genetic or developmental errors, infection, poisons, nutritional deficiency or imbalance, toxicity, or unfavorable environmental factors."

What about the several hundred thousand people who are born each year with a cleft palette? Do they have a disease?

What about a rare disorder known as congenital adrenal hyperplasia? That sure sounds like a disease, and not one you want the children to get. Nevertheless, each year, according to the *Los Angeles Times*, a few pregnant women learn they are carrying a baby "at risk" of having congenital adrenal hyperplasia.

Congenital adrenal hyperplasia (CAH)—clinical description alert—"causes an accumulation of male hormones and can, in females, lead to genitals so masculinized that it can be difficult at birth to determine the baby's gender."

Not pleasant, but fortunately, the same ingenuity in man that produced fire and Dolly has produced a hormonal treatment for CAH.

But now it gets complicated. The treatment for CAH may *re-duce*—repeat: *reduce*—the likelihood that a female baby who receives the treatment will be a lesbian. And so—you know where this is going—the "gay" community is outraged.

That community is outraged because the "rights" they have persuaded a majority of the Supreme Court to "recognize" depend on homosexuality's being a genetic condition (you know, like being black), not an impulse control disorder. Justice Kennedy, whose untimely demise is no longer possible, has not, yet, led the court to protecting the kleptomania lifestyle.

But what happens in say, fifty years (a hundred?), when genetic conditions, like congenital adrenal hyperplasia, cleft palette, and homosexuality can be cured in the womb? Some people may say that it would be improper to tinker with nature and eliminate homosexuality: that nature created homosexuals for a purpose. Really? Is it that they are disproportionately artistic? Or disproportionately attracted to betraying their country, like the Oxford–Cambridge traitors whom Christopher Andrews calls the "Homintern"?

And what about people born with cleft palette? There are many more of them born each year than there are homosexuals. Is it just the paucity of our imagination that has prevented us from figuring out why nature vouchsafed them to us?

In fifty years or so, when a doctor tells expectant parents that their child will be a healthy boy, but a homosexual, how many of those parents are going to say, "Oh goodie"? And how many are going to ask the doctor to "cure" the genetic condition, even if they have to learn Chinese?

If homosexuality really is a genetic condition, not an impulse control disorder, homosexuals are slated for extinction, like Tyrannosaurus rex, and in the future will be seen only in science fiction movies—think Jurassic Park XXIII.

The same desire to tinker that led man to discover how to make fire will eliminate abnormalities like homosexuality—unless the desire to burn people at the stake intervenes.

Wm. F. Buckley Jr. on Justice Scalia's Death
February 23, 2016

"Despair is a mortal sin" is the only phrase I remember Bill Buckley ever repeating to me—aside from "What'll you have?" in the evening.

Conservatives are understandably saddened by the death of Justice Scalia. He was a beacon of good sense, good constitutional sense, in a political world seemingly besotted by heavy-booted ubergovernment.

Adam Smith said, "There's a lot of ruin in a nation," by which it is generally thought he meant that a lot could go wrong before a nation finally collapsed. Surely that is true of America.

If the only thing that has been standing between the survival and the collapse of constitutional government and freedom in America is a single court or a single Supreme Court justice, then we're closer to running out of ruin than we thought.

Despite the long Obamanian winter of our discontent, there are signs of spring—though it is true that the success of Donald Trump may make us think it is only "Springtime for Hitler and Germany." And while we're on the subject—how to put this delicately?—springtime for liberal Justice Ruth Bader Ginsburg it is not.

Across the land—or as the politicians say, sometimes even at dinner, "across this great country of ours"—people have rejected Obama and the philosophy he represents, which is the philosophy of the Democratic Party, which is the politics of identity and envy, anti-Western Civilization multiculturalism, class conflict, and Marxist redistribution of private property.

Thirty-one states now have a Republican governor. The Democrats have lost more than nine hundred seats in state legislatures. Republicans now control both houses of the legislature in thirty states, up, way up, from 2008. That change should be seen as a political victory, which it was: it was a rejection of the politics of Obama and the Democratic Party. A political renaissance. It is true that you might not know it by looking at the Republicans in Washington. But out in fly-over land, Republicans are changing the way government operates.

In a recent speech, Charles Murray gave three reasons for being optimistic about the cause of freedom. The first is the demise of the intellectual concept that central planning works. People have discovered that the market doesn't have to work perfectly to work better than government. Millions and millions of people around the globe have been lifted out of poverty by the market. Where there is still mass poverty, there is still mass government, meddling in the economy. And there is the inevitable corruption that comes with mass government. Think, also, of crony capitalism.

Murray's second point is the widespread understanding "that the government is no longer an extension of us. It is us versus them." People have come to realize that President Obama is wrong when he says, "We're all in this together." (What do you mean "we," kemosabe?) Government feathers its own nest while it regulates the nest-building of the people. The average wage of federal employees in 2014 was 78 percent higher than the private-sector average.

Murray's third point is that we are realizing that the happiness we are pursuing is gained by taking responsibility, and that the welfare state, by providing goods, services, and security, eliminates the need to take responsibility. That deprives us of our humanity.

Not everyone will agree with Murray. Or agree that we have turned the corner necessary to see what he says is there to see.

But there are other reasons to be optimistic. Science (where computing power doubles every two years) will continue to disclose amazing secrets—like, say, that boys and girls really are different, and that humans are hard-wired to achieve happiness by taking responsibility—even to those who don't want to hear them. Hillary may try to stand athwart science yelling "Stop!" even as she wants to stand on, throttle, and bury the First Amendment. But science, and scientists, will go where they are welcomed. In the end, they will bury her.

Conservatives should be of good cheer and raise a helluva ruckus over the confirmation of Justice Scalia's successor. The more politicized the event is, the less hoary legitimacy the Supreme Court will have. The elites have trashed the law and the culture of this country, and the Supreme Court, amending the Constitution with abandon, has been one of their implements. As a joke might ask, What do you call it when (as a Gallup poll showed in September) 50 percent of the people disapprove of the job the Supreme Court is doing? Answer: A beginning.

Justice Scalia said that the process for amending the Constitution is now infinitely more difficult than it was when the provision was written (he concluded that an amendment today could be blocked by about 2 percent of the population), and that he thought the provision itself should be amended. That difficulty may be only one reason why the liberal members of the court now perform the politically controversial amending function themselves. Justice Scalia, who stated that he would like some popular control over the process of nominating justices, was asked if, therefore, Supreme Court justices should be elected instead of appointed. He answered, dismissively, "No!" Given the prospect of a Justice Donald Trump, he may have been right.

But he may have been wrong. If we are to be self-governing, we should elect those who write our rules, as judges now do.

And we must also remember, always, Abraham Lincoln's warning: "If the policy of the Government upon vital questions affecting the whole people is to be irrevocably fixed by decisions of the Supreme Court . . . the people will have ceased to be their own rulers." Repeat three times. And make the children memorize it.

A knock-down-drag-out fight over the confirmation of Scalia's successor, and its timing, is exactly the catharsis the country needs.

We must be of good cheer. We are not yet old and fragile. Constitutional governance is, Scalia himself said, "worth fighting for, *win or lose*." The struggle availeth—and even if it doesn't, it is our responsibility to struggle anyway, and it is responsibility that makes us human. We will make new friends in the battle. Write new stories, sing new songs, find new heroes.

And remind our grandchildren that despair is a mortal sin.

Harvard Law School Chases the Seal of Good Identity Politics

April 4, 2016

With a self-congratulatory whack on the back that would break the spine of a more modest institution, Harvard Law School has announced that it is "retiring" the school's seal because of its association with slavery. The seal, which was adopted only in 1936, depicts three bundles of wheat, and is based on a bookplate used in the distant past by Isaac Royall (1672–1739). It was Royall's son, Isaac Jr., who in 1781 devised land to Harvard for the purpose of establishing a professorship of either law or science. That endowment was used to help fund a professor in law, who went on to create the law department at Harvard in 1817.

The problem is that Royall Sr. ran sugar plantations in the Caribbean where he kept slaves. Subsequently, he moved to Massachusetts, bringing some of his slaves with him, and raised wheat. The son bequeathed this "plantation" to Harvard. Hence the images on the bookplate, incorporated into the law school's seal.

The decision to stop using the seal was made in response to protests by students, some of whom may have been as much as *twenty-three* years old. We might ask, or their tuition-paying parents might ask, What could twenty-three-year-olds so steeped in wisdom possibly learn from a professoriate that until only a few months before had happily collected their salaries and consulting fees without, apparently, noticing anything amiss in the moral climate of the prestigious law school?

In her letter announcing the decision to discard the seal, Harvard Law School Dean Martha Minow wrote: "I am profoundly grateful to Professor Mann and all members of the committee for the exceptionally thoughtful, inclusive, and responsive process they led."

It would be pointless to pretend that anything Harvard does in the political realm is not freighted with progressivism and authoritarianism; even so, whenever you see the word "inclusive" you should reach, if not for your gun, at least for a stiff drink, regardless of how many you've already had or what your doctor says. Oh, what the Hell, go ahead and reach for your gun if it makes you feel better—but not if you've already had those drinks, and for Heaven's sake ("Heaven" and "Hell" are capitalized because they're places, like Washington): don't shoot at anybody!

Until you get the word.

How inclusive was the process? Not just "inclusive," but, according to Dean Minow's description, "exceptionally inclusive." Well, stone the crows! That's good to hear, isn't it?

But what does "inclusive" mean? Does it mean listening to people who don't agree with you? Well, maybe one or two, but surely never a majority—i.e., not enough to derail a freight train. If Dean Minow's process had started out with listening to a black, a woman, two Jews, and a cripple, all of whom were against retiring the seal, raise your hand if you think the Powers that Be would not have been sure to include at least six other people in the process who were in favor.

Did Professor Mann's exceptionally inclusive process include listening to slaveholders? Presumably not—too expensive to fly them over from Africa.

A homosexual? Who knows, but why not? (And so surely yes.) To whom, after all, does "inclusive" generally refer if not to people with, er, unattractive sexual practices? And remember, this committee was "exceptionally inclusive."

Did the process include listening to a pair of one-eyed non-bathing Hispanic Rosicrucian transies who thought the whole business was just an exercise in moral posturing and self-congratulatory swill?

Let's go with the transies. Even people who can't keep their gender straight can, like a slow clock, be right once in a while.

But, of course, the whole business is more complicated. It always is. The law school is old, but the shield is new. Why shouldn't it go?

One dissenting member of the committee wrote: "Maintaining the current shield, and tying it to a historically sound interpretive narrative about it, would be the most honest and forthright way to insure that the true story of our origins, and connection to the people whom we should see as our progenitors (the enslaved people at Royall's plantations, not Isaac Royall), is not lost." Thank Heaven for Marxists, who would see no value in either the financial or intellectual capital of the Royalls.

There were other dissents as well. But the train rolled on.

Retiring the shield was the easy solution to Harvard Law School's problem, a solution as easy as sewing fig leaves together. The visible sign of the Royalls is gone. And although the financial fruits of their largess remain, the people who voted for the cover-up, and who agree with the decision, can feel gooood about themselves.

The hard solution would have been to divest the funds realized from the sale of the Royall land. The value of those funds, $2,938 in 1796, might be $5 million today, or even $50 million, a minor part of Harvard's $37.6 billion endowment, but still real money. One can be excused for thinking that divesting the funds might have seemed to the exceptionally inclusive committee to be morally superior to discarding a small symbol no one knew anything about until practically yesterday. Of course, there is the problem of who would have been the recipient of the divested funds. Yale?

Perhaps the Powers that Be at Harvard know that Harvard's history, perhaps even its modern history, is full of other Isaac Royalls, and that if they disposed of his gift, they would have to dispose of others. And then there might be No Endowment Left.

In the past year, Harvard has also disposed of the term "housemaster" because (you can't make this stuff up) its supposed connection with slavery upset some of the college students, some of whom were said to be *eighteen* years old—and who therefore may never have heard the word "schoolmaster" or "headmaster," and may also not have known that the word "master" comes from the Latin word *magister*, which means "teacher."

And while we're on the subject of teachers, surely not all of Harvard's previous teachers can be acceptable to the current guardians of her moral purity. Harvard professors Charles W. Eliot and A. Lawrence Lowell were both supporters of the eugenics movement— we might not unfairly call them the intellectual Isaac Royalls of their time. Both were also presidents of Harvard, and both have houses (student dormitories) named after them. What to do?

A hundred years from now, what will Harvard's guardians do about Harvard's decision, way back in 2009, not to keep calm through the storm of gender-identity politics, but to institute a professorship in lesbian, gay, bisexual, and transgender studies?

Is promoting eugenics really a lot worse? What to do?

Indeed, what *are* we to do with the age that is past?

Perhaps learn from it. And learn especially that man is complex, filled with the potential to do both good and evil, to succeed and to fail, to see truth and to practice error. To sin and to repent.

And to be redeemed.

Why did Isaac Royall Jr. give his land to Harvard anyway? Do we know? Do we care? Perhaps it was to aid the pursuit of knowledge. Perhaps it was to expiate the sins of his forebears. Or his own. Maybe that was his way of choosing between Heaven and Hell.

Why do people give to Harvard today? That *is* a puzzler. Surely not for educational purposes. What Harvard can't teach with $37.6 billion it won't be able to teach with $37.6 billion plus a few extra million in annual giving. It's a good guess that many people give to Harvard in order to be *seen* giving to Harvard. That is not a sin anywhere nearly as great as Royall's sin of holding slaves, or Eliot and Lowell's sin of supporting eugenics, but it should be sufficient to cause them to rethink being the first to throw stones, from the safety of a quarter of a millennium's distance, at people they believe to be their moral inferiors.

What was really going on at Harvard was not about the seal or even about money, whether it's five billion or five million or five thousand dollars. The whole seal business was really about identity politics. Harvard's guardians spent four months producing a ten-page report, which said, *inter alia*: "The Committee was unanimous in recognizing that modern institutions must acknowledge their past associations with slavery, not to assign guilt, but to understand the pervasiveness of the legacy of slavery and its continuing impact on the world in which we live."

That sounds suspiciously like saying that the problems today's blacks face are the direct result of slavery. Please! The black illegitimacy rate in 1940 was about 15 percent. In the mid-1960s it was 26 percent. Today, fifty years after the Civil Rights acts and the Great Society programs so championed by Harvard professors of progressivism and authoritarianism, it's about 75 percent. What are the chances an illegitimate black child will prosper in today's world? Slim to none.

Harvard's contribution to solving that problem is to dispose of a symbol practically no one had ever noticed, *and to pretend that that act will do something about the legacy of slavery!* You can't make this stuff up.

If Harvard doesn't want to divest itself of five thousand or five million or five billion dollars—it could give the funds to charter schools in poor black neighborhoods—at least it could refrain from encouraging the breakdown of Western Civilization's family culture by keeping two lesbians as the housemasters of Lowell House. (You're right: "housemaster" is an odd term for a brace of lesbians.)

Harvard would have done better to let the past be the past.

The Progressive Media's Crocodile Fears over Donald Trump

April 13, 2016

Life is rich, especially when you can watch the progressive media have a meltdown over the success of Donald Trump—even if it's a faux meltdown.

Colbert King writing in the *Washington Post* quotes, approvingly, Amanda Taub writing on *Vox*, who says Donald Trump is an authoritarian. E.J. Dionne also plays the authoritarian card in a February column. The gist of the *Vox* piece is reminiscent of the 1964 *Fact* magazine article that proclaimed: ". . . 1,189 Psychiatrists Say Goldwater Is Psychologically Unfit to be President!"

What are the authoritarian supporters of Trump accused of wanting? The Taub piece says policies such as "prioritizing military force over diplomacy against countries that threaten the United States; amending the Constitution to bar citizenship for children of illegal immigrants; imposing extra airport checks on passengers who appear to be of Middle Eastern descent; and requiring all citizens to carry a national ID card to show a police officer on request."

Not everyone will agree on the desirability of those four proposals, but it's not clear how approving of them is evidence of authoritarianism. Reasonable people *may* differ on the question of birthright citizenship, but the better argument is that the Fourteenth Amendment does not confer US citizenship on the children of illegal aliens.*

* For a short debate on the issue, see http://bitly.com/chavez-versus-eastman-on-birthright-citizenry.

Even if all the policies cited were evidence of authoritarianism, they are hardly more authoritarian than the 82,000-page Federal Register, which imposes a burden on the American people of $1.8 trillion a year, according to Wayne Crews of the Competitive Enterprise Institute. Or President Obama's mandate that everyone must buy health insurance. Or that Roman Catholic nuns must have health insurance that covers contraceptives and abortifacients. Or that disoriented boys who see themselves as girls must be allowed to shower with girls. And what about former New York City Mayor Michael Bloomberg's war on sodas and other sugary drinks larger than 16 ounces?

Progressivism—the proper name for the governing philosophy of those people who used to be called "liberals"—is inherently authoritarian, and its primary products are lamentation, and mourning, and woe.

The *Washington Post* complains that Trump "applauds the prospect of twisting the Constitution to limit First Amendment freedom of the press." But has the *Washington Post* objected to the proposal of Sen. Sheldon Whitehouse (D–RI) to have the US Department of Justice use RICO (The Racketeer Influenced and Corrupt Organizations Act) against people who deny climate change—the First Commandment of progressivism? Or Hillary Clinton's proposal to amend the First Amendment in order to curtail individual contributions to political campaigns?

You have to marvel at *New York Times* columnist Timothy Egan's comment that Trump "wants to apply a religious test for entry into a country whose founders were against any such thing." Appealing to the Founders is like turning a light on and off. What would Mr. Egan say about the Founders' thinking on, say, the tangled web of sexual pathologies celebrated by progressives, or abortion which they refer to as "reproductive rights"?

And you have to love this from the *Washington Post* editorial team. Beating up on Republican National Committee Chairman Reince Pribus, who said, "Winning is the antidote to a lot of things," the *Post* wrote: "So it falls to other leaders to decide if their party will stand for anything other than winning. A political party, after all, isn't meant to be merely a collection of consultants, lobbyists and functionaries angling for jobs. It is supposed to have principles." This from the people who are salivating to have Hillary Clinton elected; Hillary Clinton, the most corrupt person on the planet—with the possible exception of Equatorial Guinea President Teodorin Obiang Nguema Mbasogoea, Africa's longest serving ruler. He has ruled the tiny, oil-rich West African country since he overthrew his uncle, Francisco Macías Nguema, in a bloody coup d'état in 1979, the year Carolyn Moffet, a legal secretary in Little Rock, Arkansas, said she was sexually abused by Bill Clinton.

Here's what Republicans and conservatives need to understand: the left-wing media's attack on Trump is not just an attack on Trump. It's really an attack on anyone who doesn't hew the progressive line. A March editorial in the *New York Times* gave the game away: "Last week Marco Rubio and Ted Cruz, elected to the Senate partly on their appeal to extremists, seemed. . . ." Catherine Rampell wrote in the *Washington Post*, "Is Donald Trump really so much crazier or more extreme than the other Republican presidential candidates?" E.J. Dionne wrote that the Republican Party "has subtly and not so subtly played on racial resentment—. . . Ronald Reagan's famous 'welfare queen'—for decades." A man who'll accuse President Reagan of racism will (does it need to be said out loud?) accuse whoever the Republican nominee is of racism, and probably also of wanting to take us back to the darkest days of history—and you know what that means.

These comments are NOT an endorsement of Donald Trump. Why would a conservative endorse Trump when the rightward-most viable candidate since Barry Goldwater and Ronald Reagan is a major contender, and now doing better than ever? This is simply a reminder to conservatives, and Republicans, that whatever the progressive media are saying about Donald Trump today they will be saying tomorrow about the Republican nominee, whoever he is. And as Mary McCarthy said of Lillian Hellman, everything they say is a lie, including the words "and" and "the."

They're all in for Hillary—the second most corrupt person on the planet, just after Equatorial Guinea President Teodorin Obiang Nguema Mbasogoea.

If Hillary Clinton is elected president, life will be a lot less rich for those who are already suffering under the policies of progressivism and authoritarianism, the socialist twins. And that will be true even if Hillary does not engage in her hallmark corrupt practices, and even if she is only the 242nd most corrupt person on the planet.

Drew Barrymore, Donald Trump, Scrooge, and the Pope, or Dearly Beloved

April 27, 2016

Dearly beloved, Drew Barrymore is getting divorced. Again. Some of the sad details are in the current issue of *People* magazine.

However, independent research would show that readers of this column spend little time reading the popular culture magazines—the Gossip Glossies—and so as a service to them, we are providing a taste of that slice of the culture.

It is not an insignificant slice. The circulation of the popcul Gossip Glossies is huge: *InStyle* magazine (thirteen issues a year) boasts a readership of 9.542 million, of whom 92 percent are female; *Marie Claire* (a monthly): circulation 1,012,048, highest readership of any magazine among women aged 18 to 34; *People* magazine (a weekly): circulation 3,486,478; *Entertainment Weekly*: circulation 1.8 million. And there are others.

Compare those numbers with some of the publications that support the country's traditional culture: at the top, *National Review* (a fortnightly), with a circulation of ca. 150,000. At the other end, *The New Criterion* (ten issues a year): circulation 6,000.

We will make a foray into pop culture easy for you.

Drew Barrymore's first husband was Tom Green, "a Canadian actor, rapper, writer, comedian, producer, director, talk show host, and media personality" it says on Wikipedia, and I have no reason to doubt it. And isn't that the kind of man every mom wants her daughter to marry?

The marriage lasted five months.

Number two was Jeremy Thomas, a man described by *Us Weekly* as "the Los Angeles bar owner." The lovebirds were married (the details are from *People* magazine) at 5 a.m. in "Thomas's dimly lit bar, the Room. And the presiding official was a minister–psychic–private detective who arrived with her English bulldog, Jimmy. 'He snarled at everybody,' recalls an amused Thomas. 'Then he took a pee in the corner. It was quite surreal.'" Yes. But the romance—married in a bar! And the security—he owned the bar! What more could a mother want for her child?

The marriage lasted two months.

We should pause to note that one of Barrymore's problems was that, as Flanders and Swann put it in their Hippopotamus song, "She hadn't got a ma to give her advice." (More later.)

The third time never fails, they say, and in a way that was true for Drew: her third marriage, to Will Kopelman, lasted almost *four years*, which, compared to two months, must have seemed like *forever*.

People magazine says: "Drew Barrymore's marriage did not start as a whirlwind fairytale." That actually sounds promising. "According to *InStyle* magazine she didn't originally realize that Kopelman was 'the one.'" It can be difficult to tell, as Drew now knows. Besides, Kopelman was not only "the one." He was also the third.

"The couple married in 2012," *People* continues, "and has two daughters together 3-year-old Olive and 1-year-old Frankie. [*People* doesn't use the parenthetical comma after "together"—it's probably a Gossip Glossy style thing.] Barrymore also credits her daughters as part of the reason she doesn't discuss previous relationships in her new memoir *Wildflower*."

" 'I felt it was inappropriate to discuss relationships and encounters I have had with another person,' she says." Drew's phrasing makes it difficult to tell whether she is referring to numerous relationships and encounters she had with one person ("another person"), or to one or perhaps more relationships and encounters she had with numerous people. The smart money is going with the second interpretation, and you may want to too.

" 'I consciously chose not to include those. I want this book to be a love letter to my daughters, Frankie and Olive. They don't need to know about my sex life.' "

Of course, there's not much danger that her children (now two and four) will read the GGs any time soon. But when they get older they will be able to pull up all the titillating details of Drew's sex life on Google. Still, we have to admire her decorum. And her restraint.

And her courage in the face of adversity. At the Pebble Beach Food and Wine Festival on April 2, when she introduced her new rosé (from Barrymore Wines), she "poured glasses of wine, gave out hugs and posed for selfies with festivalgoers. 'She was simply a ray of sunshine the entire time,'" said one onlooker. And not only that. "'She was happy and giggly and self-deprecating and sweet with everyone she came in contact with.'"

"No one would have guessed," continues *People*, "that Barrymore, 41, had publicly confirmed that morning that she and her husband . . . were ending their marriage."

"Sadly," *People* quotes her as saying (but clearly not so sadly that people would guess her sadness), "our family is separating legally, although we do not feel this takes away from us being a family." Interesting point, actually.

"A stable, happy family unit had eluded Barrymore until she met Kopelman," according to *People* magazine. That's putting it mildly: *Us* tells us that "back in the late '80s, the precocious *E.T.* actress famously entered rehab at age 14 and, at 15, successfully petitioned for juvenile emancipation from her parents, moving into her own apartment; her relationship with [her mother] Jaid . . . has been rocky ever since." Barrymore told *Marie Claire*, "Ugh, I mean, my relationship with my mom is so complicated." Ugh, yes.

Most of the readers of this column aren't used to seeing this sort of copy. Just think of this as research into American culture, and keep reading: there may be a pop quiz.

A friend of Barrymore's reported that their decision to get divorced "was not an overnight decision. They both really wanted to make it work." You can tell: four years is a long time.

Popsugar quotes Barrymore as saying, "I had a really hard time a couple of months ago and kind of knew life was heading in a different direction." She asked a friend what to do and he gave her the kind of advice you want to put on the fridge: "You put one foot in front of the other."

People reports that a Barrymore "insider"—inside what isn't clear—says Barrymore is optimistic for the future (being worth twenty, thirty, or fifty million dollars can do that for a girl, even for one who was in rehab at age fourteen and whose relationship with her mother is, ugh, complicated). The insider goes on to say about Drew—this is the part almost worth waiting for—"She still very much believes in love."

Ooooh. She still believes in love.

Well, Scrooge didn't. When he asked his nephew, Fred, why he had gotten married, Fred replied, "Because I fell in love." Scrooge mocks him, growling: "Because you fell in love."

Scrooge is always vilified, of course, but he was on to something. Marriage may be partly about the love Barrymore still very much believes in. But marriage's primary glue is commitment. Puppy love won't get anyone through a siege of forty winters. Married people have to learn how to deal with the deep trenches time can dig in their lives.

Pope Francis, in his recent apostolic exhortation on family life ("Amoris Laetitia," "The Joy of Love"), says, "As Christians, we can hardly stop advocating marriage simply to avoid countering contemporary sensibilities, or out of a desire to be fashionable or a sense of helplessness in the face of human and moral failings." Those sensibilities and failings are exemplified by Drew Barrymore as well as, of course, by Donald Trump, to whom an invitee to his third wedding replied that he couldn't make that one but would try to catch the next one.

With the popular magazines endorsing serial fornication hiding under giggly veils of matrimony (if you call mumbling some words in a bar at 5 a.m. in front of a minister–psychic–private detective "marriage"), it does not surprise that young people now endorse even homosexual "marriage" by an ever-increasing margin. Or that mega-corporations use their economic clout to dissuade states from passing commonsense laws that support not requiring boys and girls to shower together.

Marriage was once seen by most people in this country as an honorable estate, with divine significance, not to be entered into unadvisedly or lightly. No more. Today's popular culture, nurtured by the progressives, trashes that concept, with terrible consequences for ordinary people—people who don't have their very own brand of rosé or live in fifty-million-dollar bubbles, like Drew Barrymore.

Voting and the Fire Next Time
May 1, 2016

Last Monday a federal district judge in North Carolina upheld changes in the state's election laws, including voter identification provisions, that were opposed by civil rights activists. The changes followed the Supreme Court's 2013 decision that struck down a restriction in the 1965 Voting Rights Act which imposed on nine states (mostly in the South) a requirement that any proposed changes in voting practices be "pre-cleared" by the Justice Department to determine whether they had any discriminatory purpose or effect. Predictably, the Left is having a cow, and crying "racism."

The new provisions in North Carolina include such draconian, and obviously racist, requirements as having a photo ID and registering before Election Day. They also reduced the number of days before an election during which people could vote, and ended the practice of allowing people to register before they turned eighteen. The governor compared the voter ID requirements to those necessary for "common practices like boarding an airplane and purchasing Sudafed."

A correspondent who wrote to me a while ago, in response to some observations* on why blacks don't vote Republican, claimed that "the GOP of 1964 is not perceived as the GOP of today. Blacks today perhaps draw cynical conclusions from current GOP efforts to cut back on black voting rights."

His term "blacks today" presumably means at least a majority of blacks. But it is not at all clear that a majority of blacks "draw cynical conclusions from current GOP efforts to" introduce voter ID laws, which he characterizes as attempts to "cut back on black voting rights." In fact, just the opposite appears to be the case.

The Roper Center at Cornell University reports that a 2013 poll "found non-whites as supportive of voter ID laws as whites." The report continues, "but a 2015 CBS News poll found a difference in attitudes about voter ID laws; 83 percent of whites and 66 percent of blacks supported them." Nevertheless, only a minority of blacks

* http://bitly.com/donald-trump-believe-black-voters-are-stupid

opposed voter ID laws, which is contrary to our correspondent's assertion.

The Roper report continues: "When a 2012 CBS News/NYT poll presented respondents with arguments for and against voter ID that mentioned the possibility of minority vote suppression, 53 percent of blacks supported such laws and 45 percent opposed."

We don't know how the question was worded, but according to Roper, even though the possibility of minority vote suppression was mentioned as a reason for voter ID laws, a majority of blacks still supported them.

And also, according to Roper, "A July 2015 CBS News/NYT poll found that 46 percent of blacks, but only 20 percent of whites, thought shortening voting hours and reducing time for absentee and early voting was an attempt to make it harder for minorities to vote." That's quite a difference between whites and blacks. But even so, a majority of blacks thought shortening voting hours and reducing time for absentee and early voting was *not* an attempt to make it harder for minorities to vote.

The statistics raise several questions. First, why is it that liberals like my correspondent (a highly educated, serious, and thoughtful individual of exceptionally generous spirit—and a valued friend) are so out of touch with blacks? My correspondent assumes that blacks are solidly opposed to voter ID laws, which clearly they are not.

Second, what is it that blacks do want from the political system? A majority, it seems from the polls cited above, do not pine for making the process "fairer"—i.e., making it easier to vote. Is what they want a different result from the voting—i.e., different policies promoted by the people they vote for?

That would make sense, but there's no evidence for it. We've had fifty years of voting since the enactment of the various civil rights laws of the 1960s. Yet for fifty years blacks have voted overwhelmingly, at the local, state, and federal levels, for Democrats—and never more so than for Barack Obama: 99 percent in 2008; 95 percent in 2012.

And yet, those Democrats, year after year, decade after decade, produce policies that keep blacks down on the farm, down on the liberal plantation, the liberals' vote-harvesting plantation, freeing them only once a year: to go to the polls and vote. Or if you find that too harsh, think of it this way: the Democrats not only have not promoted policies that would deliver blacks from the bondage of their previous condition of servitude; the policies they have enacted have improved the condition of blacks relative to that of whites *not at all.**

Fifty years after the civil rights acts, blacks are disproportionately poor, disproportionately uneducated, disproportionately unwed, and disproportionately illegitimate. Disproportionately underlings. *Fifty years after the civil rights acts!*

Would blacks be better off today if they couldn't vote—if they hadn't been able to vote for the last fifty years? That would presumably have resulted in more Republicans being elected; and that would presumably have resulted in a stronger tendency toward free market approaches to public policy questions, as well as a more vigorous defense of traditional morality. What do Detroit, Baltimore, New Orleans, Cleveland, and Atlanta have in common? They're all disaster areas; they're all cities run by liberal Democrats; and those liberal Democrats would not have been elected without the black vote. And neither would Barack Obama, who has been the worst president for blacks since the racist Woodrow Wilson. QED. And so, for all their voting, blacks have made no progress at all.

Where is the fault for that lack of blacks' progress? Not in their stars, of course, but maybe also not in an easily criticized, perhaps thoughtless, perhaps selfish, anti-black attitude among non-blacks that doesn't quite amount to racism.

Bathroom Bills Stall amid Shower of Criticism
May 17, 2016

We may miss the nasty vulgarities that the pivoting Donald Trump is said to be leaving behind. Now we're stuck with the bathroom bills— and Trump's own comment that people should "use the bathroom they feel is appropriate." So: the mighty-handed Donald Trump, whose wrinkled lip and sneer of cold command beat back Mexican rapists, Muslim terrorists, and black murderers, is—let's not beat around the bysshe—shrinking like a shriveling shrinking thing before the

---

* See the piece that provoked my correspondent's remarks at http://bitly.com/donald-trump-believe-black-voters-are-stupid.

NewYorkTimesie pushers of gender-neutral bathrooms and showers for high school kids. Look on my works, ye mighty, and despair!

The bathroom bills, which push back against this latest insanity, bring to mind Randall Jarrell's quip in *Pictures from an Institution*: "You have to see it not to believe it." What astounds is that the transies aren't just interested in bathrooms, *qua* bathrooms, as they probably say in the tony gender-free aeries of progressive liberalism. What they want is to destroy convention itself. Not just marriage and family: they want to integrate—though they haven't got around to stealing that word from the civil rights campaigns yet—they want to integrate high school locker rooms and showers. As almost any normal child would say, "Gross!"

Dozens of bathroom bills have been introduced into state legislatures, and the long knives of progressive liberals are starting to flash. A Kansas bill provides that "in all public schools and postsecondary educational institutions in this state, student restrooms, locker rooms and showers"—don't skip over that too quickly: *"locker rooms and showers"*—"that are designated for one sex shall be used only by members of that sex." Could you imagine, last year, having to legislate that?

Indiana is considering a bill that contains the provision: "As used in this chapter, 'female' means an individual who: (1) was born female at birth; or (2) has at least one (1) X chromosome and no Y chromosome . . . [and] 'male' means an individual who: (1) was born male at birth; or (2) has at least one (1) X chromosome and at least one (1) Y chromosome." What kind of a world do we live in where men and women have to be defined by lawyers in terms of their chromosomes? It's a good bet the Founding Fathers never thought it would come to this.

Here's the long knife the US Civil Rights Commission flashed last week about one of these state bills: "Critically, the new legislation also forces transgender people to utilize public bathrooms and changing facilities based on the sex issued on their birth certificates [oh, the indignity], and not according to their gender identities. This jeopardizes not only the dignity, but also the actual physical safety, of transgender people whose appearances may not match societal expectations of the sex specified on their identification documents." Who says we can't cut the federal budget by 10 percent?

After North Carolina passed a bill last month, The Department of Justice notified the state that the law violates Civil Rights Act legislation, which forbids discrimination based on sex. The state thereupon filed suit against the federal government contesting the Justice Department's warning, whereupon the feds brought a suit against the states.

The federal government's threat is that it will withhold some of the $4 billion in aid that goes to the state. It's time for North Carolina, and any other state inhabited by sane people, to focus on how much of that "federal" money actually came from their own citizens.

Big corporations also threaten economic sanctions. States will have to decide whether to sell out Western Civilization for a few coins. Conservatives, often seduced by the promise of economic success, will have to decide if there are higher goals.

Truly, this could be closing time for Western Civilization. Bathroom bills may be the Battle of the Morannon in the culture war.

When did this war begin—this war that has replaced freedom with compulsion (masquerading as tolerance) as the highest value in American society? Probably (HEALTH ALERT: Doctors recommend assuming the seated position before reading this sentence) in 1964, which is when the Civil Rights Act with the public-accommodation provision that Sen. Barry Goldwater objected to was enacted. Goldwater voted against it and argued, essentially, that Americans would lose their freedom *not* to associate with people they didn't like. In the heyday of the civil rights era, when the issue was equality for blacks, Goldwater's was not a winning argument. And now that it is, it may be too late.

Following the Supreme Court's decision on homosexual marriage last year, a number of states passed, or tried to pass, bills making exceptions for people with particular religious objections and exempting them from having to serve homosexuals (e.g., baking cakes for their weddings). But religion was never a sufficient reason, as those who thought it was a high-card argument discovered. The culture vandals (a.k.a. the progressive Left) don't much care about religion. They aren't going to let oddball religions rewrite society's general rules so as to exempt themselves from obeying them. What, you say, Roman Catholicism (with 69 million US members) is an oddball religion? Well, yes. To the culture vandals all religions are oddball.

The proper ground for allowing people not to serve homosexuals is the *general* (classical liberal, and First Amendment) rule of the right to associate or not to associate, *not* an exception to a rule of the prescriptive progressive state. It follows, therefore, that people should be free not to associate with other people for any reason, whether they're homosexuals or Zoroastrians.

Even so, there is a public carrier/public accommodation exception to that rule that comes from the common law. The common-law rule required that only public carriers and innkeepers accommodate all comers (or at least not unreasonably discriminate against them), because their businesses tended to be monopolies that had been granted by the state. However, a coffee house was not considered an inn, and neither was a tavern or a bar or a restaurant. There is no reason in a free society to apply the public carrier/public accommodation exception in a town that has a dozen bakers. One of the thirteen is likely to be willing to do whatever any customer wants. And if none will, requiring the customer to bear the inconvenience of going to a neighboring town is better than violating the general right to free association.

What's the difference between a Soviet commissar's telling a citizen he can't see a priest, and a progressive Democrat's telling him he must serve a homosexual? That would be a good question for a reporter to ask President Obama the next time he talks about his new pals in Cuba. Or Donald Trump, that colossal wreck of American politics, boundless and bare.

Monkey Time—and Monkey Business—at Harvard

May 18, 2016

In China, it's the year of the monkey. It's monkey time here too. The monkeys on the back of the political system this year are Donald Trump and Bernie Sanders.

But there are other monkeys loose as well. Harvard University has a barrel of them on its own back: a slate of five insurgent candidates running for the position of Overseer. The Board of Overseers at Harvard is one of two governing bodies, the other being the President and Fellows, also known as the Corporation. The Corporation is self-perpetuating, which limits change. But one power the Overseers have is to consent, or withhold consent, to the election of Corporation members.

Three of the five insurgent candidates are Ralph Nader, Ron Unz, and Stuart Taylor. They are part of a group known as "Free Harvard/ Fair Harvard." Their primary goals are to abolish tuition and increase transparency in the admissions process at Harvard College.

The group's website says: "Harvard is now one of the world's largest hedge-funds, with its $38 BILLION portfolio tax-exempt because of the college it runs as a charity off to one side. The university's annual investment income is twenty-five times larger than its net tuition revenue. Meanwhile, thousands of student families are forced to spend most of their life-savings on $180,000 of total tuition, while relatively few non-affluent students even bother applying. Paying tuition to a giant hedge-fund is unconscionable, and Harvard should immediately abolish all college tuition."

The insurgents claim that the admissions policies favor "the wealthy and the powerful over more able students from ordinary American families" and that "there is also strong evidence that Harvard has a system of 'Asian Quotas' just like the 'Jewish Quotas' of the 1920s." The insurgents want to do away with the quotas. How do you say "Amen" in Asian?

But the Free Harvard/Fair Harvard candidates are being opposed, according to the *Harvard Crimson,* the college newspaper, by a pro-affirmative action group of nearly seven hundred alumni. The only surprise there is that the group doesn't number seven thousand . . . or seventy thousand.

The insurgents have other ideas too, and some of them can be found in the answers to a questionnaire sent to them by ACTA, the indispensable American Council of Trustees and Alumni.

Asked about academic freedom, Stuart Taylor wrote, "Civil liberties, academic freedom, and intellectual diversity are in deep trouble on America's campuses, including Harvard." Ron Unz answered, "I am completely appalled at some of the current trends of ideological suppression by activist groups at Harvard and as an Overseer would strongly oppose them."

Asked about due process in cases of alleged sexual assault, Taylor wrote: "As 28 Harvard law professors said in October 2015, Harvard University's new disciplinary procedures 'lack the most basic elements of fairness and due process, are overwhelmingly stacked against the accused.' The law professors urged Harvard—in vain—to stand up to the Obama administration's pressure to eviscerate due process, and 'stand up for principle in the face of funding threats.'"

Asked about ROTC cadets' receiving no academic credit for military-science courses, Lee Cheng, another insurgent, wrote: "Military science courses should receive academic credit and cadets on campus should receive the same level of protection, tolerance and welcome, if not more, than any other group of students."

There are other issues at Harvard, but the Free Harvard / Fair Harvard folk can't take them all on—yet. Harvard, flexing its mussolinis, is forcing the private single-sex clubs on campus (known as "final clubs") to take members of what in olden times was known as "the opposite sex." The ostensible reason is that too many sexual assaults are occurring at parties at the clubs.

According to the *Wall Street Journal*, "a survey of Harvard students conducted last year found that 47 percent of senior women who participated in final club activities experienced 'non-consensual sexual contact,' compared with 31 percent of all senior women at the school."

Hmm. That just seems . . . unlikely, and for a different take, see "Why Harvard Shouldn't Push Its All-male Final Clubs to Go Co-ed" by Caitlin Flanagan in *The Washington* Post, April 22, 2016.*

However, if it is true, it sounds like a separate admissions problem. But think about it: Harvard's dormitories are coed; the uber-enlightened Harvard administration, fellow-traveling with the zeitgeist, surely sees nothing wrong with premarital sex; the students go to parties where both boys and girls drink too much; and—stuff happens. Is that good? Of course not. Is it predictable? Please. Perhaps the admissions problem is that the wrong people have been admitted to the Board of Overseers.

And, uh, excuse me, but, uh, what were the girls wearing? A

---

* https://tinyurl.com/w9dy8xv

scandalous question, no doubt, but look: if you were one of the brightest senior coeds on the planet and knew that 47 percent of the milk for sale in your neighborhood was contaminated and would make you sick, wouldn't you take steps to see that the milk you bought was potable? That's just common sense, which, the survey is telling us, appears to be in short supply at Harvard.

What Harvard needs is to be shaken upside down by its toes, paddled on the behind, ridiculed, dunked in a barrel, and told to fly right. That, roughly, is the process the Free Harvard/Fair Harvard crowd is trying to begin. Even if you don't favor free tuition or unbiased admissions policies, it's worth voting for the insurgents just to shake things up. Harvard graduates are hereby urged, therefore, in the good Boston tradition, to vote early, and often, for the insurgents.

So kids: What time is it at Harvard? It's monkey time!

Roll out the barrel, we'll have a barrel of fun.

Donald Trump, Congress, and the American Tradition

June 22, 2016

The Republican Party set its life upon a cast, and must stand the hazard of the die. The die's come up Trump. Even those who think they hold the indoor and outdoor records for opposing Trump in the primary season should, and can without modifying their principles, support the GOP primary system's selection, if only because of the alternative.

In 2014, at the fiftieth anniversary of the Philadelphia Society (the nongeographical clubhouse for the intellectuals of the conservative movement), the Society's president and fourteen of his predecessors spoke for three minutes each about "the Future of the Philadelphia Society in the Light of Its Past."

One of them made these two points:

The conservative movement began almost sixty years ago, in 1955, when Bill Buckley launched *National Review* magazine. Since then, with a few notable exceptions, it's been downhill all the way. The state has grown relentlessly, and our freedoms have been curtailed.

In tennis and squash, and probably most other sports, the rule is: If you're playing a winning game, keep it. If you're playing a losing game, change it. We have been losing for sixty years. We are losing today. We need to change our game.

Now, two years later, we see that Donald Trump may be the game changer. He's a one-man earthquake that may shake the voting blocks off their traditional shelves. Economically marginalized blue-collar workers, the unemployed, the disenchanted, the fearful, the resentful, and minorities may flock to the anti-Washington, anti-PC candidate. Voting patterns could be changed for generations. That would be great news.

But there is no doubt that many of the people who were at that Philadelphia Society meeting are dismayed by the rise of the horrible and seemingly unstable Donald Trump. Many will sit out the election. A few will make their peace with Hillary Clinton.

One conservative movement intellectual has written:

> Hillary Clinton, while definitely no angel, is more predictable, will be less dismissive of the Constitution, will promote policies that are more rooted in reality, will be less insecure in office, and has a greater understanding of how to get things done (even if you don't like them) than Donald Trump.*

True or not, that represents, more or less, the position of some conservatives today. Still, that is a program only for sticking out your chin and hanging on, not a call to arms befitting a free people. And it is certainly not a call that remembers the central role of Congress in the American tradition. We can do better.

We need to behave like adults and ask ourselves which of the two—*and only two*—candidates on offer would we rather have as president: an anarchist in the world of taste and judgment and the nation's most conspicuous vulgarian (which is how William F. Buckley's described Harry Truman), whose behavior, if not his principles (always assuming he has any), requires us to despise him,

* http://t-c-a.info/james-burnham-political-economy

or a liberal-socialist-progressive—who in her spare time just happens to be, with her husband, the world's most conspicuous liar and crook (think Juanita Broaddrick, Kathleen Willey, Paula Jones, Filegate, Chinagate, Travelgate, cattle futures, the Marc Rich pardon, and stealing everything from the White House that wasn't load bearing)?

Washington Post columnist Richard Cohen, a liberal Democrat, has fumed that Trump's remarks disparaging Mexicans, women, prisoners of war, and the disabled "evince a man who lacks empathy. This—not his narcissism, not his lying, not his unfathomable ignorance—is his most dangerous characteristic."* Whoa, Nelly! Who knew? Who knew that empathy was the *sine qua non* for public office?

But notice: all the characteristics that Mr. Cohen and many others who oppose Trump object to are just rhetorical noises. What about substance? What about Hillary Clinton's substance?

A President Hillary Clinton, working with, let's assume, a Democratic Congress, is a guarantee of the continuing growth of the state and the continuing loss of freedom. Riding high on the triple-crown steed of identity politics (race, gender, and, er, sexual orientation), Hillary Clinton will seriously diminish our freedom to enjoy and preserve the culture of Western Civilization, by a thousand rules enforced by liberal-progressive judges. Our freedom to do business (and support our families) will be diminished by a myriad of monumentally oppressive regulations enforced by busloads of bureaucrats. Our freedom to live in peace will be diminished by perpetual war, goaded by the immensely incompetent Benghazi bungler who decided to depose an aging Libyan dictator who was no threat to the people of this country, a decision that has left another part of the Middle East in chaos. The Supreme Court will be packed with liberal progressives, hot to reinterpret the First Amendment to ensure freedom from religion, to restrict free speech and democracy, and to restrict the right not to associate with people we don't like (and don't want our children showering with), and cocked to reinterpret the Second Amendment to disarm the citizens. And socialized medicine will, finally, come.

Yes, Hillary knows how to get things done all right, and for four (maybe eight) more years government would continue to grow, and

---

* http://t-c-a.info/reince-priebusfool

freedom to shrink. How can the anti-Trump people be sure there'll be enough tinder left then to reignite the flame of liberty?

Conservatives who posit that Donald Trump, with either a Republican Congress or a Democratic Congress, could be worse than Hillary Clinton have a case that even O.J.'s lawyers couldn't make.

Could Trump build a wall all by himself, or might he need Congress's approval? Could Trump deport a million illegal immigrants all by himself, or might he need Congress's approval? Is there, really, anything Trump could do all by himself, without Congress's approval? Is there anything he could do that would not be subject to being undone, or prohibited, by Congress?

The answer is twofold. First, Trump would clearly have some power to act unilaterally by Executive Order—and Democrats, having for seven years cheered on the extravagant use of that power, are understandably apoplectic as they contemplate Trump's using the same tool. (We will now pause for five minutes of smirking.)

Second, whatever the president does, Congress, *if it has the will*, can amend or undo. With a lot of empathetic Democrats in Congress, Republicans, whether constituting a majority or not, should have little trouble managing a President Trump.

The point is this: if Congress ceases to be an actively functioning political institution, political liberty in the United States will come to an end.

All Americans, and especially conservatives, need to understand that if a Trump presidency is a constitutional or military disaster (to be distinguished from a disappointment), the real fault will lie, not with President Trump, but with Congress, which holds the high card and will need to remind Donald Trump of that every day: unlike Annie's tomorrow, always a day away, impeachment can be voted on *today*.

Donald Trump too, like Richard III, has set his life upon a cast. Conservatives must see to it that the hazard he will stand is Congress.

Note to reader: This piece begins and ends with a quote from Richard III, *which is revealed to the reader in the second usage, in last paragraph.*

In the opening paragraph, the phrase "indoor and outdoor records" is a reference to George Will who at the 2008 Conservative Political Action

Conference urged conservatives to support John McCain because the process had produced him. George said that he held the "indoor and outdoor record for opposing" McCain but would now support him because the process had produced him. George has now recommended trying to make Trump lose in all fifty states.

There is also a reference to Charles Murray's recent piece in National Review Online, *where he asks if conservatives can support Trump whose principles require us to despise him without modifying our principles.*

There are two references to the musical "Annie": stick out your chin and hanging on, and the reference in the penultimate paragraph.

But the real fun is in the opposing of "young" Jim Burnham (my high school classmate, whose quote I introduce with "One conservative movement intellectual") with his father, James Burnham (we were colleagues at National Review), *the title of one of whose books,* Congress and the American Tradition, *is part of my title (I inserted the obligatory serial comma after the word "Congress" in the title of this piece to postpone the reader's recognition of the title of Burnham's book). The central message of the book is summarized in the antepenultimate paragraph of the piece.*

Let's Play "Pin the Mustache on the Donkey"
July 14, 2016

Vilification of Donald Trump continues as the mainstream media's favorite sport. Leading the pack are the cartoonists, who wallow in depicting him as the authoritarian National Socialist Adolf Hitler. The funny little führry mustache is easy to draw, easy to recognize. These liberal-progressives, who are so quick to condemn Trump for his foul mouth, are willing to link Trump to the Nazis more quickly than you can say "hypocrite" auf Deutsch.

But Donald Trump, who certainly has a foul mouth, isn't channeling the Third Reich. Trump is showcasing only . . . Donald Trump.

Not so Bernie Sanders. He is pushing the ideology of socialism. And socialism is essentially what Hillary Clinton is selling too, when she's being serious. When she's not, it's just cheating, lying, and stealing, like Eva Perón.

Why don't the cartoonists depict the socialist Sanders as . . . well, that's the problem. Who's a recognizable socialist?

There are communists, of course, and we'll get to them, but they're different—though the difference between communists and socialists may be something like the difference between Bernie Sanders and Hillary Clinton.

Still, personifying socialism is a challenge. Karl Marx is considered the father of socialism, but how recognizable would a cartoon drawing of Marx be? Anyone who doesn't know which US president the city of Washington DC was named after is not likely to recognize a cartoon drawing of Karl Marx. But how many of even the more astute people—people who at least could answer the question: What color was George Washington's white horse?—would recognize a cartoon drawing of Marx?

Of course, the cartoonists could skip the intellectual-socialist phase of collectivist authoritarian government and go right to its brother, hard-core gulag communism, but that doesn't really solve their problem. Who's a recognizable hard-core communist barbarian? Joseph Stalin was certainly a barbarian, but is he recognizable today? Probably not. Nikita Khrushchev? Nikita who? There's Mao Tse Tung, of course, who was even more proficient than Stalin at killing people, but he was Chinese, and depicting a non-Caucasian in a funny way, even at Halloween, might encroach on the safe space so many people, most especially college students, seem to need today. So we're stuck with Hitler.

But there is this arresting fact: Hitler was a nasty piece of work, no doubt, but he was a junior, or really only a freshman, to Stalin when it came to killing people. A limerick by the late Robert Conquest is pertinent:

> There was a great Marxist named Lenin,
> Who did two or three million men in.
> That's a lot to have done in,
> But where he did one in
> That grand Marxist Stalin did ten in.

Robert Conquest's estimate was that Stalin probably killed not less than thirteen to fifteen million people. In pursuit of Marx's socialism.

Given socialism's history, you might have thought Sanders would have come up with a different name for whatever his philosophy is.

Margaret Thatcher famously said, "The problem with socialism is that you eventually run out of other people's money." Oscar Wilde said the problem with socialism was that it took too many evenings. That line may not seem quite so funny to people who spent twenty years of evenings in the gulag.

Running out of other people's money is certainly one problem with socialism, but not the only one. Socialism is inherently authoritarian, which is why it is the younger brother of communism and a first cousin of the authoritarian progressivism of Wilson, Roosevelt, Johnson, and Obama. And Bernie and Hillary. After all, how do the socialists *get* other people's money? They take it. Which means people will hide their money. Which means the state must employ spies and guys, and guys with guns—and crooked agents like Lois Lerner to run crooked agencies like the Internal Revenue Service.

Even in socialism's most benevolent form it brings suffering. In Canada, from 1993 to 2009, an estimated 25,000 to 63,000 women died prematurely, from having to wait for medical treatment, according to the Fraser Institute, a Canadian think tank. The number for men is lower, which means socialism may be worse for women than for men.

Of course, 25,000 Canadians isn't in Hitler's league (six million Jews); and Hitler wasn't in Stalin's league (thirteen million Russians); and Stalin wasn't in Mao's league (65 million Chinese). But do numbers count? Was Stalin really worse than Hitler? 2.167 times worse?

Canada's socialism is as benevolent as it gets. But most socialism, however innocently conceived, grows up to be like the rabid Cold War socialism of Russia and Eastern Europe, and China. The suffering then was legendary. But legends don't travel well in 140 characters, and so that suffering is almost unknown to the iPhone generation, who are Bernie Sanders's, and also probably Hillary Clinton's, supporters.

The socialism of Sanders and the progressivism of Clinton are inherently authoritarian, which is why, if any of the current presidential candidates deserve to be depicted as the German house painter turned National *Socialist* monster with the funny little mustache, those two do.

Schadenfreude and the *New York Times*
November 22, 2016

I am just back from Europe, where the Germans are preparing to sing a Christmas favorite, the MAGA version of which goes: "O Schadenfreude, O Schadenfreude, Du bringst ein schoen November." Which means, roughly: O Schadenfreude, O Schadenfreude, Thanks, pal, for the election result.

It's a result that has made it fun to read the *New York Times*—at least for a while.

Paul Krugman, who spent "the DAY AFTER avoiding the news," is suffering from "this terrible shock." "Everyone," he writes, "needs to face up to the unpleasant reality that a Trump administration will do immense damage to America and the world." And not just for four years. "The political damage will extend far into the future too. The odds are that some terrible people will become Supreme Court justices too." Courage, man.

Contributing writer Timothy Egan is also traumatized by Trump's victory. "It feels, in much of the nation, like the death of a loved one—the sudden unexpected kind. I haven't felt this way since the nuns told our second-grade class that John F. Kennedy had been assassinated." Grow. Up.

And *NYT* columnist Frank Bruni wrote ominously: "But there are darker implications here, too. After all the lies he told, all the fantasy he indulged in, all the hate he spewed and all the divisions he sharpened, he was rewarded with the highest office in the land. What does that portend for the politics of the next few years, for the kinds of congressional candidates we'll see in 2018, for the presidential race of 2020? I can't bear to think about the conflagrations to come."

For lighter *New York Times* fare, there is Vanessa Friedman's column, "Is Fashion's Love Affair with Washington Over?"

"More than any other industry, fashion had pledged its troth to Mrs. Clinton. *Vogue* magazine formally endorsed her, the first time it had taken a public stand in a presidential election. The *W* magazine editor, Stefano Tonchi, declared his allegiance in an editor's letter. Diane von Furstenberg, the designer and chairman of the Council of Fashion Designers of America, and Anna Wintour, the editor of *Vogue* and artistic director of Condé Nast, had aggressively raised funds for her, during fashion weeks and beyond," Friedman noted. "In understanding how she could use fashion to 'express ideas'—as Joseph Altuzarra, who made clothes for Mrs. Obama and contributed a T-shirt to Made for History, said—Mrs. Obama elevated the industry beyond the superficial to the substantive." Dear reader: You are not going to believe *how* substantive. "She framed clothing as a collection of values: diversity, creativity, entrepreneurship. Mrs. Clinton seemed primed to continue that trend. The Trumps, however, may not."

Stop, Schadenfreude, stop. Please stop!

A calmer David Brooks writes: "Trump's main problem in governing is not going to be some fascist ideology; his main problem is going to be his own attention span, ignorance and incompetence." Pop quiz: How many billionaires are ignorant and incompetent? "Trump's bigotry, dishonesty and promise-breaking will have to be denounced. We can't go morally numb." But then, looking on the bright side, "After all, the guy will probably resign or be impeached within a year."

Loyal readers know that we discussed this issue back in January. Because impeachment is possible (in the next Congress, if every Democrat were to vote for impeachment in the House and conviction in the Senate, only twenty-five House Republicans and nineteen Senate Republicans would be needed to remove Trump), a President Trump will have to behave himself. The clue that he intended all along to behave was his selection of Gov. Mike Pence as his running mate. The impeachment-assurance VP selection would have been Sheriff Joe Arpaio.

The over-the-top frenetic reporting on the Trump election, here and abroad, has already been acknowledged to have been manifestly inaccurate. It followed years of over-the-top imputations and insinuations directed at conservative politicians and thinkers of all stripes. For some in the media, every Republican is "extreme." In which case, why shouldn't Americans, and Europeans too, conclude that the press's reporting on, say, Marine Le Pen, the "far right" candidate for the president of France, is equally inaccurate? She may well be a new Hitler (her father, whom she has denounced, is a Holocaust denier), but the progressive liberal press has lost its credibility to make that case. Jean-Pierre Raffarin, a former center-right French prime minister, has warned that Le Pen could win the French election next year. If that's a terrible outcome, the now patently irresponsible press will bear a large share of the blame.

And Schadenfreude will have to give way to more serious activity.

Donald Trump Brings Season of New Hope
January 2, 2017

Samuel Johnson famously said that a second marriage is a triumph of hope over experience. Each ballot cast in November by a middle-class working man or woman in America, especially an unemployed working-class man or woman, and most especially an unemployed worker in Michigan, Ohio, Pennsylvania, or Wisconsin in yet another presidential election might also be seen as a triumph of hope over experience.

After all, Barack Obama ran on the slogan "Hope and Change," a slogan so beautifully mocked by Gov. Sarah Palin's quip, "How's that hopey-changey stuff workin' out for ya?" Gov. Palin, for all her faults, was on to something: that hopey-changey stuff hasn't worked out well at all. Search the internet for "President Obama's failed economic record" and you will get about 4,020,000 results in 0.56 seconds.

Unemployment may be down but the number of people who have dropped out of the work force has gone up: Labor force participation has fallen to a level not seen since March 1978. Gross domestic product growth has been anemic: Mr. Obama is the only president in history not to have a single year of growth of 3 percent or more. Meanwhile, poverty is up, as is the number of people on food stamps. Median income is down.

Could that failed record have been what drove Michelle Obama to say recently on the *Oprah Winfrey Show*, "We feel the difference now. See, now, we are feeling what not having hope feels like"? Probably not.

Probably she was simply expressing her disappointment and misgivings at Donald Trump's victory, though President-elect Trump graciously said, "I actually think she made that statement not meaning it the way it came out, I really do." Mr. Trump continued, "I assume she was talking about the past, not the future—'cause I'm telling you, we have tremendous hope, and tremendous promise."

Certainly that's what the country seems to think. The stock market has shot up since Trump was elected, a rise that mirrors the mood of the people. Hope and change are in the air again, but their progenitor isn't Barack Obama. Maybe that's what Mrs. Obama meant, that there was no longer any hope that her husband would be the agent of the change so desperately wanted by so many. For so long.

We should hope that Mrs. Obama's statement meant something different from what it seemed to be saying, coming as it did in the midst of the Christmas season. That season actually began on Advent Sunday, about four weeks before Christmas Day. For Christians, Christmas is a season of hope. And in the coming year, Americans—70 percent of whom identify themselves as Christians—may get some of what they hoped for. It's easy to understand why people care so much about politics, why they need to feel so much hope—about what the government does and, therefore, about who is in charge of deciding what government does. It matters. And it matters especially to people who have to make a living in the marketplace, and who can't insulate themselves from the unattractive parts of life, whether it's their boss, their neighbors, their health care system, or their failing schools.

Because government is now so large, it affects almost everything everyone does. During Mr. Obama's presidency, twenty thousand new regulations were added to the Code of Federal Regulations, a huge net of rules to catch, penalize, and ruin the unsuspecting. Harvey Silverglate wrote a book called *Three Felonies a Day*—that's what almost anyone who is doing anything in America is committing. For all the accusations of "fascism" leveled at Mr. Trump, it's the progressive liberals (the kind of people who govern with pen and phone instead of representative assemblies) who are the real authoritarians. They're the ones who want everyone to follow orders. "Hey, you. You can't limit adoptions to married couples." "Hey, you. You can't order that large soft drink." "Hey, you. Take your own bag to the supermarket." "Hey, you. Bake a cake for those homosexuals."

People have to care about government because government doesn't care about people. And they have to care so much that there's less time for caring about other things, like faith, hope, and charity, and the obligations they impose and the joys they impart.

But there seems to be a new kind of government coming, one that promises to eliminate 90 percent of regulations, cut taxes, make America prosperous again, and appoint judges who will preserve the culture for which generations have fought.

Americans, when freed from the tyranny of excessive government, will have more time and money for the spiritually rewarding tasks of working with and supporting the hallmarks of a civil society, the mediating institutions that minister—in ways that government never can—to those who are in necessity and tribulation. To prisoners and captives. To fatherless children and widows. To the desolate and oppressed. To the sick in mind, body, and estate. To the homeless and the hungry. To the forgotten old and the abandoned young.

To the least of the brothers and sisters of Him who came so silently, one night years ago, giving all the world hope.

That is the change some people were hoping for this Christmas season. That is the change they hope to experience in Anno Domini 2017.

Donald Trump and the Art of the Possible
January 5, 2017

On one of William F. Buckley Jr.'s *Firing Line* shows, Clare Boothe Luce intoned—as only someone who had seen the rise and fall of empires could—that "politics is the art of the possible." The sarcasm in Buckley's reply is unmistakable, though restrained, so taken aback must he have been by hearing such a cliché from a woman who took credit for FDR's phrase "A New Deal" and Churchill's "blood, sweat, and tears."

It went something like: "Oh really, Clare. That's so interesting." But Clare was not one for flinching. She might even have taken credit for that line, but then Bismarck's use of it, in 1867, would have revealed her to be rather older than she wanted to seem.

But *is* politics the art of the possible—the art of only the possible?

Jim DeMint, the president of The Heritage Foundation, has suggested that the phrase traps us in the amber of yesteryear, where conservatives have been stuck for decades.

In Buckley's 1955 mission statement for *National Review*, he described conservatives as, essentially, people "who have not made their peace with the New Deal." But people calling themselves conservatives, by the score, by the hundreds, by the thousands long ago made peace with the New Deal, as they accepted not only the programs but the premise of FDR's game-changing political and social policies: government knows best; therefore government will direct the economy and redistribute wealth in a more equitable fashion than the market or civil society can or will.

The New Deal was expanded by Lyndon Johnson's Great Society. We now have eighty programs costing more than $700 billion a year fighting poverty. Reagan was right: We waged war on poverty and poverty won. There has been no net decrease in poverty since the sixties.

Then came Nixon, and then went Nixon, but leaving us, before leaving himself, a slew of New-Deal-Great-Society-type programs: the Occupational Safety and Health Administration, the Environmental Protection Agency, the National Oceanic and Atmospheric Administration, the 1972 Noise Control Act, the 1972 Marine Mammal Protection Act, the 1973 Endangered Species Act, the 1974 Safe Drinking Water Act, and probably more regulations than had been imposed on the economy since the New Deal.

Remarkably, after all that, the liberal-progressives did him in anyway (he'd nailed Alger Hiss), prompting the late, great M. Stanton Evans to remark that he was never *for* Nixon, *until* Watergate. Evans said that when you looked at wage and price controls, OSHA, EPA, détente and Kissinger, going to China, and all the other stuff Nixon was doing, Watergate was like a breath of fresh air.

But the smog returned, and we had the Bushes. And then Obama, and his more than *twenty thousand* regulations. The National Association of Manufacturers estimates that regulations today cost $18,000 *per job*.

So it's easy to understand why many conservatives abandoned any plan of making no peace with the New Deal: politics is the art of the possible.

Until it isn't.

Which looks like now.

The Republicans have won all three houses, which is more than Ronald Reagan did in 1980, and which gives Trump a better chance to enact his programs than Reagan had. Maybe he *can* make America great again—a phrase no doubt whispered to him in his baby carriage by Clare Luce.

Trump has said he plans to appoint as federal judges people who will uphold and defend the Constitution; repeal Obamacare; secure the border; fix the tax code; promote school choice; make war on the regulatory state; defund Planned Parenthood; eliminate Dodd–Frank and perhaps Sarbanes–Oxley too; and on and on and on. The more he does at once, the easier it will be: newspapers have only one front page.

At a recent gathering of conservatives and people close to the Trump transition team, the talk was of reducing the corporate tax rate to 15 percent and lowering the personal income tax—and perhaps stuffing a far-smaller IRS into a room at the Department of the Treasury. One said the Trump administration would promote the building of pipelines to make the country's supply of natural gas more available—it's the ultimate infrastructure project and isn't financed by government. They estimate that each of those policies would increase GDP by 1 percent. GDP has been flat for the seven long years of the Obama Recession.

One panelist suggested eliminating the payroll tax, which only Al Gore (inventor of the internet and man who once said E Pluribus Unum means "Out of One, Many") thinks goes into a lockbox where it waits, safe from political hands, to be returned to the workers who paid it.

The policy people spoke of Trump's endorsement of the "penny plan", under which Congress would reduce discretionary spending by 1 percent each year (excluding defense, Social Security, Medicare, and Medicaid).

There was even talk of returning to the gold standard, one panelist saying that you can't have free trade with floating currencies—a position Donald Trump seems instinctively to have understood, if not articulate. He focused on NAFTA, but the real problem, the panelist said, is that the peso went from being worth 33¢ in 1994 to 5¢ in 2016.

Will Trump do it all? Probably not. Trump is not a conservative, after all. He's a maverick. But the lefty, progressive great-grand-children of the New Deal fear he'll do it all. They know now, if they didn't before, that Trump has a backbone like the Washington Monument, an army of free marketeers and socially conservative policy people that could fill the Washington Mall, and a MAGAphone that lets him ignore the media.

Soon, sooner than they think—or conservatives ever dreamed—the art of navigating within national policies that allow freedom, opportunity, prosperity, and civil society to flourish may be the only politics that's possible.

Hillary Clinton and the Rule of Law
February 2, 2017

> *"A contempt of the laws is the high road to anarchy."*
> —Alexander Hamilton

Hillary Clinton's email scandal and the Clinton Foundation scandal are back in the news, as they are likely to be for years to come. At his confirmation hearing, Attorney General–designate Jeff Sessions said he would recuse himself from all investigations involving the Clintons.

Last November, President Donald Trump said that his preference was for no further investigation of Hillary Clinton or the Clinton Foundation. A decision (which does not seem to have been made yet) not to continue any investigation raises at least three concerns:

1). Deciding whether to prosecute someone isn't normally the president's decision to make. It's the job of "the system."

"The system" may sound amorphous, but in fact "the system" is what we call "the rule of law." That rule is not just an arcane concept that interests lawyers and public policy mavens. The rule of law is probably the single most important governing concept we have—far more important than democracy. The rule of law elevates the weakest citizen to the level of the most powerful.

In this case, the rule of law would see the FBI and the Justice Department make the determinations whether or not to continue investigating and to prosecute. Nevertheless, the attorney general can always exercise prosecutorial discretion and decide to drop an investigation without necessarily traducing the rule of law. And if the AG (in this case, the deputy AG, Mr. Sessions having recused himself) can make that decision, so can his boss, the president.

2) Dropping the case raises the question of fairness.

Fairness may be an elusive concept; even so, we tend to know it's missing when we don't see it. It is true that it's not always possible to be fair. Sometime it's necessary to be just. But in this case, there are people who have done far less than what Mrs. Clinton has already been shown to have done and who have been punished for it. Why should they have to pay a price if she does not? The response that life is not fair does not entirely satisfy.

In 2009, Kristian Saucier, a Navy machinist, took six photos labeled "confidential/restricted" of the nuclear submarine USS *Alexandria*'s classified propulsion system. Saucier was sentenced to one year in prison and six months of home confinement following his release, and to perform one hundred hours of community service.

In 2015, Bryan H. Nishimura, a naval reservist deployed in Afghanistan in 2007 and 2008, pleaded guilty to unauthorized removal and retention of classified materials. There was no evidence, however, that Nishimura intended to distribute the classified information to unauthorized personnel. Nishimura pleaded guilty and was sentenced to two years of probation, assessed a $7,500 fine, and ordered to surrender his security clearance.

And Gen. David Petraeus, hero of the Iraq War, gave classified material to another person who had a security clearance but no "need to know." Gen. Petraeus was sentenced to two years probation and ordered to pay a $100,000 fine.

3) Danger lurks in curtailing the investigation.

Who knows what evils the Clinton Foundation engaged in? The answer is: many people know—the many people who have been investigating it. They know things. And it is almost inconceivable that there will be no leaks. Those leaks would embarrass Donald Trump for letting Mrs. Clinton escape, even as they would embarrass Mrs. Clinton—always assuming it's possible to embarrass a Clinton.

One can argue that continuing to investigate and perhaps prosecute Mrs. Clinton would continue to divide the nation, though we should note that it appears to be the hard-core Left that is foment-ing the divisive activity. Even so, one can argue that trying to heal that divide is more important than strictly observing the rule of law. Perhaps. People will differ.

What is more difficult to differ on, however, is how people like Nishimura and Saucier, and probably dozens like them, should be treated if Mrs. Clinton et al. are allowed to escape investigation, and perhaps prosecution and punishment.

If Mr. Trump decides to stop the investigation of the Clintons, he should also pardon all people currently in situations similar to those of Nishimura and Saucier. Such a pardon would be both fair and supportive of the rule of law because it would tend to equalize the small fry and the kingpins.

In addition, such pardons, especially if there were lots of them, would make apparent the venality of Mrs. Clinton and make the case for her guilt, but without the trauma of another Watergate-like circus. Mrs. Clinton, though free to spend time with her loving hus-band, would appear in the public's mind to be guilty, yet would have no way of being exonerated.

That's not a perfect outcome. But it's not bad either.

Draining the Independent Regulatory Agency Swamp

February 21, 2017

One of the headlines most frightening to progressive liberals would probably be "Extra! Extra! Donald Trump to abide by Constitution!" You can almost feel them begin to shake.

One good thing President Obama taught us was never to let a crisis go to waste. (Actually it was Obama's first White House chief of staff, Rahm Emanuel, now the somewhat disgraced mayor of Chicago which on his watch has become the murder capital of the United States, who made the phrase famous, even if he didn't invent it.) Another way of putting the thought is that every crisis should be seen as an opportunity.

President Trump has a plethora of crises to manage if he is to make America great again, and one of the most important of those is taming the so-called independent regulatory agencies. There are dozens of them—perhaps scores: no one seems to know—and they wield tremendous regulatory influence and control over just about every aspect of Americans' lives, which means they will need to be reined in if Trump is to reach his goal of cutting 90 percent of regulations.

And the agencies exist essentially outside the law. At least they exist outside the Constitution, which is the highest law of the land. Or at the very least, they exist outside a strictly construed Constitution, which is the way President Trump has said the Constitution should be construed.

President Trump's first not-to-be-missed opportunity to deal with the "independent" agencies is presented by the Consumer Finance Protection Bureau described by House Financial Services Chairman Jeb Hensarling, a Texas Republican, as "arguably the most powerful and least accountable Washington bureaucracy in American history."

Established as part of the Dodd–Frank law after the 2008 financial crisis, the CFPB has only a single commissioner. And because the CFPB was established as a unit within the Federal Reserve System, it gets its funding directly from the Federal Reserve, which in turn gets its funds from its own operations.

So, in this great democracy of ours, who's in charge of the CFPB? In theory the people are, but only, of course, through their representatives in the legislative branch who raise funds for the operations of the government, and through the executive branch which supervises the work of the agencies. But the people are not in charge of the CFPB since their elected officials control neither the CFPB's budget nor the actions of its chairman.

This situation is made for Donald Trump.

In a recent case involving an enforcement action brought by the CFPB against mortgage lender PHH, PHH challenged the CFPB's action in US Court of Appeals for the District of Columbia Circuit, where a three-judge panel reversed the enforcement action. The court said, among other things, that "the CFPB's order violated bedrock principles of due process." That's about what you'd expect from an agency not subject to any political control. Two of the three judges ruled also that the structure of the agency was unconstitutional.

Now the Trump administration is said to be looking for reasons to justify firing CFPB Chairman Richard Cordray, who can be removed, according to statute, only for cause ("inefficiency," "neglect of duty,"or "malfeasance"). It is extremely unlikely they will find such cause.

What Trump should do is stop looking for cause and simply deliver to Mr. Cordray his iconic phrase: "You're fired!" (Just because your goal is to drain the swamp doesn't mean you can't shoot a few alligators along the way.)

The problem is not just the CFPB. It's the whole concept of independent regulatory agencies. The Constitution provides for only three branches of government: congress, the executive branch, and the judiciary. Independent agencies fall into none of those categories.

Although the theory is that the agencies are independent of the executive branch, which is what makes them unconstitutional, under the Obama administration that was not always the case. President Obama instructed, or pressured, the Federal Communications Commission into a very controversial decision to protect so-called "net neutrality." FCC chairman Tom Wheeler resigned as soon as Trump became president, but suppose he had not? Should Trump have been saddled with a commissioner who had been doing President Obama's bidding?

The Obama–Wheeler partnership is actually the way the system *should* work: the president should make the decisions and then be held accountable for them. And if a commissioner of an agency doesn't do what the president wants, he should be fired.

Of course, at the moment it's slightly more complex than that. In 1935, the Supreme Court held that President Roosevelt did not have the authority to fire a commissioner of the Federal Trade Commission.* The decision is clearly wrong. The Supreme Court said that the debates over the creation of the Federal Trade Commission demonstrated that the commission was not to be subject to anybody in the government, but only to "the people."

Please. On its face, that upends the whole constitutional scheme. By attempting to make the commission subject only to "the people," Congress made it subject to no one. Being free from legislative or executive branch (i.e., political) domination or control means being

---

* http://t-c-a.info/obama-undermines-so-called-agencies

free from democratic accountability. That may please the kind of people who like government by pen and phone, but not, probably, the people who are so governed.

A few good appointments of strict constructionists to the Supreme Court could go a long way toward helping President Trump meet his goal of eliminating 90 percent of the country's regulations—as well as rattling and rolling the progressive liberals. The Court wouldn't have to eliminate the so-called independent regulatory agencies altogether. It could just hold, as the court of appeals did in the CFPB case, that they are not independent, but subject to the control of the president, a ruling that just might produce the headline, "Extra! Extra! Supreme Court Follows Constitution."

Drain the Research Swamp
March 13, 2017

President Trump has made it reasonably clear that he is not concerned about the deficit, though he hasn't gotten around yet to appropriating Ronald Reagan's quip that the deficit is big enough to look after itself. As if thumbing his nose at the deficit, Trump plans to reduce the corporate income tax to 15 percent. The respected and nonpartisan Tax Foundation estimates that, even scored dynamically, the new rate will reduce federal revenue by $1.54 trillion over the next decade, or an average of about $154 billion each year. Even in Washington, that's serious money.

Like the deficit, the corporate tax revenue shortfall also may be big enough to look after itself, but that's no reason not to give it some help. And help is only a research grant—or ten thousand research grants—away. The federal government gave out an estimated $147 billion in research grants in 2016: $79 billion for defense, $68 billion for non-defense.

So: PRESTO! Cancel all the research grants and the net loss to the federal treasury from the corporate tax cut becomes manageable. Corporations can spend on research however much of their tax savings they want to and in whatever ways they deem useful.

Defense mavens would not be happy. They would say it is unlikely that the country's defense needs could be met by industry's developing adaptations of civilian sector technology for the government. Not wishing to pick a fight with people who spend billions for bombs, let's just eliminate, for now, the spending on non-defense research.

Adult readers know intuitively that much of the research money granted by the federal government is probably nothing more than political payola.

A case in point: in 1982 the federal Department of Education sought to run an actual competition for the "research" funds it was supposed to award on a competitive basis to "labs" and "centers" (as they were called) that did research on educational issues. The labs and centers would submit proposals, and the department would fund the best of them. When Congress got wind of the scheme to go back to competitive bidding, it attached a rider to a bill that required the department to continue to give the funds to the same organizations that had been receiving them for years. It became embarrassingly apparent (if Congress is capable of being embarrassed) that the grants had nothing whatsoever to do with quality research. They were pure payola from the congressmen to their constituents.

Who doubts the situation is the same with much of the $68 billion of non-defense research grants that will be dispensed this year? And who doubts that privately directed research would be more useful than government-funded and controlled research?

One who says he doubts that is L. Rafael Reif, who, writing in the *Wall Street Journal*, says, "The qualities that make industry good at applied research and development—an appetite for immediate commercialization, a laser focus on consumer demand, an obligation to maximize short-term returns, and a proprietary attitude about information—make industry a bad fit for supporting basic scientific research." Mr. Reif is the president of MIT, and readers with a laser focus on full disclosure will want to know how much money MIT gets from the federal government, a datum not vouchsafed to us by Mr. Reif.

Serious doubters are urged to read *The Evolution of Everything: How New Ideas Emerge* by Matt Ridley. He quotes Terence Kealey, a biochemist turned economist, who says that when you examine the history of innovation, you find that scientific breakthroughs are the results, not the causes, of technological change. "It is no accident," writes Ridley, "that astronomy blossomed in the wake of the age of exploration. The steam engine owed almost nothing to the science of thermodynamics, but the science of thermodynamics owed almost everything to the steam engine. The flowering of chemistry in the late nineteenth and early twentieth centuries was driven by the needs of dye makers. The discovery of the structure of DNA depended heavily on X-ray crystallography of biological molecules, a technique developed in the wool industry to try to improve textiles."

Adam Smith noticed the same flow, reporting in *The Wealth of Nations* that "a great part of the machines made use of in those manufactures . . . were originally the inventions of common workmen."

Ridley writes, "In the late nineteenth and early twentieth centuries, Britain and the United States made huge contributions to science with negligible public funding, while Germany and France, with hefty public funding, achieved no greater results in science or economics."

"In 2003," Ridley reports, "the OECD [Organization for Economic Co-operation and Development] published a paper on 'sources of growth' in OECD countries between 1971 and 1998, finding to its explicit surprise that whereas privately funded research and development stimulated economic growth, publicly funded research had no economic impact whatsoever. None."

Mr. Reif, and no doubt others, will point to discoveries that resulted from federally funded projects. But given the amount of taxpayer money—billions and billions of dollars—granted by the federal government over many decades, we should be surprised, and appalled, if it had produced *nothing*. That argument would convince only a grant recipient.

Donald Trump is the perfect change agent for draining the research swamp, and the perfect time is now, when he's cutting the corporate income tax, and cutting it by more than 57 percent! Draining the research swamp immediately, thereby maximizing the long-term returns, is a breakthrough government could justly take pride in producing.

Billionaires for Deregulation

April 4, 2017

The *New York Times* is having a hissy-fit over billionaire "investor" Carl Icahn's being named as President Trump's special advisor on regulatory matters, which many hope means *deregulatory* matters. What's troubling the *Times* is that Mr. Icahn has been working on deregulating the Environmental Protection Agency and particularly a regulation that governs the way corn-based ethanol is mixed with gasoline. The problem, for the *Times*, is that Mr. Icahn owns a company that would have saved a couple of hundred million dollars last year if the fix Mr. Icahn is recommending had been in place. Is that a conflict of interest?

No doubt it reminds the *Times* of the Maryland liquor magnate who was appointed head of the state's alcoholic beverages control agency and was accused of having a conflict of interest. He responded, indignantly, that he had no intention whatsoever of running the government agency in a way that would conflict with his business interests.

The real problem is that a billionaire, almost by definition, has investments, essentially, everywhere. Which means that if President Trump can make America great again, billionaires are going to profit like gang busters, or, the way the *Times* tends to view billionaires (except George Soros), like economic gangsters.

There's a huge opportunity for growth in the economy because the Obama crowd, the regulatory-state progressives, adopted a slew of anti-growth policies that prolonged the Obama Recession.

It's called the Obama Recession because growth was so slow during Obama's time in office, and that wasn't because of the alignment of the stars or the collapse of the Peruvian anchovy harvest. It was because the economy was overregulated by progressive legislation like Dodd–Frank. In the recession of 1982, unemployment reached 10.8 percent in December. The highest it reached in Obama's time in office was 10 percent, in October 2009. GDP growth averaged 2.2 percent through the first 25 quarters of President Obama's "recovery," whereas GDP advanced at a 4.6 percent annual pace during the comparable period for President Reagan.

What's a poor billionaire like Icahn to do if he wants to help his country? Sell all his stocks and buy an index fund? But if the economy improves the way Trump and Icahn (and maybe even George Soros) hope, index funds will go up too. It is too much to expect that the *Times* will not object to Icahn's owning an index fund.

Where is he supposed to hide his money? In his socks—designed by Ivanka Trump? According to *Forbes* magazine, Icahn is worth $16.6 billion, making him the twenty-sixth wealthiest person on the *Forbes* 400 list. If Icahn bought enough of Ivanka's socks to store that much money, she'd make a killing—and then what would the *Times* say?

The problem with the *Times'* scare piece—and this should be obvious even to *Times* readers—is that Carl Icahn is surely not the first nor the only person to say that regulations governing the way corn-based ethanol is mixed with gasoline should be changed. This is not a policy Icahn thought up solely to benefit his companies. And probably all the rest of the recommendations he will make will have been written about and recommended by a slew of public policy organizations over a number of years. Icahn is simply organizing the deregulatory effort.

Mr. Icahn isn't being paid—what do you pay a man who has $16.6 billion?—so that can't be an objection. Come to think of it, what do you give a man worth $16B for his birthday?

Nor can President Trump be stopped from conversing with Mr. Icahn. Both of them retain their First Amendment rights—Hillary Clinton having lost the election—which means that after a round of golf at Mar-a-Lago they can discuss matters like . . . regulations governing the way corn-based ethanol is mixed with gasoline.

What the *Times* really doesn't like, of course, are the recommendations—any recommendations—for deregulating the economy. For reasons known only perhaps to the Peruvian anchovies, the Democratic Party has abandoned the working men and women of America by signing on to the left wing's crazy anti-economic agenda, including most especially their anti-energy policies. As a result of those policies, some Americans have lost their jobs, and the average American hasn't seen a pay raise in fifteen years. That's why they voted for Trump. And they would surely rather have even a self-interested billionaire help jazz up the economy than a penniless socialist promote the kind of anti-job economic policy nostrums favored by the *New York Times*.

Those are the policies Trump has said he wants to change, and he is likely to enlist anyone willing to help. Even your local friendly billionaire.

Love the socks, Carl.

Advice and Consent in the Time of Obstruction
April 25, 2017

Desperate times call forth diabolical pleasures, and what could give more pleasure than stopping the obstructionist Democrats dead in their tracks.

There are more than five hundred unfilled executive branch positions and more than 120 judicial vacancies. If the Democrats decide to require a minimum of thirty hours of debate on *each* nominee, as they are entitled to do under Senate rules, confirming all of President Trump's nominees could take, essentially, *forever*—i.e., for President Trump's whole first term. This is the revenge of the sore losers.

President Trump has said he doesn't need to fill all the positions, and that is technically true. But he has to fill many of them if he is going to get control of the federal bureaucracy, which he must do if he is to fulfill his oath to take care that the laws be faithfully executed.

The solution to the problem is simple, unconventional, and not without precedent. President Trump should, pursuant to Article II, §2, cl. 3 of the Constitution, simply appoint hundreds of people to the vacant positions during a congressional recess.

It is true that recess appointments are normally thought of as one-off operations. But there is no reason why five hundred people couldn't be appointed during a recess.

In 1903, more than a half century before modern cesium atomic clocks (which are accurate to one second in 1.4 million years), Teddy Roosevelt made 193 recess appointments during—and "during" is a generous word under the circumstance—the fractional nanosecond when, as the gavel hit the desk, one congressional session ended and the next began. Congress was not amused.

Barrack Obama tried the recess appointment gambit, but if he spent more than a nanosecond studying the rules it didn't show—though, more likely, he did know the rules but thought he could get away with breaking them. He didn't. His recess appointment of three people to the National Labor Relations Board while the Senate was on a three-day break was invalidated by the Supreme Court in *National Labor Relations Board v. Noel Canning*. The court held that the three-day break was not a recess. The vote was 9-0, the kind of lopsided decision that stimulates Hillary Clinton to tweeting. The Court indicated that the president may use the recess appointment power only during a Senate recess of ten days or longer.

So: President Trump can ask the Senate majority leader, Mitch McConnell (R–KY), to recess the Senate for eleven days (one day extra to play it safe) and on day eleven appoint five hundred people to executive branch positions, and perhaps a few to the federal bench as well.

The recess appointees could serve until the end of the next session of Congress, i.e., almost two years, which is about as long as many executive branch appointees serve anyway.

Even though the solution to the problem is easy, we should ask, Is this a good idea? In a better world, the answer would certainly be, No. Conservatives should always be suspicious of the exercise of power by the executive.

But the unhinged Democrats' obstruction is quite beyond normal and calls for a similar response. For years—decades, actually—a liberal Supreme Court by its decisions has "enacted" legislation that Democrats were unable to get Congress to enact. Now, as the Democrats are loath to give up the legislating power of the Supreme Court (hence the stonewalling of Judge Gorsuch), so are they loath to allow the executive branch to function properly.

Of course the real problem is that the country is seriously divided. It no longer has a common politics. The progressive liberals, heirs of Wilson, Roosevelt, Johnson, and Obama, devotees of the administrative regulatory state and the sixties' counterculture, just don't have the same concept of government and its proper role as the conservative Trump people, heirs of Coolidge and Reagan, and free marketeers tempered by concerns for neighborhood, custom, and social stability. The progressive liberals have lost the confidence of the country, as is demonstrated not just by the 2016 presidential election but by state and local elections over the last six years. Their time is over. They are going.

But they are not going quietly. Instead, they are obstructing the governing process which is supposed to carry out the will of the people as expressed at the ballot box.

That is why President Trump, channeling his inner Teddy Roosevelt, should take the desperate measure of appointing executive branch personnel wholesale. He can revel diabolically in the discomfort of the sore losers who seek to obstruct (the duration of which discomfort, and the attendant Schadenfreude, will be measurable by a ticktockingly dillydallying pendulum clock) while teaching them the lesson that obstruction has a price: losing the opportunity to have the Senate advise and consent.

Oilman Rex Tillerson and Ukraine
April 26, 2017

"Why should US taxpayers be interested in Ukraine?" Secretary of State Rex Tillerson was heard, or overheard, to ask at a recent meeting of the Group of Seven foreign ministers. The remark sent the usually astute Anne Applebaum into medium dudgeon.

Writing in the *Washington Post*, she commented, snidely: "Unlike everyone who has held the job for at least the past century, he has no experience in diplomacy, politics or the military; instead he has spent his life extracting oil and selling it for profit."

Whoa, Nellie. Extracting oil indeed.

Does the description conjure up a vision of a man in overalls digging in the sand? I forget: Do we have it in for people in overalls now? Or people who dig for a living? Or are the overalls meant only to be contrasted with the pinstriped suits diplomats wear—the kind of diplomats who effected the removal of all chemical weapons from Syria and prevented North Korea from getting the bomb?

And what is the problem we are meant to infer from "selling it for a profit"? What should Tillerson have been doing all those years he was at Exxon? Selling oil for a loss?

Saying Tillerson has spent his life extracting oil without listing his very considerable executive experience is not even like saying Jack Kennedy and Bill Clinton spent their lives messing around with girls while omitting to say also that they were US presidents because it's true that those two did fool around with girls. Lots of them, apparently. Whereas there's no indication in Tillerson's biography that he himself has ever actually extracted oil. Nor are there any readily available photos of him in overalls.

It is possible, of course, that he was occasionally espied in overalls at the University of Texas at Austin, from which he received a bachelor's degree in civil engineering in 1975, but we have no evidence of that. We do know, however, that later that year, at the age of twenty-three, Tillerson joined Exxon as a production engineer.

In subsequent years, Tillerson became (deep breath): general manager of the central production division of Exxon USA; president of Exxon Yemen Inc. and Esso Exploration and Production Khorat Inc. (in Thailand); a vice president of Exxon Ventures (CIS); president of Exxon Neftegas Limited with responsibility for Exxon's holdings in Russia and the Caspian Sea; executive vice president of ExxonMobil Development Company; president and director of ExxonMobil; and, on January 1, 2006, chairman and chief executive officer of ExxonMobil.

ExxonMobil has 83,700 employees and its revenue is $246 billion, making it the world's seventh-largest company by revenue.

By contrast, the State Department has 69,000 employees and revenue of about $47.4 billion, making it the 192nd largest operation by revenue, just behind FedEx.

Oh, no. Wait a minute. The State Department doesn't have revenue. The $47.4 billion is the amount it spends. Whew! Anne Applebaum might have accused them of doing something for profit.

Overalls or no overalls, Tillerson's real skill, of course, is managing. His experience so exceeds the experience of the last two occupants of the office, Hillary Clinton and John Kerry, that we (including Applebaum) should assume that he can manage the job at least as well as they did—admittedly, an embarrassingly low bar.

Secretary Tillerson's remark, "Why should US taxpayers be interested in Ukraine?" was sufficiently provocative to cause the State Department to describe it as a "rhetorical device."

But Applebaum saw it as a gaffe, prompting her to say that selling (promoting) something intangible, like American values and influence, can't be achieved using the tactics of selling oil. Are we sure about that?

And just what, actually, is the US taxpayers' interest in Ukraine? Applebaum's answer is: the principle of border security. That, she says, is what turned Europe into "a safe and peaceful trading alliance," which made it rich and, inter alia, made the United States rich as well.

Funny: that sounds like the kind of thing a businessman, even one with less experience than Secretary Tillerson, might understand even better than a seasoned diplomat who had spent a lifetime in think tanks and government. Or a columnist.

It's a good guess that the gravamen of Applebaum's complaint is that Tillerson was not as verbally anti-Russian as she would like. But Russia, with its many nuclear weapons, is not Secretary Tillerson's only problem: he has to deal also with North Korea and Iran—and a shrunken US military that is not currently prepared to fight a three-front war. The US taxpayers' resources and patience are not unlimited (see: election of Donald Trump), raising, if not answering, the question, Why should US taxpayers be interested in Ukraine?

Trump's 100 Days vs. Democrats' 100 Days of Resistance: A Progress Report

April 29, 2017

There's no magic to the first hundred days of a president's administration, other than the memory—sacred to liberal progressives—of the fundamental changes to America that Franklin Roosevelt made in his first hundred days.

Roosevelt was inaugurated on March 4, 1933. (The date of inaugurations was moved to January 20 by the passage of the Twentieth Amendment in 1933.) By the 104th day of his presidency, Roosevelt, aided by his advisor, Harry Hopkins (the most important of all Soviet wartime agents in the United States), had signed, among others, the Agricultural Adjustment Act, which paid farmers not to farm; the Truth-in-Securities Act; the Glass–Steagall Act; the

National Industrial Recovery Act, later struck down by the Supreme Court; and bills creating the Federal Deposit Insurance Corporation, the Tennessee Valley Authority, and the Home Owners Loan Corp. It may be a stretch, but not a big one, to say Roosevelt created the welfare state in a hundred days.

Liberal progressives are now hugely enjoying (and fooling) themselves at what they claim is the lack of legislation enacted during Donald Trump's first hundred days—and chastising him for getting so little done.

Of course, the less legislation there is, the happier they are, since they do, or will, oppose most of Trump's proposals, as they have opposed most of the president's nominees to executive branch positions.

Joe Peyronnin writes in *The Huffington Post* that "Trump has had the worst first 100 days of any modern-era president."

MSNBC analyst Jonathan Alter said, "This is the worst, least successful, first 100 days since it became a concept in 1933."

Charles Blow writing in the *New York Times* pats himself and others on the back saying, "The resistance to the travesty of Donald Trump's presidency is holding up just fine, thank you very much." (Actually, it isn't.)

The Nation ran a piece that said, "The great lesson of these first 100 days is that, even when Republicans control Washington, resistance is possible."

The *New Yorker* even ran a piece on April 17 by John Cassidy entitled "The Trump Resistance: A Progress Report." This is all catharsis for Hillary's supporters, the non-deplorables. That's OK. We're a rich country. Everyone can have something. Hillary's supporters have Resistance as Catharsis. Trump's have Schadenfreude. Both are growth stocks.

But the catharsis is taking a toll on the political integrity of the Trump opposition. How else to explain this line from Cassidy's piece: "To the extent that the goal of the resistance is to make sure the checks and balances in the American political system work as intended, and to prevent the emergence of an overweening presidency, or a potential despot, it seems to be succeeding." Are the *New Yorker* and John Cassidy turning their backs on the way Barack Obama governed? By pen, and phone, and executive order? That (if true—and it isn't) would suggest Donald Trump has already been more successful than even his own supporters dreamed—and well before a hundred days were up.

Trump supporters need not despair at the lack of major legislation so far. The hundred-day mark is purely arbitrary. A more meaningful period is the one that starts on the day of the inauguration and goes to the beginning of Congress's summer recess (July 28, 2017). But even that is an arbitrary timeline. Trump's stated goals are to make fundamental changes in the way the country has been governed since Harry Hopkins was whispering communist nostrums into Roosevelt's ear.

Despite the resistance's claim that they seem to be succeeding, all is not well for them. President Trump has already, inter alia: signed twenty-five executive orders (the most of any first hundred-day period in more than fifty years); gotten a Supreme Court nominee confirmed; instituted immigration policies that have driven illegal border crossings to a seventeen-year low; and removed job-killing regulations.

Adam Cohen, author of "Nothing to Fear: FDR's Inner Circle and the Hundred Days That Created Modern America" says, "Even if there are not many major tangible accomplishments, [Trump's] administration has changed the political and cultural trajectory of the country—not as much as FDR did following Herbert Hoover, but more than the average new president does."

What President Trump hasn't accomplished, yet, is getting enacted the big ticket items he campaigned on: repealing ObamaCare, restructuring the tax code, building the wall, rebuilding the military, and deconstructing the administrative state.

But those items are hugely controversial, even among Republicans. They will take time. Fortunately, there is time. Trump still has a thousand days to go . . . in his first term.

The bad news for the resistance is that if the election were held (again) today, Hillary would still lose. That means Resistance-as-Catharsis will be big business for a long time to come.

But not as big as Schadenfreude.

John Jimenez Built That

May 4, 2017

"You didn't build that!" may be an iconic Obama phrase, but a lot of Americans *have* built a lot of businesses and are proud of it.

Calvin Coolidge said famously that the chief business of the American people is business. And the chief kind of business of the American people is small business. In 2010 there were 28 million small businesses (not including John Jimenez's because he hadn't started his yet) but only 18,500 firms with five hundred employees or more. According to the Small Business Administration, the 28 million small businesses in America account for 54 percent of all US sales. Small businesses provide 55 percent of all jobs and have provided 66 percent of all net new jobs since the 1970s.

Those figures mean that across America, every day, people like John Jimenez are starting businesses to make a living for their families and to provide a product or service for their fellow Americans. Stop for a moment and consider the vastness of America. That small business creativity is truly a wonder of the modern world.

But starting a business usually requires more than just an idea and the drive to realize it: it requires capital too. That's not hard to get, at least not if you're a Harvard dropout.

But suppose the spoon in your mouth when you were born was made of McDonald's plastic: then how do you get your start-up capital (even if you don't need very much of it)?

Go to a bank for a small business loan? Dream on! And what you're dreaming of is the pre-Obama-regulated world. Banks don't lend to small businesses any more. It's too risky—not the loans themselves, but the response of the Obama bank regulators—which is why small regional banks are either going out of business or stopping lending to people who want to start small businesses, like John Jimenez.

John Jimenez had a very simple idea: cut busy executives' hair in *their* offices instead of making them come to *his* office—which we call a barber shop. That may not be the next Windows, Google, or Uber. But it is, sort of, Haircuts 2.0.

So Jimenez entered a young entrepreneurs competition run by the Network for Teaching Entrepreneurship (NFTE). NFTE's mission statement is: "to provide programs that inspire young people from low-income communities to stay in school, to recognize business opportunities and to plan for successful futures." But NFTE doesn't just provide programs: they also give out money to aspiring young entrepreneurs who win an NFTE competition, like John Jimenez.

Jimenez won a total of $4,000 from NFTE. With that seed capital he started and built his business, which with luck will take him far—or at least away from the streets of Harlem, New York, where he was recently robbed of a day's take.

Jimenez's family situation is precarious, and it's really not necessary to describe it in detail here. If you're reading this you probably have little or no experience with the kind of low-income family life Jimenez has had. He is probably the first in his family to graduate from high school (which he will do in a few weeks). He is certainly the first in his family to go to college—where he intends to continue his business.

And he'll continue working on developing an app, for both barbers and customers. He wants to become the Uber of barbering. You see, Jimenez is not just a barber or an app designer. He's an American entrepreneur.

The numbers he gave to NFTE for the competition have to make you smile. And they should make his college professors smile too.

Investment Opportunity: $4,794
Annual Operating Costs: $47,497
Annual Sales: 2,559 Units of Sale (i.e., haircuts!)
Annual Profit: $46,685
Return on Sales: 46 percent
Return on Investment: 974 percent (!)

An investment of $4,794 isn't a whole lot, but a return on investment of 974 percent is likely to beat Microsoft, Google, and Uber this year.

The take-away from the Jimenez story is how little money it took to launch this young man on the path to independence—$4,000! That money has changed his life and likely the lives of other young people he meets, to whom he can tell his story of entrepreneurship and hope. And American generosity.

You can find John Jimenez's business on the web. It's called GroomedOnTheGo.com.

John Jimenez built that.

Saying Goodbye to Grandma
May 10, 2017

In his first month in office, Donald Trump delivered on his promise to be an anti-abortion president and help stop our national shame. He reinstated the "Mexico City Policy" that bans federal funding to international groups that provide abortions.

Then, second, he appointed two people opposed to abortion, Charmaine Yoest and Teresa Manning, to positions at the Department of Health and Human Services.

Now he's rounding third with his executive order on religious freedom which will provide regulatory relief for religious objectors to Obamacare's burdensome preventive services mandate, a position supported by the Supreme Court's decision in *Hobby Lobby*.

If he is able, in September, to defund Planned Parenthood, that will make it a homerun. Donald Trump will go down as a great anti-abortion president.

The country needs that, given that Democratic National Committee Chairman Tom Perez has announced that being pro-abortion is now "not negotiable" for Democrats. If abortion weren't such a serious matter, the Democrats' position would be almost comical.

Bryce Covert, the economic policy editor at ThinkProgress and a contributor to *The Nation*, wrote nine hundred words on the topic for the *New York Times*. He picked on Bernie Sanders for supporting a candidate for mayor of Omaha who is not pro-abortion.

Covert describes how abortions can be economically beneficial to women, especially working women. Covert writes: "The glaring mistake they [i.e., miscreant Democrats] all make, however, is thinking that there is any way to disentangle reproductive rights from economic issues."

For serious people, the debate over abortion is not about economic issues. It's over whether what actually happens during an abortion is good or bad.

Suppose we substitute killing a grandmother for abortion in Mr. Covert's article. Some of Mr. Covert's sentences would read as follows:

> Economics reverberates throughout women's lives when they can't terminate their grandmothers. In a study of women who sought to terminate their grandmothers, those who were unsuccessful were three times as likely to fall into poverty over the following two years as those women who were able to terminate, despite beginning in comparable financial situations. They were also more likely to wind up unemployed.
>
> A woman in a precarious financial situation who knows she can't afford a grandmother can easily fall farther behind if she has to care for a grandmother, something that costs the average person thousands of dollars a year. In a country that offers little to no paid leave, grandmother-care assistance, or other supports, a grandmother who needs care can make it impossibly difficult to hold down a job or get a higher degree.

There you have the case for terminating grandma. Air-tight!

If it weren't so tragic, it might be comical. It reminds one a bit of movies that have cross dialogue: two characters think they're talking about the same thing but aren't, as in this scene from *Moulin Rouge*.

(Christian is trying to read his poetry to Satine, but she thinks he's talking about something else.)

Satine: A little supper? Maybe some champagne?
Christian: I'd rather just, um . . . get it over and done with.
Satine: Oh! Very well. Then why don't you . . . *(lies on the bed)* come down here. Let's get it over and done with.
Christian: I prefer to do it standing.
Satine: Oh!
Christian: You don't have to stand, I mean . . . It's sometimes . . . it's quite long. And I'd like you to be comfortable. It's quite

modern what I do and it may feel a little strange at first, bu—,
but I think if you're open, then . . . then you might enjoy it.
Satine: I'm sure I will.

But I'm not sure grandma will.

Although a majority of millennials now support increasing re-
strictions on abortion, it is nevertheless still supported by a majority
of people in this country. That should not surprise given the way
mainstream media discuss abortion: as no more significant than, say,
buying a car.

The real issue, of course, is: Is what the procedure terminates a
person? Every day modern science takes us to a fuller understanding
that the small living thing, from day one, is in fact a person. But also,
every day, modern liberal progressive politics takes us in the opposite
direction: that there's nothing wrong, really, with terminating those
who undoubtedly are persons but who are, you know, helpless and
useless, like, well, you know, grandmothers, and grandfathers too.

With the election of Donald Trump, Planned Parenthood (which
runs the nation's preeminent abortion mills) is on the run—reason
enough to have voted for Donald Trump over Hillary Clinton. And a
Supreme Court refurbished by Donald Trump, now a real possibility,
could, literally, save lives.

But in the meantime, the national shame continues, which
should scare the living daylights out of old people we used to honor
and protect.

Goodbye, Grandma.

Boarding School Daze
May 12, 2017

Bob, that's great news about your Belmont High son being accepted
by that swank New England boarding school, well known as a feeder
to the Ivy League. The sticker price of $56,500 a year (not includ-
ing athletic equipment), is not a problem for *you*. I mean, $169,500
for three years at a tony boarding school, with a *very* good chance
of getting into Harvard, Yale, or Princeton is a bargain. I'd have to
stretch—no new Mercedes each year!—but I guess I could ask my

Swarthmore wife to leave Planned Parenthood for a few years and get a job downtown worthy of her JD from Duke. But can you imagine the agony of paying all that money to a second rate boarding school and then having your son only get into f—ing Rollins?

Your son will make new friends, and many of them will be foreign, mostly, of course, from the Orient, or the oil countries—I wonder why! But some of them will be bright kids from, you know, Fishtown—about 35 percent of the students at your son's new school receive financial aid. They'll be great for your son to mix with, but your house probably isn't quite big enough for them to come and visit over Thanksgiving.

You and your wife lead a pretty straight-laced life, notwithstanding your intellectual and serious financial support for the important causes: abortion (right, "reproductive health and freedom"), the climate, and social justice. Those issues are appropriate for you, but your children's lives so far have been a bit more contained.

Now, however, your son will be branching out. His new school puts a big emphasis on diversity, at least in the traditional sense—socioeconomic, ethnic, religious, gender, sexuality, and political—though there probably won't be many fans of George Bush or Donald Trump there! Some of the official language is posted in the "Diversity" section of the school's website.

Several transgender and gender-nontraditional students have graduated from the school in the last ten years. And it's an issue current students are well aware of. In fact, recently the student council opened up the election for Head of the Student Council to accommodate students who don't identify as gender binary (boy or girl), or students who identify as trans but aren't ready to "come out." A prominent East Coast newspaper wrote a piece about the decision last year titled "Swank Academy Ends Gender Rule."

The piece quotes Ibn Saud "Sandy" Faisal, a senior and cochairman of the student council who, writing in the school newspaper, said no particular student was the reason for the change but that they acted because "we discerned that, demographically, gender would likely become a factor and that it would be fair to act now."

"Times have changed," Faisal said. "We no longer live in a world in which identity is seen through an old-fashioned, overly simplistic lens.

"We, as a modern-age community, have grown out of these archaic norms and have learned to accept the world, and the people within it, the way they are now."

Faisal said that the new rules would help make transgender students, or those who are "grappling with their identities," feel included.

The school's dean of students, Imabita Confusio, lauded the students' initiative as "responsible, thoughtful, [and] thorough. As an institution which values diversity of all kinds, we support the students' effort to create a more inclusive student government," Confusio said.

The school's motto is "Be Brave. Be True." and in his article Faisal asked, "How can we be brave or true if we require other people to be people they are not, solely for getting a position on the student council?"

Of course, you don't have to worry about all that gender stuff. It's not likely *your* son is confused. Still, I'd wait till his bridal dinner to resurface those photos of him at age three prancing about in the pink tutu.

Incidentally, if you and your wife are really committed to diversity, you might want to attend the school's alumni day program in June. They have a very diverse panel to discuss diversity! There's a female Washington journalist who hates Trump, a black woman pundit who helped shape two major pieces of Obama legislation, a writer for *The Nation* and *Mother Jones* who used to work for John Kerry, and a lawyer who aided the successful challenge to California's prohibition of same-sex marriage. Quite a diverse group.

You've got a winner of a school for your son. There hasn't been a sexual molestation scandal there for several years, and they've certainly updated some of their other requirements to match their diversity policies: chapel is no longer required (I think they store athletic equipment there now). So: praise the lord and pass the hockey sticks! Your son will have a blast.

Piling On: The Desperation of the Left
May 17, 2017

Advocates have a rule when making a case: don't pile on. But the columns against President Trump for firing FBI Director James Comey are piling on and spilling over the top—and are losing their punch.

Here's a list of titles from just one day of the *Washington Post*:

- *Comey's firing was about Russia (duh!). Why can't Republicans admit it?*
- *The White House's laughable spin about Comey now lies in smoking ruins.*
- *Trump is at war with the nation he is supposed to lead.*
- *Everything is backward with Trump.*
- *It's impossible not to compare today to Watergate. And our officials are falling short.*
- *Trump seems to be staging a coverup. So what's the crime?*

But for sheer cake-taking, cup-retiring nonsense, it will be difficult to top the column the *New York Times* ran two days after Comey's firing: *American Fascism, in 1944 and Today* written by Henry Scott Wallace. Wallace is the grandson of Henry A. Wallace, vice president of the United States during President Franklin Roosevelt's third term. (He also made a fortune developing a very successful hybrid seed company.)

We don't know for certain if Wallace was a communist. According to Conrad Black, writing in *National Review*, FBI Director J. Edgar Hoover told Roosevelt that Wallace was close to communists in Hollywood and "had inappropriate connections with overseas communists, including in the Soviet Union."

In 1944, Wallace toured the Soviet Union with communist Owen Lattimore and was taken to a labor camp where he was told, and apparently believed, that all the work was done by volunteers.

Black also writes: "Eminent Cold War historian John Lewis Gaddis has written that 'there is Soviet documentation that Wallace was regularly reporting to the Kremlin in 1945 and 1946 while he was in the Truman administration,' and that later, when Truman was considering a secret effort to approach the Soviets, his effort was 'blown wide open by Wallace when he was running for president on the Progressive Party ticket' in 1948. This was after Truman fired Wallace for giving an address in Madison Square Garden attacking the Truman administration for excessive anti-communist zeal."

It's fair to conclude that Wallace was either a fool or communist knave.

Grandson Wallace says that the *New York Times* asked his grandfather in 1944 to write about whether there were fascists in America. Grandson Wallace writes: "His article . . . described a breed of super-nationalist who pursues political power by deceiving Americans and playing to their fears, but is really interested only in protecting his own wealth and privilege." And then the clincher: "In my view, he predicted President Trump."

Is it possible to keep a straight face reading that? Young Wallace has now made the whole Trump experience worthwhile—even if Trump had not nominated Neil Gorsuch to the Supreme Court.

"To be clear," young Wallace retreats just bit, "I don't think the precise term 'fascism'—as in Mussolini and Hitler—is fairly applied to Mr. Trump" (e.g., no gas chambers). But by then the damage is done.

What young Wallace actually meant, he says (raising the question, why didn't he say it to begin with?), was that "Mussolini was a proponent of 'corporatism,' defined by some as 'a merger of state and corporate power.' And through that lens, using that term, my grandfather's warning looks prescient."

It does?

"They [hucksters spouting popular themes] invariably put 'money and power ahead of human beings,' he continued. 'They demand free enterprise, but are the spokesmen for monopoly and vested interest.' "

Does that really describe the Donald Trump who beat up the Carrier Corporation when they threatened to move some of their manufacturing facilities out of the United States? And who has threatened massive tariffs on corporations that move their manufacturing facilities abroad? Whatever the wisdom of that policy, it would seem, at least on its face, to be a policy that puts "human beings" ahead of "money and power."

"And what is the ultimate goal [of these fascists]?" young Wallace asks. "Their final objective" the grandfather wrote, "toward which all their deceit is directed is to capture political power so that, using the power of the state and the power of the market simultaneously, they may keep the common man in eternal subjection."

Grandson: "That sounds like Mussolini and his embrace of 'corporatism'—the marriage of government and corporate power. And it also sounds like President Trump."

No it doesn't. What absolute rot. It sounds like your average anti-Trump liberal progressive Democrat hugely enjoying himself at the expense of his intellectual reputation—assuming he had one.

We don't know for sure if Henry A. Wallace was a communist. We can be reasonably certain that his grandson is a windbag enjoying his fifteen minutes of fame in the *New York Times* by piling on.

Flied Lice and Golden Visas
May 23, 2017

Poor Nicole Meyer, Jared Kushner's sister: she's had to pretzelize herself because she mentioned that she was . . . Jared Kushner's sister when she was pitching a real estate deal to a group of Chinese businessmen. Denizens of the left-wing fever swamp, taking time out from incessant complaining about President Trump's governing process, have spent the last week beating up on her and other Kushners because the sister was dangling EB-5 visas, known colloquially as "golden visas," to Chinese businessmen if they invested the EB-5 statutory minimum requirement of $500,000 in a US project.

For the Left there were, apparently, two scandals: the EB-5 program and Jared Kushner's sister. She actually mentioned that President Trump's son-in-law and advisor, Jared Kushner, was of the same Kushner family that was pushing the real estate deal.

It is worth pausing a moment to compare China with Russia. Russia is a backward country: it's had a major recession, and without even a high level to recess from. Its gross domestic product fell during 2015–16 by more than 4 percent. Real incomes declined by 10 percent. Its population is declining, and its annual GDP is on par with far smaller and less populated Italy, which, as a wit remarked years ago, isn't really a country—it's just a geographical location.

China, on the other hand, is, relatively speaking, booming. According to the World Bank: "Since . . . 1978, China has . . . experienced rapid economic and social development. GDP growth has averaged nearly 10 percent a year—the fastest sustained expansion by a major economy in history. " The Chinese aren't just making pretty paper parasols anymore, and they're not having flied lice for lunch either—unless that's what you're having, because it's your lunch they're eating.

Basically, the Russians are incompetent; the Chinese, super-competent. Yet the media have ascribed to the Russians the ability practically to manage the US presidential election by remote control. But the Chinese, we are led to believe, weren't even able to figure out that Nicole Kushner Meyer, who was making the pitch in Beijing, was Jared Kushner's sister.

Somehow that just seems . . . improbable. A stretch, for the purpose of venting anti-Trump frustration.

Second: What's wrong with Mrs. Meyer's discussing the EB-5 visa program with the investors? Critics say the program is just a way for rich people to buy their way into the United States. But that's not correct. The program is also, or at least in theory is also, a way to create jobs in this country by encouraging rich people to invest serious money here.

If an application is approved, the investor and "derivative family members" will be granted conditional permanent residence for a two-year period. The investment must be either $1,000,000, or $500,000 if it is to a "Targeted Investment Area."

There must be evidence that the new commercial enterprise will create at least ten full-time positions and that the number of existing employees is being or will be maintained at no less than the pre-investment level for a period of at least two years.

Last year, ten thousand green cards, the statutory maximum, were granted under the EB-5 program, 9,128 of which went to people from China—where, incidentally, according to a former US ambassador to China, there are more people who speak English than there are in the United States.

Senator Chuck Grassley (R–IA) has said, "The EB-5 regional center program has been plagued by fraud and abuse," and that "it poses significant national security risks."

That may be, though Sen. Grassley voted for the provision in 1990 as did then Rep. Chuck Schumer (D–NY), now the Senate minority leader. And it may be a terrible program for other reasons not mentioned by Sen. Grassley. But as of now, which is when Mrs. Meyer was pitching to the Chinese, the EB-5 program is the law of the land. If it's a bad law, that's not her fault.

It is reasonably common for countries to grant citizenship to wealthy people who will invest in the country. Only on the American Left is there a sense that immigration should be restricted to the tired, the poor, and the huddled masses (whether or not they can learn to speak English, so long as they'll vote for Democrats).

The whole attack on the Kushners has been nothing other than more resistance by the tired, poor, and huddled Democrats—the same people who were shocked that Donald Trump took all the deductions the law allowed on his income tax returns.

If Donald Trump sang, "José, can you see by the dawn's early light?" the Resistance would accuse him of having cut off nighttime electricity to Mexican communities.

That may seem like good partisan politics to Democrats, but it's not clear how their conduct helps the governing process—about which they complain, incessantly.

Comey, Flynn, Trump, Brutish, and Short
May 25, 2017

That pretty much describes the first 125 days of the Trump administration.

James B. Comey, Michael T. Flynn, and of course President Donald Trump himself have been the marquee names during the first four months or so of this drama-filled administration.

Comey, the former FBI director, recommended on July 4, 2016, that no criminal charges be brought against Hillary Clinton for her handling of classified information while she was secretary of state, and since then he has been on center stage in the Trump saga. In his second act, on October 28, 2016, Comey said the investigation into Hillary Clinton's conduct was back on. Then, three days before Election Day, Comey cleared Mrs. Clinton again. Then on May 9, Trump fired him.

Flynn, a three-star army general with thirty-three years of military service, was said to have been considered by Donald Trump as a candidate for vice president before Mr. Trump decided on Mike Pence who was the governor of Indiana. After Trump's inauguration, he named Flynn national security advisor. Shortly thereafter—remarkably shortly thereafter—Trump dismissed Flynn because he had misled Vice President Pence about communications he had had with Sergey Kislyak, the Russian ambassador to the United States.

President Trump himself is also, obviously, a star of the show, both because of his modus operandi, including his tweeting, but also because of the unhinged desire of the progressive liberal Left to make sure that he gets nothing done. There is very little, if anything, on Trump's wish list that corresponds to what's on theirs. The carping and sniping have been incessant, and will continue.

This presidency has been brutish: Comey dismissed. Flynn dismissed. And now Trump mentioned in the same sentence as "impeachment" because of asking Comey to end the investigation of Flynn, and also, perhaps, because of firing him, and maybe even because of revealing classified information to the Russians.

David Gergen said last week, "I think we're in impeachment territory." Democratic Rep. Al Green of Texas has called for impeachment, and other Democrats, Reps. Maxine Waters (D–CA), John Yarmuth (D–KY), and Mark Pocan (D–WI), have also mentioned the "i" word. Most likely, it's just talk for the purpose of neutralizing President Trump. If they really believe it, they dream, for three reasons.

First: Do Democrats really want to impeach President Trump? He is probably the best fundraising tool they have. They are already raising money on his name in order to win elections for seats vacated by people who have joined the Trump administration. Donald Trump—*President* Trump—is for the Democrats what Obamacare and the threat of losing gun rights have been for Republicans. Democrats need President Trump.

Second: If Donald Trump were impeached, Vice President Pence would become president. How is that an improvement for the Democrats? Pence is well liked, well spoken, and well versed in the ways of Washington. He would be at least as capable of getting legislation through Congress as Trump is.

Third: How would impeachment work? Only a simple majority of the House of Representatives is needed to impeach the president, but a vote of two-thirds of the Senate is required to convict. Although the Republicans hold a majority of House seats and could therefore vote to impeach without any Democrats, the Republicans (assuming all of them voted for impeachment) would need fifteen Democrats to join them in order to convict in the Senate.

So: Republicans in the House, crumbling under unbearable pressure from their good friends in the liberal progressive media whom they admire so much (joke alert), vote to impeach. Then the Senate votes and—whaddya know?—the Democrats don't go along!

Now what?

Now Trump and the Republicans are at war with each other. And maybe the Democrats have made a deal with the president: they won't vote for impeachment if he promises to, say, nominate their candidates for Supreme Court vacancies. That would make today's Washington seem tranquil, and give new meaning to the term "brutish."

Thomas Hobbes in his *Leviathan, or the matter, forme, and power of a commonwealth, ecclesiasticall and civill* (1651) described the state of nature (i.e., before government) as "solitary, poor, nasty, brutish, and short"—which an American wag changed to "solitary, poor, nasty, British, and short."

Life before government, according to Hobbes, was "warre of every man against every man." That would be Trump's Washington, and ours, after a failed impeachment attempt, and it is not certain that any success the Trump administration might subsequently have—even brokering peace in the Middle East—would end that "warre." Republicans can be expected to figure that out and not, under any circumstances, go to war against President Trump.

Which is why one thing in this world is absolutely certain: Donald Trump will not be impeached.

That is the short of it.

Fear of Flying

May 26, 2017

How lucky can Donald Trump get? He now has another chance to tick off the liberal progressives, and in particular this time, *Washington Post* columnist Dana Milbank, who's probably written more than a hundred anti-Trump columns. All Trump has to do is make sure that Makan Delrahim, his pick to be assistant attorney general in charge of the Antitrust Division of the Department of Justice, plots a free-market course.

Mr. Milbank doesn't like the way the airlines run their businesses. He thinks Congress can do a better job. Seriously.

"Washington," Milbank says, "in its wisdom deregulated the airline industry and later looked the other way as it underwent a series of mega-mergers leaving a four-carrier oligopoly controlling 85 percent of the market. And what do we have to show for it? Reduced competition; packed cabins; tiny seats; proliferating fees for food, bags and flight changes; outsourcing of maintenance; boarding delays; higher fares in many cases; labyrinthine contracts that protect airlines rather than consumers; and routine overbooking.

He claims that four carriers are insufficient for competition to work for the benefit of consumers. But what is his evidence for that? How many carriers does he think are necessary? He says the mega-mergers that followed deregulation have "reduced competition." Yes. And if we had gone from a hundred carriers to ninety-nine, competition would also have been reduced. The question is, how many carriers do you need in order to produce adequate competition? Mr. Milbank hasn't a clue.

Then he lists eight or so gripes that undoubtedly annoy passengers, except those who fly in premium classes. What he has forgotten—perhaps he is too young—is that in the good old days of flying it was all premium class. Spacious cabins. Big seats. Hot meals. Fancy cutlery. And lots of personal attention. Verrry fancy.

And very expensive.

Deregulation has enabled many people to fly who had not been able to afford it under the old pre-deregulation command-and-control system. Grandparents can now fly across the country to see a new grandchild or attend a graduation. Or see friends. Or go to a medical specialist—the kind of thing rich people like Mr. Milbank do without thinking.

There are at least two problems with regulation. One is what is known as "regulatory capture." The industry writes the rules. Nobel Prize–winning economist George Stigler said that "regulation is acquired by the industry and is designed and operated primarily for its benefit." Why would Mr. Milbank think otherwise?

But even assuming Congress could write regulations uninfluenced by airline corporations (and that pigs could fly), what is Mr. Milbank's evidence that Congress could do a better job than the market?

Congress, in its wisdom, has given us 92 poverty programs that cost, in 2012, $799 billion (about $9,000 per person or $36,000 for a family of four) and $22 trillion since the inception of the war on poverty. As President Reagan said, we declared war on poverty, and poverty won. And Mr. Milbank wants those same people to run the airline industry?

Mr. Milbank doesn't like having to pay a fee for checking a bag. But bag checking costs money. Milbank wants to socialize the cost. He wants passengers who are not checking bags to pay for his checked bag. Why is that an improvement?

And why should someone who has packed his own sirloin steak sandwich have to pay extra so Mr. Milbank can be served a meal? Milbank wants to socialize the cost of meals too.

Overbooking enables the airlines to fill more seats and keep fares lower. It is true that when too many people show up for a flight the airlines should offer passengers whatever cash is necessary to persuade enough of them to give up their seats so the ticket holders who are not willing to take a subsequent flight can be accommodated—instead of dragging them off bloodied and bruised. But is it clear that an inflexible government rule would work better?

There are other effects of deregulation Milbank doesn't mention: the decline of small and midsized airports. But the problem there is economy of scale: small airports have to spread over far fewer passengers the cost of the air traffic control tower, the runway, ticketing, and baggage handling. Who's going to pay for that? Mr. Milbank would probably say that the government should pick up the tab. He'd socialize that cost too, to the whole US population.

During the Reagan years, the Federal Trade Commission had a slogan: "The market doesn't have to work perfectly to work better than government."

Donald Trump, who famously repaired New York City's beloved Wollman Skating Rink in six months (after the city had tried for five years) probably knows that instinctively. Mr. Milbank apparently has yet to learn it.

Health Care Reform: Not in God's Lifetime
May 31, 2017

One gets the sense that Congress's trying to craft a healthcare bill is like trying to play the piano in mittens.

Why should it be so difficult? Because Congress is trying to command and control the actions and interactions of millions of people. That can't be done—which means it's not possible to agree on how it should be done.

And so the left-wing media and the Democrats blame President Trump, as always. What do they expect him to do, if his predecessor couldn't even slow the rise of the oceans and heal the planet? Don't they know that market forces are even more powerful?

Have you ever seen Grand Central Station at rush hour? Thousands of people running for trains and rarely, if ever, crashing into each other.

Now picture Congress trying to legislate the paths of all those frantic people: citizen 011-22-3333 should head 2 degrees left, at a speed of not more than 3 mph but not less than 3.34 mph, for 16.7 feet toward track 26; whereupon said party should vector right 4.85 degrees toward track 27 (to miss the oncoming commuter); but immediately pause for .8 seconds to allow small woman carrying baby barreling along to pass uninterrupted. . . .

Only Congress and the Kremlin would think they could manage that from Central Headquarters by legislating today how all those people should catch their trains next week, next month, next year!

It can't be done. And neither can all the actions and interactions of patients, doctors, hospitals, and myriad other health professionals be prescribed years in advance and miles away by Washington legislators and bureaucrats. They are trying to legislate what only the market can produce. This can only end in tears.

In their saner moments, Republican legislators recognize this. Democrats, who are essentially socialists, cannot.

That is why it is so difficult for Congress to pass a healthcare bill: most Republicans want something entirely different from what most Democrats want. Democrats want socialized medicine, but socialized medicine—socialized anything—is a politically lascivious way of pleasing voters: candidates can always promise to increase benefits—viz, food stamps or disability payments.

Many (but not all) Republicans, on the other hand, want a free-market health care system, or at least a freer market, with government intervention (i.e., government assistance—health stamps?) for people who can't afford adequate health care.

Because there really is no common ground, Democrats will attack everything Republicans propose, as Republicans attacked Obama's attempt to socialize the system.

In a freer-market health care system people who have the ability and the financial means to look after themselves (i.e., most Americans) would be allowed to do so. But that means the country needs a competitive marketplace where competition can work its magic, the same way it does in the market for houses, automobiles, food, or beer. People should be allowed to buy policies that cover only what they want, with whatever deductible amount they choose.

They should not be required, as they are now under Obamacare, to buy coverage they don't want or for events that will never occur to them. Women don't need insurance for prostate cancer. Men don't need maternity coverage. Those kinds of requirements, imposed by Democrats, have nothing to do with insurance. They are really just hidden taxes: they force A to pay for something he will never use so that B's insurance premium for that good can be lower.

But unlike the market for, say, beer, there's a free-rider issue in health care: people who don't buy insurance when they're well, but expect Cadillac care when they get sick. They're a problem: and they will get some care. But if they are scheming shirkers, they should also pay a price for free riding—perhaps forfeiting their drivers' licenses.

What's the value of the health stamps poor people should receive? That also would be a hot political issue, but more manageable because it can be designed so there's really only one variable—the dollar amount to assist in buying insurance. This much is certain, however: a free-market system combined with health stamps would provide quality healthcare to those paying the freight, and be cheaper and more efficient than the socialized system we've been suffering under since Obamacare was enacted.

But Democrats and Republicans will never be able to agree on these matters. And without an ECON 101 lecture from a stern Donald Trump—and the threat of expulsion of recalcitrant students—nothing good is likely to come from Congress.

And so . . . spring will turn to summer without a replacement for Obamacare, and summer to fall, and then we will be headed into a long, cold winter of discontent, and then congressmen really will put on their mittens.

And when they sit down to play, we won't be able to tell the difference.

Closing Time for the Episcopal Church?
June 13, 2017

The Episcopal Church must take immortality seriously. How else explain the amazing things it does which will certainly hasten its demise?

Washington DC has two prominent, historic Anglo-Catholic parishes: the Church of the Ascension and St. Agnes, and St. Paul's Parish, known colloquially as St. Paul's K Street. An Anglo-Catholic parish is one that continues to accept much of the Catholic (sometimes called "Roman Catholic") faith and doctrine as well as its liturgical form, while tending, as Catholic theologian Ronald Knox conceded, to be better at liturgical drama.

But Washington's two Anglo-Catholic parishes have now gone over to the dark side. Ascension and St. Agnes has just "called" a homosexual priest to be its new rector, and St. Paul's has decided to bless homosexual "marriages." A notice in a recent bulletin read: "Flowers on the High Altar this Sunday are given by Samuel Smith and Michael 'Tricks' Moon [names changed] to the greater glory of Almighty God and in thanksgiving for the Blessing of their Civil Marriage which will be celebrated in this parish . . . to which all members of the parish are invited."

Your servant was unable to attend the ceremony due to a subsequent engagement as well as his inability to lay his hands quickly on a neutron bomb—one benefit of which would have been (*inter alia*, as the prosecutor at the trial might have put it) to relieve the parish from the embarrassment of performing a vain, insulting, and frankly ridiculous act. Two men can't enter the state of holy matrimony any more than two screwdrivers can.

The Episcopal Church began losing its way in the sixties with the move to ditch Archbishop Cranmer's *Book of Common Prayer* in favor of a newspeak version, and it fell into the identity politics trap when it decided that women could be priests. There are still a few hold-out parishes, but they are under heavy assault.

Parish activity expands to spend all funds available. Parishes are therefore always in danger of not making their budgets. If there are two or three big donors who say they'll go elsewhere if the parish doesn't accept women priests, what's a poor rector to do? Should he, like Samson, pull the temple down on all heads? How does he argue with the big pledgers who say that the women in town "feel" the parish is anti-woman because it won't allow women priests? Most of the other Episcopal churches allow women priests: Why not St. Phillinthename's?

Here are two arguments a rector could try:

Look, I've studied this for my whole life. I know more about the substance of this issue than you do. Do you really want to be out of step with the Catholic church? If you accept women priests, you can't describe yourself as any kind of Catholic, which you do every time you say that part of the Nicene Creed which reads: "I believe in one holy, catholic, and apostolic Church."

There are 1.2 billion Catholics, 260 million Eastern Orthodox Christians (give or take 50 million), 83 million Anglicans, but only 3 million Episcopalians—about 0.2 percent of all Christians. That same percentage of Americans lives in Denver, Colorado.

What would you say about a Hilton Hotels VP who told a

civil engineer hired to design a hotel in Vermont, "Don't build in any margin of safety. We don't care what the practice is in the rest of America. We want to do this the *Vermont* way." You'd say, "He must be an Episcopalian."

As his second option, a rector under assault by the women of the town might respond:

Ladies, what do the following people all have in common? Dorothy Day, Faye Dunaway, Susan Hayward, Clare Boothe Luce, Patricia Neal, Kirsten Powers, Edith Sitwell, Alice B. Toklas, Ann Widdecombe, and Katherine, Duchess of Kent?

They were all accomplished women, prominent in their fields, who converted to Catholicism as adults. Would they have done that if the church were anti-woman? The church whose first saint was a woman?

What the rector of an Episcopal church has to realize is that if he accepts women priests, the homosexual lobby will soon be all over him to force him to bless homosexual "marriages."

But, some may ask, can't homosexuals be Christians? Of course they can. And so can bank robbers. And adulterers. But they can't put on their calling cards "Christian bank robber" or "Christian adulterer." If those are their sins, they should try to deal with them, not try to normalize them.

But it's much easier, of course, to become a parishioner of an Anglo–Catholic parish that has gone over to the dark side, of which there are now, unfortunately, two more in Washington DC, for a while, anyway—until closing time.

Solving the Mueller Problem

July 4, 2017

There is a way out of the Mueller problem after all.

Robert Mueller, the special counsel appointed to look into Russian influence in the 2016 election, is an honorable man. He is—or at least was—highly regarded. He was once known for being above the fray. But as Americans are learning, past performance is no guarantee of future performance. Mueller, so well known as an honorable man, is now being condemned by some as being, if not thoroughly partisan, at least negligent in giving the appearance of impartiality. His critics have a legitimate gripe.

Mueller himself may be non-partisan, but the people he has hired are liberal Democrats to the core. At least four of them, Andrew Weissmann, James L. Quarles III, Jeannie Rhee, and Elizabeth Prelogar, contributed to Hillary Clinton's campaign, and Rhee represented the (almost certainly corrupt) Clinton Foundation.

The Resistance holds that Justice Department rules prohibit Mueller from taking ideological or political views into consideration when deciding whom to hire. But even if those rules did apply to Mueller, the proscription must be observed prudentially. Presumably he could not hire ten unrepentant communists—even if they had voted for Hillary.

Mueller's job is not just to investigate: it is, in the end, to produce results that can be considered acceptable by fair-minded people, which means, among other considerations, that it must be non-partisan. If Mueller's staff consists of hard-core lefties, the conclusions Mueller comes to are not likely to be accepted by fair-minded people. Mueller faces a dilemma.

A. If he finds no wrongdoing on the part of President Trump, his having hired a slew of hard-core lefties will make that conclusion more palatable to the Democrats. But even if they think Mueller's conclusions are correct, how likely is it that they will cool their criticism of President Trump?

It is possible that Mueller has already concluded that Trump has done nothing improper and so is staffing his team with lefties precisely to make his conclusion more saleable to the Left. Somehow that just seems . . . as unlikely as coming across three white leopards sitting under a juniper tree.

B. Mueller's larger problem is that if he does find fault with President Trump, Republicans are not likely to accept his conclusions given the staffers he has hired. If Mueller's instincts told him that President Trump had done wrong, he should have hired primarily Republicans.

If Mueller has, and has had, no idea what the investigation is likely to reveal, he should have picked a more neutral team. If, with the team he has hired, Mueller condemns Trump, the howls from Republicans are likely to be vastly louder than the howls from the Democrats would have been if he had found no fault with Trump. His conclusion will not be accepted by Republicans and there will therefore be no closure on the issue—*which is the whole point of having a special counsel.*

Mueller has brought this on himself. If he had the courage he is reputed to have, he would now resign, realizing that everyone makes mistakes, and the best course of action is to acknowledge them rather than persevere in a fruitless course of action. He would preserve his reputation for another day—and for history. But there is no indication Mueller is contemplating that course of action.

What to do?

Simply firing Mueller will not do. All Hell would break lose ("Hell" is capitalized because it's a place, you know, like Chappaqua). The Never-Trumpers and the Sore-Loser Democrats, with their Main Stream Media allies, would shut down the government (hmm). Much as Trump's base might like that, it is probably not a wise course of action. There is a better way.

President Trump should fire Mueller AND at the same time instruct Deputy Attorney General Rod Rosenstein to appoint another special counsel. And, not incidentally, part of the new special counsel's assignment should be to investigate the leaks at the Justice Department and the FBI. Whatever work has been done will be available to the new team so there will be no need to start over from scratch.

Trump could list Mueller's mistakes and say, quite correctly, that because of the bias of his hires, Mueller's conclusions, if critical of the president or any other Republicans, would simply not be accepted by the country.

Yes, the Democrats would howl and the media would have a meltdown—and the price of schadenfreude (SCHDF) would decline ever further.

But justice would be served. A different special counsel could reach a conclusion that would be acceptable to fair-minded Democrats (and unicorns) and Republicans alike.

It was Mueller's job to be, *and to appear,* fair-minded. He has

failed. It is now up to President Trump to step in and correct that
failure.

Obamacare Forces Policyholders to Pay for Health Risks They Don't Have

July 19, 2017

Gail Collins writes in the *New York Times* that "while Ivanka has been
making mewling noises about working moms, the Trump White
House has appointed people to major health care policy jobs who
don't appear to believe in contraception."

What does she mean? (And why "mewling? What's Ivanka ever
done to Gail Collins?) Does she mean that the Trump appointees
have religious beliefs (horrors!) that contraception is wrong? Then
she should say that. But that wouldn't sound quite as scandalous.
There are seventy million Catholics in the US, and while not all of
them may "believe" in (i.e., accept) the church's conclusion and
teaching that contraception is wrong, and others may believe it but
use contraceptives anyway, the concept of "not believing in contraception" loses its scandal value in light of that number.

Perhaps what she means is that the Trump people don't believe
that government should subsidize contraception. That makes sense,
but, unfortunately for Collins, that belief also can lead to a debate
among reasonable people—which would spoil her game.

It is reasonable to ask, should government (the taxpayers) pay for
contraception? Put more personally, should A be required by government to pay for B's contraception?

There are two issues. One is the religious issue. Should people
who think contraception is contrary to their church's teaching be required, through their tax payments, to pay for it? The answer to that
question is obvious—unless you write for the *New York Times*—No.

The other issue is, should a routine expense like contraception be
covered by health insurance? Birth control pills cost about $600 a year
(without insurance). The average household wastes about $600 each
year throwing away unwanted food, spends about $850 each year on
soda, and the typical American spends about $1,200 on fast food each

year. If contraceptives were subsidized through insurance, wouldn't that just enable people to buy more fast food or soda? Is that good public policy? Mayor Bloomberg wouldn't approve.

Why don't the Gail Collinses lobby for government subsidization of toothpaste, too? That would raise the real question, which is, what should insurance cover? Or more precisely, who should decide what an insurance policy covers—the government or consumers who buy insurance?

Ms. Collins writes: "Insurance is all about sharing risks. If people who didn't require maternity coverage, i.e. men, were able to save money by forgoing it, the price for the women who did need it would skyrocket." Maybe, but the price of that insurance—if it covered all illnesses—would be offset by women's not having to pay for prostate cancer expenses. More importantly, to require insurance to cover a risk that the policy holder does not face is to force him to subsidize the people who do have that risk. It is just a form of off-budget, hidden taxation.

It's surprising how many people don't understand what insurance is for. The basic goal of insurance is to spread the risk of (the possibility of suffering) (1) an unlikely but (2) serious, perhaps even catastrophic expense, over many people who are exposed to that same risk (not to people who are not exposed to it), so that no single person who suffers it has to bear the whole cost alone.

There are two separate issues in the public policy debate that need to be untangled: (A) coverage of wholly predictable expenses that the insured will incur, and (B) cross-subsidies for other peoples' risks, whether normal or not, that the insured does not risk incurring.

A person should be free to buy insurance (if it's available) that covers such predictable events as oil changes or toothpaste, but that is different from that person's being required to buy insurance for oil changes or toothpaste if he doesn't want to—if he only owns a bike or has false teeth.

Of course, the premium for insurance for oil changes or toothpaste would be high because the events insured against are certain to occur. The premium is really just a prepayment of the expense.

Contraceptives are also a routine expense—more than 60 percent of women of childbearing age use contraceptives—as are pregnancies.

Ms. Collins seems to consider getting pregnant a risk, implying that it is also a disaster. Try telling that to the 6 million women in the United States ages 15–44 who have difficulty getting or staying pregnant.

People should be free to buy whatever health insurance they want, whether low deductible or catastrophic. Poor people can be subsidized as necessary, but not to the extent of making them better off than the people who pay the taxes that subsidize them. The inevitable free-riders should be dealt with sufficiently harshly to . . . discourage free-riding.

The market will work, if we let it. But Gail Collins, and her friends, will never understand that.

Prep Schools Like Milton Not Teaching Political Diversity

August 2, 2017

"Dare to be True" is the motto of beautiful and stately Milton Academy, established in 1798 and located at the other end of the subway line from Harvard University. Milton prides itself on its commitment to diversity. On the school's website there is a page titled "Embracing Diversity" which tell us: "Milton has long fostered critical thinking and has understood how important diversity is for learning."

Whether diversity is in fact important for learning is debatable (Were Watson and Crick gender sensitive? And Pythagoras?), but assuming it is, we can ask, How is Milton doing in promoting learning?

According to the website, "Students of color, who define themselves as African-American, Asian-American, Latino, indigenous or bi/multi-racial, are 41 percent of Milton's student body" (don't miss "who define themselves"). Thirty-five percent receive financial aid. Faculty members of color are 19 percent of the faculty.

Milton has a number of student groups: among others, an Asia Society, a South Asian Society, a Caribbean Student Association, and a Christian Fellowship. And also GASP! (Gender and Sexuality Perspectives). "GASP! provides a safe space for LGBTQ people and their allies to discuss issues of sexual orientation and educate others, and provides support to people of all orientations."

Clearly, Milton has embraced the trinity of identity politics: race, gender, and sexual orientation. But what about learning at Milton? Is that diverse too?

One of Milton Academy's traditions is a War Memorial Lecture. The official description is: "The Alumni War Memorial Foundation was established in 1922 to honor those Milton Academy graduates who gave their lives in World War I. In recent years those graduates who have sacrificed their lives in subsequent wars have also been honored by the memorial."

The last twenty-three of the forty-nine speakers have been: The Lady Barbara Ward Jackson, The Honorable Charles E. Wyzanski Jr., J. Robert Oppenheimer, Edwin O. Reischauer, Jean Mayer, Ralph Nader, William F. Buckley Jr., Ivor Richard, Lord Caradon, Lt. Gen. James M. Gavin, Soedjatmoko, Maya Angelou, Bruno Bettelheim, William Manchester, Helen Suzman, Stevan Dedijer, Amory Lovins, Oscar Arias, Togo West, Kenneth H. Bacon, David McCullough, Randall L. Kennedy, and Vivek H. Murphy.

Some of those speakers may not have been known primarily for their political views and not all may have been card-carrying liberals. But the only recognizable conservative in the entire group is, of course, William F. Buckley Jr. One out of twenty-three. Diversity?

As part of Milton's reunion day activities this June, the school scheduled a discussion titled "Alumni Panel: Politics and Policy." The listed panelists were a man who helped lead the team that challenged and overturned California's prohibition of same-sex marriage; a man who served as executive editor of *Foreign Policy* and *The New Republic* and who was the chief foreign policy speechwriter for John Kerry; a woman who is the head of a left-leaning research and advocacy group who served in 2008 as John Edwards' Deputy Policy Director; and a reporter for *The Hive*, a *Vanity Fair* operation. Diversity?

Just inside the front door of the library there is a stand showcasing books described by a big sign, "Milton Students / Literature to Change." On the stand are: *Their Eyes Were Watching God; The Michael Eric Dyson Reader; How the Garcia Girls Lost Their Accents; We Should All Be Feminists; Invisible Man; Dear Ijeawele, or A Feminist Manifesto in Fifteen Suggestions; Roots; Everyday Sexism; Malcolm X; Symptoms of Being Human; My Beloved World; Why Are All the Black Kids Sitting Together in the Cafeteria: And Other Conversations About Race; Speak;* and *Men Explain Things to Me.*

Eighteen books. You may not know them, but they are a veritable bible of identity politics. How much would you pay to read, or have your child read, *Symptoms of Being Human?* It's a novel about Riley Kavanagh, who, according to the Amazon blurb, "is many things: Punk rock. Snarky. Rebellious. And gender fluid. Some days Riley identifies as a boy, and others as a girl."

Tuition at Milton is $55,410, and bright students have an excellent chance of getting into Harvard: sixteen of this year's graduating class of 184 students are going there, more than to any other college. It's not likely there are many Riley Kavanaghs in that group.

Can it be worth it? Who really wants to pay $221,640 for four years of gender fluidity? A whole lot of people, apparently: Milton's acceptance rate is 16 percent.

And it's a good guess that, with the exception of explicitly Catholic schools like Portsmouth Abbey in Newport, Rhode Island, all the other tony prep schools are just like Milton, busily preparing students to take their places among the nation's intellectual elite, training them for diversity. And for the Resistance.

Milton's beautiful and stately campus is far from the heartland of America. And it does not seem likely that these students will be leaders in making America great again.

Dare to be true indeed. Where gender is fluid, there is no truth. And what is truth, anyway? And didn't some historical figure ask that once? Do Milton students learn who he was?

Who Promoted Emma Lazarus?

August 7, 2017

It's time to send Emma Lazarus home. That may not be fair to her. All she did was write the sonnet "The New Colossus," from which the lines, put on a plaque and installed at the base of the Statue of Liberty years later, were taken:

Give me your tired, your poor,
Your huddled masses yearning to breathe free,
The wretched refuse of your teeming shore.

What was she thinking, and whom was she writing about? She may have had in mind the Jews fleeing from the pogroms in Russian, but not many of them had come to the United States by 1883.

And why were her lines selected for the Statue of Liberty? Who promoted Emma Lazarus? And does her description fit the typical immigrant to America?

Not even a poetic license issued in 1883 should have allowed Lazarus to insult the hard-working immigrants by describing them as tired, huddled, wretched, and refuse. Refuse!? The condescension reeks.

America has since its early days been the new home of the en-ergetic, the brave, the daring, the fearless, the entrepreneurial, the risk-taking. Though the immigrants Lazarus knew may have been poor—few immigrants came with much money—certainly not all of them were wretched. They came seeking opportunity. And they found it. They worked hard. There was no welfare program to sus-tain them. They built communities all over this land. They built America.

And the hard work of those early immigrants, and the insults of Lazarus's lines, should make us think about the kind of immigration policy we want today.

Whom is our immigration policy meant to benefit? The potential immigrant or America?

Does anyone have a *right* to come to America? Do we have an obligation to take in anyone who wants to come? Are we obliged to take all refugees from war-torn areas? Some refugees? Which refugees? Who decides? In theory, we want only the best and the brightest. That's what President Trump, quite sensibly, has said, thereby earning the usual derogation from the Resistance. He wants to change our immigration system to one based on merit. "I want people to come in on merit. I want to go to a merit-based system. Actually two countries that have very strong systems are Australia and Canada. And I like those systems very much, they're very strong, they're very good, I like them very much. We're going to a much more merit-based system."

President Trump has said that he wants immigrants to commit to not receiving any form of welfare for their first five years in the country. That's hardly an original thought. The Immigration Act of 1882 made several categories of immigrants ineligible for citizenship, including people likely to become public charges.

We in America (and elsewhere) are fixated now on immigrants from terror-infected countries, for obvious reasons. But we need to think more comprehensively about immigration. And certainly the immigrants we allow to become citizens should at least, as President Trump has said, be good for America. The minimum official requirements for naturalization are being able to read, write, and speak basic English; having a basic understanding of US history and government (civics); being a person of good moral character (that would eliminate the Clintons); and demonstrating an attachment to the principles and ideals of the US Constitution (that would eliminate most of the Democratic Party).

One aspect of America that immigrants should understand is that America has a heritage and a character: its heritage is European, with a particular emphasis on fidelity to the rule of law, and its character is the product of Western Civilization and the Enlightenment. Multiculturalism is not the culture of America. Indeed, multiculturalism cannot, by definition, be a culture at all.

Lazarus, in her sonnet, misses the boat. Immigrants to this country, if oppressed in their native countries, may appear to be tired, poor, wretched refuse. But by coming to America, they wipe away that past and get the chance to lead a new life, to be bold and resourceful.

It's too late to send Emma Lazarus home now, and not only because she died in 1887 before the plaque with her words was installed at the base of the Statue of Liberty, but also because she was already home when she died, at the age of thirty-eight, in New York City, where she was born.

But it's not too late to correct the false impression made by the plaque that bears her lines, not too late to put up a new plaque (even if we let the old one remain) that will teach Americans here, and would-be Americans everywhere, that America is a land of opportunity. But the opportunity is for the brave and resourceful: to rise early, work hard, and trust in Providence.

Summer Games for the Resistance

August 16, 2017

What would the Resistance and the Never Trumpers do without white supremacists and neo-Nazis? Well, a lot, actually: and that's what they've been doing ever since Trump won the election. They even *call* themselves the Resistance. They are resisting a duly elected president: they write editorials in the nation's major newspapers and news networks, and they stonewall the president's actions in Washington. Those activities of the Resistance have real consequences. They affect the political business of the nation. They impede the operation of our democratically elected government.

Line them up against a handful of nasty people promoting white supremacy and neo-Nazism and it puts—or to any fair-minded person should put—the president's statements about the weekend events in Charlottesville, Virginia, in perspective.

Which is not to suggest—obviously—that there should be any condoning of the killings or the violence that occurred there. And there hasn't been.

But the Resistance was not satisfied with the wording of the president's statement in response to the weekend events. This was President Trump's first response: "We condemn in the strong possible terms this egregious display of hatred, bigotry and violence on many sides."

The anti-Trump complaint is that by saying "many sides" the president failed to limit his condemnation to the white supremacists. And that is true. But why shouldn't he condemn all violence? Do we believe that attacking white supremacists is okay?

According to the *New York Times:*

In Charlottesville, established groups like the local chapter of Black Lives Matter, as well as liberal and anarchist groups, started planning their response in June when activists learned that the Ku Klux Klan would be marching in the city . . . said Nathan Moore. . . . "It's been a real summer of hate here."

In a "real summer of hate" it might seem like a good idea to condemn all violence.

Nathan Moore, you may be interested to know, is, according to the *Times,* a member of the steering committee of Together Cville, a Resistance group that formed shortly after the presidential election.

Suppose no one had shown up to oppose the crackpot white supremacists and confront them? Put otherwise, if a tree falls in the forest and the *New York Times* and CNN fail to cover the event, has it really happened? And is there, therefore, any danger to the body politic?

According to the *Times*, Laura Goldblatt, a postdoctoral fellow at the University of Virginia, said that some kind of response in the street was necessary because history has shown that "ignoring white supremacy, in terms of shutting your doors and not coming out to confront them, has been a really dangerous strategy."

Really? Do sentient people actually think that white supremacists and neo-Nazis constitute a serious danger to the United States of America?

President Trump's second statement was more inclusive in its condemnation: "Racism is evil. And those who cause violence in its name are criminals and thugs, including KKK, Neo-Nazis, White Supremacists, and other hate groups are repugnant to everything we hold dear as Americans. Those who spread violence in the name of bigotry strike at the very core of America."

It is true that President Trump probably should have led with that statement, if only to have made it more difficult for the Left to posture. But Mr. Trump is not yet finely attuned to the wicked ways of Washington and the left-wing Resistance.

Remember that the Left, when the Black Lives Matter movement became popular, was, or pretended to be, offended when others said that white lives matter too. Inclusiveness is a one-way street, apparently.

What's going on here, obviously, is that the Resistance is trying to link the Trump Administration to whatever hate groups are successful in getting national attention. The *New York Times* even went so far as to opine that Mr. Trump has "embraced" the hate groups. And the more attention the media can give to hate groups, the more they can use them to attempt to discredit President Trump.

Nevertheless, it is fair to say: clearly the first response of the president should have been stronger.

That being said, when Merck Chief Executive Kenneth Frazier resigned from the president's American Manufacturing Council, saying he was taking a stand against intolerance and extremism, President Trump tweeted: "Ken Frazier of Merck Pharma has resigned from President's Manufacturing Council, he will have more time to LOWER RIPOFF DRUG PRICES!"

It's a bit of a stretch to say that the whole left-wing attack on the president over the Charlottesville business was worth the opportunity to get off that tweet. But if the Resistance wonders why Trump remains popular with his people, they should study his reaction to adversity.

President Trump and the Navy's Welfare
August 23, 2017

The news is just in that *another* navy ship, The USS *John S. McCain*, has collided with an oil tanker, resulting in ten deaths and colossal financial damage. No doubt President Trump was responsible—as President Reagan surely was for Hurricane Kate in November 1985.

Back in the mid-seventies when plane hijackings were new, the philosopher James Burnham (author of the seminal *The Managerial Revolution, et al*) quipped that you should always carry a bomb onto an airplane, because the chances of there being *two* bombs on an airplane were almost zero.

The wisdom behind that quip may be applicable here: What are the chances of there being *two* horrendous collisions of navy ships within two months of each other? Especially since, after the USS *FitzGerald* collided with a freighter off the coast of Japan on June 17, all navy ships were surely instructed to be extra vigilant.

Something is wrong. Two possibilities bother the layman: First, that the navy's computer system may have been hacked, allowing foreign agents to fool a ship's personnel into not sensing imminent danger; or, second, that the navy's personnel, training system, or management and command structure, or all of them, are unbelievably inadequate.

The layman wonders why, even if all the sailors on the navy ship were asleep, drunk, or watching *Gilligan's Island*, the oil tanker failed to see the USS *John S. McCain*. But the layman is quickly reminded by a former naval officer that the Arleigh Burke class destroyers that were involved in the collisions were designed to be as invisible to radar as possible. There are few, if any, right angles above the water-line of the ship, and much of the exterior of the ship is covered in soft padding. A ship that is designed to be "invisible" to a sophisti-cated enemy may not appear as a 505-foot destroyer on a commercial ship's radar.

There are other impediments the layman is not aware of. The helmsman of a destroyer is not exactly looking out a window as if he were driving a bus down Fifth Avenue. He is at the back of a room that looks more like the mission control center at Cape Canaveral, reading instruments and getting information from other techni-cians on the ship. He could see an approaching ship, if he looked, but that's not really his job. That's the function of . . . other people: a lookout, who is an enlisted person, and probably a junior enlisted person.

Whoever is in charge at that hour of night (the captain is snug abed) gives orders in order to accomplish whatever the ship's mis-sion is at that time, and woe unto him who crosses those orders. Deviating from the approved course is . . . risky.

A few years ago, a flight deck officer in charge of landing a heli-copter on a ship decided that the pitch and roll were too extreme to land an approaching chopper. The captain of the ship said to land it anyway.

What would you do? Disobey the captain and risk your career? Or give the clearance to land and risk killing the chopper crew?

Modern warfare is complicated, and perhaps too complicated for the traditional rank structure. Enlisted technicians may know more than seasoned officers. If you're in the chopper, who do you want deciding if it should land? That crew was probably lucky the naval officer maintained his position and didn't let the chopper land.

The institutional issue is how much initiative do we allow the crew, whether they are enlisted men or officers? Suppose you're a junior whatever, in charge of the USS *John S. McCain*. You have been given a mission, and dodging an oil tanker (which, hey, c'mon, isn't going to hit you anyway) may compromise that mission. What do you do?

And how well has the navy trained you and your fellow crew members? Well enough to make the critical decisions necessary to guarantee that a $2 billion destroyer can dodge freighters and oil tankers? Or has the navy spent its time integrating women into combat roles and onto submarines?

Are navy personnel, both officers and enlisted, trained to use their initiative or only to follow orders? And how much initiative do we really want people driving $2 billion vehicles to take? Would we have *more* accidents than we have had if rules were not followed, always, to the letter?

Those are questions that need to be answered. But not by the navy alone. President Trump should appoint an independent board to investigate not just the two recent collisions, but also the whole structure of training for the navy. We may discover that vastly more funding is necessary if we are to have a navy that doesn't go bump in the night—even if we have to take the funds from the left-wing history-hating Resistance's favorite welfare programs.

Remembering that the navy is one of the country's four most important welfare programs.

Sex, College Sex—and Harvey Weinstein
October 12, 2017

Several years ago, a member of a once-tony club walked into its bar and noticed that most members weren't wearing neckties, a requirement that had existed for more than a century. He asked the president, who happened to be at the bar, why the rule had been changed. The president said that a majority of the members no longer wanted to wear ties. The member replied, quicker than you could down an ameliorative shot of premium whiskey, "Sounds like an admissions committee problem." Perhaps Harvey Weinstein was a new member.

And that sounds like the problem that has troubled a number of universities too, including most especially last year, the University of Minnesota, as well as Florida State, the University of Tennessee, Baylor University, and others.

Last year's Exhibit A student sex scandal was the one at the University of Minnesota where ten students were suspended, but the plot was roughly the same everywhere, every time. A student claimed that she was raped by one or more students. They denied it. She had been drinking. They had been drinking.

What to do? How seriously do we take campus rape? How do we take campus rape seriously?

In the 1960s and 1970s most states passed rape shield laws. These laws, supported especially by feminists, were enacted to protect rape victims from having to have their prior sexual history displayed in court, which tended to make them reluctant to come forward to charge rape. The theory was that just because the accusing woman had had sex with Tom on Monday night and with Dick on Tuesday night did not mean that the sex she had with Harry on Wednesday night was consensual. Nor would evidence be admissible to show that she had had sex with Tom and his ten friends on Monday and with Dick and his ten friends on Tuesday. With this aspect of the accuser's character being inadmissible, it was easier to convict a defendant of rape.

But not easy enough for some people, which is why there was a movement to make the standard by which college rape defendants were "tried" by the schools (rather than by a proper jury) the "preponderance of evidence" standard used in civil cases rather than the "beyond reasonable doubt" standard used in criminal cases. President Obama's Department of Education decreed, and so informed educational institutions, that the civil standard should be applied in college rape cases.

The real problem, of course, is that sex has become entirely casual and recreational. Boys and girls in college—not, really, men and women—live in the same dormitories and copulate as casually as they watch TV, shake hands, or pat each other on the back. That's called the Harvey Weinstein excuse.

What if the girl at the University of Minnesota had filed a complaint saying that whereas she had willingly allowed Tom and Dick to pat her on the back, she was outraged and felt personally violated when Harry had done the same, and she was filing an action against him for battery? That is, approximately, what the University of Minnesota's Office of Equal Opportunity and Affirmative

Action found to be the situation in the Minnesota case. The details are mind-numbing and can be found in the EOAA's 80-page report.

In that case, the Minneapolis Police Department concluded that the woman's sexual contact with the first two men appeared to have been consensual. Whether the sexual contact with the subsequent ten or twenty men was consensual is disputed.

How can we possibly tell? And do we care? And is asking that question the perfect way to scandalize a postmodern progressive liberal—still smarting from Hillary Clinton's humiliating defeat?

If a female student is going to treat sex so casually, why shouldn't her own casual standards—if we can call them standards—be admissible in evidence?

And what about the ten or twenty "men" who lined up at the bedroom door waiting for their turn to have sex with her? Even if the sex was consensual, they should all be expelled. Creatures like that belong in game parks, or zoos—though animals tend not to text their friends, saying things like, "Me and the recruit finna double team this bitch" ("finna" generally means "going to") or "all 3 them n****s hitting rn" ("hitting" generally means "having sex with," and "rn" means "right now").

Betsy DeVos, President Trump's Secretary of Education, fortunately has rescinded the Obama directive to apply the civil "preponderance of evidence" standard to college rape cases. Rape shield laws tip the scales far enough in favor of the accuser. Secretary DeVos's rescission will annoy (more schadenfreude) the postmodern progressive liberals because they are concerned only with the issue of consent, not the sex.

The real problem is that students have received no teaching about sex or proper behavior, partly because their parents, if they have resident parents, have bought into the liberal zeitgeist that sex is only recreational. Ask Harvey.

In addition to being instructed to use the proper legal standard for trying rape cases, colleges and universities should also be given incentives to be more diligent in deterring campus rape. They should be penalized, perhaps losing 5 percent of whatever federal funds they receive, for each campus rape case. "Federal funds," after all, are taxpayer funds, and if they are going to be given to educational institutions—and whether that is a good idea is a separate issue—they should be used to encourage the institutions to encourage students to behave properly.

At the same time, because the possible loss of funds might tempt the institutions, even if only slightly, to hedge on reporting rape cases, girls at those institutions might have an incentive to behave rather more circumspectly, knowing that the institution might ignore any complaint of rape.

And the potential loss of funds might also give the institutions an incentive to act more in loco 1950s parentis, a task that could be made rather easier if the institutions' admissions committees tried to admit only students who seemed to have been brought up to treat sex seriously, as a gift from God to be used properly (or if they are non-believers, as a "civil sacrament"), not as mere recreation. See Harvey Weinstein.

How would a college do such screening? Who knows? But they test for everything else; why not that, too? And surely some of the institutions with the worst records, and perhaps others that didn't want to join that club, could hire Google to come up with an algorithm that would separate the people from the animals. Screening out the animals may be the only way to reduce the incidence of campus rape. Hollywood is a separate problem.

The problem for postmodern progressive liberals, who are the people running most of the institutions, is that they really don't have any grounds for taking rape seriously because they don't take sex seriously—or at least not any more seriously than they take the issue of whether members of tony clubs should wear neckties.

Roy Moore and Jeff Sessions: Two Problems— and a Solution

November 12, 2017

The problem with the *Washington Post*'s scandal story about Judge Roy Moore, the Republican candidate for the Alabama Senate seat once held by now Attorney General Jeff Sessions, is that the *Washington Post* has become one giant editorial page, with no credibility on factual matters because it is so frenetically anti-Trump. People simply don't believe the *Post* anymore. That doesn't mean that everything the *Post* writes is wrong. But it's always suspect.

The *Post*, now the plaything of fifty-three-year-old Amazon gazillionaire Jeff Bezos, has a new slogan: "Democracy dies in darkness." But that slogan can be easily reversed: "Democracy dies in blinding light." People blinded by light can't see the truth either. And the *Post* is blinded by the fierce light of its own anti-Trump mania.

The *Post* has just claimed that candidate Moore behaved in an improper sexual manner with (or perhaps "to") a fourteen-year-old girl, Leigh Corfman, thirty-eight years ago.

Moore denies it.

The *Post* says that two of the then fourteen-year-old's childhood friends claim that she "told them at the time that she was seeing an older man, and one says Corfman identified the man as Moore." Corfman's mother says, according to the *Post*, that "her daughter told her about the encounter more than a decade later, as Moore was becoming more prominent as a local judge.

Three other women, according to the *Washington Post*, say "Moore pursued them when they were between the ages of 16 and 18 and he was in his early 30s, episodes they say they found flattering at the time, but troubling as they got older."

Moore denies all, except that he may have dated teenage girls.

What should rational people, not blinded by anti-Trump hysteria, believe?

Moore makes the argument that he has run for statewide office five times and this charge has never surfaced before. The argument is compelling, but not dispositive. We are living, now, in the post-Harvey Weinstein era: it takes less courage for victims of sexual aggression to come forward with their stories. Their silence twenty years ago, ten years ago, even five years ago is understandable.

What to do? Mitt Romney, the third-rate presidential contender in 2012, announced that "innocent until proven guilty is for criminal convictions, not elections." That is a dangerous standard for a Republican to lift: Republicans live in a hostile media world—in case you hadn't noticed.

Do we really want the media, now frenetically left-wing and anti-Trump, deciding who is innocent and who is guilty of whatever charges are publicized during a campaign? Isn't a jury, in this case of the voters of Alabama, a better bet?

And whatever happened to the statute of limitations? Those statutes exist for a reason: after the passage of many years, evidence gets old, records are lost, memories fade. Even current eyewitness accounts are notoriously inaccurate, as people with only minimal knowledge of trial law know.

Leigh Corfman may, today, truly believe what she has just told the *Washington Post*. Mitt Romney, who once aspired to the highest office in the land, a position that includes overseeing the Department of Justice, said, "I believe Leigh Corfman." Really? Romney has never laid eyes on the woman; all he has to go on is an account in a notoriously anti-Republican newspaper and yet—he believes!

Statutes of limitations also reflect, if only informally, the sense that, with the passage of time, people can change: Is Roy Moore really the same man he was thirty-eight years ago? Maybe amendment of life, through grace, is a belief limited to Christians, not intelligible to the left-wing media. But then how to account for their continuing adulation of Bill Clinton and his enabler Hillary?

What to do? There are two practical solutions.

One: let the voters be the jury. That's probably best.

But there is an alternative: Judge Moore drops out of the race; Attorney General Jeff Sessions resigns and runs a write-in campaign to regain the seat he vacated to become attorney general.

Sessions's tenure at the Justice Department has—how to put this delicately?—not been a thing of beauty: much has been left undone. And because he recused himself over the Russia business (a stupid mistake), he has been impotent in dealing with the metastasizing Russia scandals. President Trump all but fired him, understandably, which would have been yet another scandal.

A new attorney general could go all out after the Clintons, now in their twenty-fifth year of villainy, and get to the bottom of the real Russia scandals. And you'd be able to read all about it in the *Washington Post*.

Maybe.

A Tale of Two Cultures—and Two Bracelets
November 21, 2017

"Prospect of New Special Counsel Rattles Justice" was the scary front-page headline on a recent, worried edition of the *Washington Post*. The faux fuss was caused by Attorney General Jeff Sessions's suggestion that after weighing recommendations from senior prosecutors, he might appoint a special counsel to investigate Hillary Clinton's role in the Uranium One deal.

The key facts of that deal, for those whose attention has been wholly absorbed by the all-day coverage of the corruption trial of Sen. Bob Menendez (New Jersey Democrat, of course), are: first, Russian interests gave the Clinton Foundation $145 million dollars; second, paid (now finally, not after Harvey Weinstein but only after Roy Moore) disgraced former President Bill Clinton $500,000 for a short speech on tying shoelaces; following which, third, the sale of Uranium One to the Russians was cleared by the State Department then run by (now mostly disgraced for covering shamelessly for the now finally and fully disgraced said Bill Clinton) Hillary Clinton.

It's true that eight other government agencies also had to approve the sale, but does anyone really think that either a low-level bureaucrat, a mid-level Democratic appointee, or a possible future Democratic candidate for any office in the land (even canine collector) would have crossed the Democratic Party's very own WW of the W*?

Democratic Louis Renaults, who are rattled at what they claim is politicization of the Justice Department, should turn the clock back (any conservative can show them how) to the Eric Holder Justice Department days for a master class on politicizing.

John Fund and Hans A. Von Spakovsky wrote a whole book on corruption in the Holder Justice Department called *Obama's Enforcer: Eric Holder's Justice Department.*

One longtime lawyer in the Civil Rights Division told the authors Mr. Holder had:

---

* Think *Wizard of Oz*.

racialized and radicalized the division to the point of corruption. They embedded politically leftist extremists in the career ranks who have an agenda that does not comport with equal protection or the rule of law; who believe that the ends justify the means; and who behave unprofessionally and unethically. Their policy is to intimidate and threaten employees who do not agree with their politics.

People may differ on what kind of actions they think rise to the level of politicization. That is not only inevitable, but increasingly likely in our increasingly polarized political world. The real issue—slouching slowly toward our conscientiousness—is: Can two major cultures coexist in our democracy? In any democracy?

American politics has always been rambunctious. One need only read accounts of some of America's early political campaigns to get a sense of the permanence of political hyperbole—doing business as mudslinging.

Even so, perhaps, but only perhaps, we think the administration of justice should be different. It would be satisfying to blame the high-octane politicization of the courts on Sen. Edward Kennedy's unspeakable campaign in 1987 against Robert Bork's confirmation to be a justice on the Supreme Court. In fact, the uber-politicization of the courts began years earlier, perhaps in 1973 with the Supreme Court's decision in *Roe v. Wade* legalizing abortion. That decision was simply legislation from the bench; divisive then, divisive now. And more legislation, and more divisiveness, came with the Supreme Court's decisions legalizing sodomy, in *Lawrence v. Texas* (2003), and marriage between homosexuals, in *Obergefell v. Hodges* (2015).

But now the party's over, for the Left. And you can see why they're worried. There are eighteen vacancies on the courts of appeals and 127 in the federal district courts. The Senate has already confirmed twelve of President Trump's nominees. He may fill most of the remaining vacancies during his first term, and will certainly fill them all if he gets a second term. Because the judges serve for life, their influence will be felt for decades to come.

But there are still two cultures. One lives according to traditional Western Civ morality, the other pushes a feel-good cocktail of new-age practices; one believes in limited government, the other that government power should reign supreme. And the struggle will continue. The leftist side has been most prominently represented by the Clintons, though it does look now as if their day, finally, is passing. It's passing because of Hillary's defeat, and because of Hollywood mogul Harvey Weinstein's behavior, and that of so many of the left-wing cinematic glitterati whose behavior was just like his and, just like his, known to the rest of the denizens of the glitterati galaxy—including, undoubtedly, the Clintons.

Is it any wonder the Deplorables say, "Lock her up"?

Lock her up, indeed. Tempting. Better, probably—more fun, certainly—to put one of those ankle bracelets on her and on Bill, and sentence them to stay close to each other, always. Till death do them part.

A better slogan might be: "Lock her up—and give culture a chance." But the rattled writers of scary headlines know that traditional Western Civ culture may now get a chance even if she stays free.

Merry Christmas, Bill Burke
December 22, 2017

Once upon a time, Bill Burke was a high school athletic coach. One day, a bit like Stephen Harkness, who was said by later generations of his family to have been so dumb that he tripped over an oil well (he was a silent partner of John D. Rockefeller), Burke stumbled onto Shakespeare. Now a scholar, William L. Burke III is the headmaster of St. Sebastian's School, an all-boys Catholic day school in Needham, Massachusetts.

As with Levy's Real Jewish Rye, you don't have to be Catholic to go to St. Sebastian's. But the chance of becoming Catholic there is somewhat greater than the chance of becoming Jewish after eating Levy's rye bread. Students don't have to be Catholic to be admitted to St. Sebastian's, but all 375 of them do have to go to chapel. Every day. Students who are uncomfortable with that rule probably . . . should go to St. Sebastian's. Despite the chapel rule, the school makes it very clear that St. Sebastian's is not arrogant about its faith. Nor is it apologetic. Catholic means "universal."

What is the stated mission of St. Sebastian's? What is the stated mission of *your* school? A typical statement reads something like: "The Hedge Fund School prepares students to seek meaningful life-time success in a changing world"; or "The Brahmin Academy (TBA) trains its students to exercise responsible citizenship through local and global engagement, service, and environmental stewardship"; or "San Dollaromo is committed to excellence in education, preparing the next generation of global leaders."

St. Sebastian's mission is probably radically different from that of every public school in the country, as well as most private schools.

> A Catholic independent school, St. Sebastian's seeks to engage young men in the pursuit of truth through faith and reason. . . . The ideal St. Sebastian's graduate will be a moral and just person, a gentleman of courage, honor, and wisdom, a life-long learner who continues to grow in his capacity to know, to love, and to serve God and neighbor.

Pursuing truth through faith and reason? Saints alive! Don't you wish you'd thought of that? Despite that / Because of that [circle one], 16 percent of last year's graduating class at St. Sebastian's went to Ivy League colleges. (Hmm . . . Is that good or bad?)

In addition to teaching reading, writing, and arithmetic, St. Sebastian's also teaches its community how to support important academic endeavors. In 1990, when Burke arrived at St. Sebastian's, its endowment was $30,000. Today it's $36 million.

Now do you believe in the efficacy of prayer?

St. Sebastian's is currently engaged in another fundraising effort. It's trying to raise $24 million, not so much to compete with the well-heeled competition (how many schools seek to engage young men in the pursuit of truth through faith and reason?) as simply to pay the faculty more and build better facilities. If your bonus is seven figures this year (c'mon, we're all going to know), and maybe even if it's not, you could do worse than give to a school that teaches students how to live a life according to the best of Western Civ.

. . . And to a school that makes a particular effort to teach students how to write—an underrated skill in the age of 280-character tweeting. The cornerstone of St. Sebastian's writing program is

Freshman Writing, a course taken by all ninth graders. One aspect of writing that students are taught is structure. Students learn that structure doesn't stifle creativity. Structure demands it. Readers who want to learn more about structure should read the absolutely unputdownable *Farnsworth's Classical English Rhetoric*.

Here's a sample writing assignment St. Sebastian gives its ninth-grade students. Give it a try.

> Write a seven-sentence paragraph in this form:
> Simple sentence.
> Complex sentence.
> Compound sentence.
> Complex/compound sentence.
> Compound sentence.
> Complex sentence.
> Simple sentence.

(If you've forgotten what those definitions mean, you can look them up on the internet.)

Here's my attempt:

It's Christmas time again. Even though we know each year that Christmas is coming, we're never prepared for it. We weren't prepared for Christmas last year, and we probably won't be prepared for Christmas this year. We are never prepared for Christmas because it is our nature to think primarily of ourselves; we tend not to think about God, and we tend not to think about others. We are human and often selfish, and we need to practice being more generous and godly. If we understand our problem, we can attempt to solve it. It's not too late to prepare for Christmas.

And it's not too late for me to thank all my readers, especially those who comment—flatteringly and unflatteringly—and from whom I take much pleasure (and often wisdom), to all of whom, as well as to Bill Burke, I wish a very Merry Christmas.

Attorney General Sessions: Call Your Office
December 26, 2017

President Trump's tweeting provides great sport for the media and for Democratic politicians, most recently for Senator Kirsten Gillibrand (D–NY) who accused Trump of a sexist smear when he tweeted that Gillibrand would "do anything" for a campaign contribution. Is that what Oliver had in mind when he sang to Nancy, "I'd do anything . . . anything for you?"

Trump's tweet may have been unwise but probably not as unwise as the texts former Robert Mueller investigator Peter Strzok sent to his mistress, Lisa Page. (Once upon a time, having a mistress was a security risk. Not anymore. CBS News referred to Page only as Strzok's "colleague.")

Ordinarily, even FBI employees can have catty opinions, but not if they are working on sensitive investigations like the Trump–Russia probe, so Special Counsel Robert Mueller, quite properly, removed Strzok from his team.

End of story? Not even close. It may be the end of only a chapter in the story as it affects the Trump–Russia–Collusion investigation.

But it is an amazing development in a different story: the Hillary Clinton private email server scandal.

The problem with Strzok is that it was he who led the FBI's investigation into Hillary Clinton's use of her private email server. When James Comey announced on July 5, 2016, that he was recommending that Clinton not be prosecuted, Comey said that she had, nevertheless, been "extremely careless." He did not say that she had been "grossly negligent." It's true that those are just words and that there isn't a dime's worth of difference between them—except that the relevant statute happens to use "gross negligence" rather than "extreme carelessness" in criminalizing the conduct.

It now appears that "grossly negligent" was the wording in a previous draft of Comey's statement. And it may have been Strzok who changed the wording to the non-criminal "extremely careless." Although Comey's announcement was damaging—it may have cost Hillary the election—it was not as damaging as "grossly negligent" would have been. That would have raised the question, Why isn't the FBI recommending prosecution? Then Bernie Sanders might have been nominated, and then Trump probably *would* have won the popular vote that he said he did win.

A reason has been advanced for the change in wording: Mr. Comey had concluded that Mrs. Clinton had done nothing illegal and needed to have his statement reflect his decision.

But there's a problem with that explanation: Comey's original statement exonerating Clinton was drafted two months *before* she was even interviewed by the FBI. Which, among many other indicia, makes it look as if the fix was in from the beginning: the highly partisan Obama Democrats in the FBI had no intention of prosecuting Clinton.

That raises the question, Why did Comey make his damaging announcement about Clinton on July 5 which, even though it stated that she would not be prosecuted, may have cost her the election? The answer, probably, is that it wasn't at that time conceivable to a single one of the pro-Clinton FBI Democrats that Clinton could lose the election.

In retrospect, however, it does seem . . . extremely careless of the FBI's partisan Democrats to have left the paper trail that has now been discovered.

What is now publicly known about the FBI's Clinton investigation begs for congressional investigation.

But these revelations should also lead the FBI, now under the guidance of Attorney General Jeff Sessions, to reopen the investigation of Mrs. Clinton's use of her private email server. The Democrats would cry foul, of course, and claim that only banana republics investigate people who lose elections. But unlike banana republics, America is a country that believes in the rule of law, and believes that it should apply even to people who (or whose charitable foundations) can afford to buy whole banana companies.

What the president should do is instruct Attorney General Sessions to reopen the investigation into Hillary Clinton's email server scandal, and the Uranium One scandal as well (and ask him why he hasn't already done so). If Sessions interprets his recusal from the Russia investigation so broadly as to limit his power to investigate other matters, then Trump should replace him because

Sessions would be admitting that he is not able to see that the laws are faithfully executed.

Meanwhile . . . you can almost hear Bill and Hillary back in Chappaqua singing, "I'd do anything, anything for you." And, *pace* Kirsten Gillibrand, it would not be obvious that the song of the nation's most corrupt couple, who raked in millions in dodgy contributions to their family foundation, was laced with sexual overtones.

June 30: Pumpkin Time for Robert Mueller
January 7, 2018

Coins have two sides. So do most decisions evaluating risk. Look before you leap, *but* he who hesitates is lost. People who drive instead of fly because they think flying is dangerous haven't looked at the other side of the coin: statistics clearly show that flying is much safer than driving.

And so it is with Robert Mueller's investigation into connections between the Trump campaign and efforts Russia made to interfere in the 2016 election.

The country wants, or should want, to find out if impeachable offenses were committed. Even Trump supporters should not condone impeachable behavior. It is surely not necessary to find a crime—the violation of a specific statute—in order to impeach the president. Wouldn't his attempting to get, or actually accepting, Russian "assistance" in winning the election, coupled with an effort to hide it, be an impeachable offense, even if not technically a crime or treason?

The suspicion that Trump may have engaged in such activities may be justification enough for the current investigation. But investigations, including this one, are not cost-free. This investigation, ongoing and ongoing, casts doubts every day on the president's legitimacy and, by extension, on the acts he and his administration take.

The country should be willing to pay some cost for the investigation, but not, surely, *any* cost. Not the cost of paralyzing the president in dealing with an immediate threat from, say, North Korea. Or the economy.

The Left sees it differently. Their goal is precisely to paralyze President Trump. The Left has even given a name to its obstructionism: they call themselves "The Resistance." If there were not even gossamer hints of penumbras formed by emanations of suggestions that something had been amiss during the campaign, the Left would still be claiming treason or fraud. Some of them call regularly for Trump's impeachment. Rep. Maxine Waters (D–CA) has even called for Vice President Pence's impeachment.

The Resistance needs to be reminded that Robert Mueller's investigation is not like the Starr investigation into President Clinton's behavior. Everyone, even Democrats, knew Clinton was lying about Monica Lewinsky—and everyone was right. Senator Kirsten Gillibrand (Opportunist–NY) has now admitted as much. She has said that President Clinton should have resigned during the Monica Lewinsky scandal. "Things have changed today," she said. Oh, please.

What has changed is that the Clintons no longer have potential power and so there is no downside to Gillibrand's pushing them off the platform into the path of an oncoming Washington DC metro train—assuming it's running. For Democrats it's now safe to be anti-Clinton. And that makes being anti-Trump look (vaguely, somehow) nonpartisan.

But there is a downside to Mueller's investigation, at least in the view of people who care how the country is governed: how the American eagle flies in all its glory. The investigation calls everything President Trump does into question. The unending innuendoes from the left-wing press cast a pall over all the actions of the administration—from NATO to the tax cut, deregulation, Obamacare, and most perilously, North Korea. That may warm the hearts of lefties in Congress and the media, but it is not good for America.

It is, therefore, time to call the question. Robert Mueller, appointed on May 17, 2017, needs to produce evidence that foul deeds were done or close the investigation. That, unfortunately, is not likely. He is an honorable man, if flawed—flawed for insufficient attention to how the perceived bias of some of his investigative attorneys would taint his findings. But he is likely to drive on forever until he finds . . . something.

Forever is too long for the country.

If after thirteen months Mr. Mueller hasn't found anything substantial, he should close up shop. Yes, that means some impeachable behavior by Mr. Trump might go undiscovered. But rational people will understand that such behavior is not likely to have occurred if Mr. Mueller hasn't been able to find it after thirteen months of searching.

After thirteen months, it will be fair to say that the *risk* that Mr. Trump engaged in impeachable behavior is not as great as the *risk* to the country of continuing the investigation.

Therefore, the Republicans in the House and Senate should send a letter to President Trump requesting that he notify Special Counsel Robert Mueller of his intent to close the investigation on June 30, 2018. That will give Mr. Mueller a sense of urgency to find impeachable behavior—i.e., acts committed by the president, not just routine illegalities committed by staff and associates (lying to the FBI, money laundering, failing to disclose lobbying activities) that he has revealed so far.

Mr. Mueller's writ is not to collect injustices. There is a country to govern.

And flying is still safer than driving.

DACA for Dummies: Nightmare for Dreamers
January 16, 2018

DACA, "Deferred Action for Childhood Arrivals," is an Obama pen-and-phone program, not one created by legislation. It was simply a policy announced by President Obama on June 15, 2013. The date was chosen because it was the thirtieth anniversary of *Plyler v. Doe*, a Supreme Court decision that barred public schools from charging illegal immigrant children tuition.

Speaking in the Rose Garden, President Obama said: "These are young people who study in our schools, they play in our neighborhoods, they're friends with our kids, they pledge allegiance to our flag. They are Americans in their hearts, in their minds, in every single way but one: on paper."

Some people take paper seriously, and one could be excused for thinking Barack Obama would be one of them: he had to produce a Hawaiian birth certificate in order to put to rest the claim of the "birthers" that he was not an American.

Now, four and a half years after President Obama created DACA, there are about eight hundred thousand DACA people in the United States. They are often called "Dreamers" after the title of an act first introduced in 2001 (i.e., long before President Obama used his pen to create DACA), called "The Development, Relief, and Education for Alien Minors (DREAM) Act."

A fair question is, did Obama have the authority to create the DACA program? On twenty-two separate occasions, Obama said he couldn't create his own immigration law, even going so far as to assure nervous conservatives, "I'm president; I'm not king"—a wise act of humility: the birthers would have demanded to see his crown.

Nevertheless, he said that "what we can do is to prioritize enforcement, since there are limited enforcement resources, and say we're not going to go chasing after this young man or anybody else who's been acting responsibly and would otherwise qualify for legal status if the DREAM Act passed."

Fair enough, perhaps, but if so, then surely President Trump could use a similar rationale to cancel DACA (a nightmare for Dreamers). Obama focused his policy on deporting only people "who are really causing problems as opposed to families who are just trying to work and support themselves." But even those families are using services (education, medical care) which the states are required under *Plyler v. Doe* to provide.

Last September, the Dreamers' nightmare became reality: President Trump ordered that the DACA program end in March 2018, saying he was driven by a concern for "the millions of Americans victimized by this unfair system." Attorney General Sessions was more specific, saying the program had "denied jobs to hundreds of thousands of Americans by allowing those same illegal aliens to take those jobs." As of March 6, DACA permits will begin to expire.

Unless Congress can make a deal with President Trump.

A comprehensive deal would have three other, non-negotiable, parts: building the wall, ending chain migration, and ending the lottery system. The wall needs no comment—except to say that in past (pre-Resistance) years a number of Democrats have supported building at least sections of a wall.

Under chain migration, citizens and green-card holders can sponsor extended family members to get their own green cards, who in turn can sponsor *their* extended family members, and so on, *ad infinitum.* The White House estimates that as many as 930,000 chain migration immigrants (more than 70 percent of all new immigrants and more than the total number of DACA people here now) come to this country *every year*!

Under the visa lottery system approximately fifty thousand immigrants receive lifetime US work permits without regard to their skills (or, in most cases lack of them) or how they affect American workers.

What to do? It looks as if President Trump is determined to do something for the DACAs. It is true they are here illegally, but most of them came before reaching the age of reason. It was their parents who broke the law.

One obvious compromise is: let the DACAs stay, but not become voters. The Democrats can be expected to balk at that, and the president may decide to allow the DACAs to become citizens (assuming, of course, that the other three *sine qua nons* are agreed to). His calculation might be: the DACAs are more like ordinary Americans than other immigrants because they have been here since childhood—which means they will be both Republicans and Democrats, and may have some understanding of the genius of our constitutional system. And if, in the deal, the country can cut off chain migration—of 930,000 people a year!—that will be a terrific benefit to the country.

Failing a compromise now, action will be deferred for voter consideration in 2018, and perhaps again in 2020. Will the voters get it right? We can only dream.

Snow White Didn't Come from Burkina Faso
January 25, 2018

The Left Thinks DNA Stands for "Does Not Apply"

In 2015, approximately 17 percent of people in the United States married someone of a different race. Putting it ever-so-slightly differently, in 2015 approximately 83 percent of the people in this country married someone of the same race. What are we to make of that?

If you listen to the left-wing media and most Democrats, you'd expect them to say that those figures indicate that 83 percent of the people who got married in 2015 are racists. They haven't said that—yet. But we don't know they don't think it.

President Trump has been accused, but only by a Democrat, of calling some unfortunate countries "ess" holes, which by any objective standard they certainly are. The countries weren't named, but they appeared to include Haiti and a number of African countries, probably the five poorest: the Central African Republic, the Democratic Republic of Congo, Burundi, Liberia, and Niger. How many people do you know from those countries? How many times have you vacationed in one of those countries? With the children? Are you ashamed?

Trump was immediately called a racist by twice the number of usual suspects, who would probably also call him a racist if they caught him reading *Snow White and Her Seven Vertically Challenged Friends*.

A more charitable, and objective, view of Trump's comment is that he didn't have race in mind at all but was focusing only on the poverty of those countries, and what the typical immigrant from any one of them would be likely to bring to the United States.

Of course there is always the exceptional immigrant from, say, Guinea-Bissau, inevitably located by the media, who has rescued small children from a burning building on a wintry night while holding down two jobs that support a family of nine, several of whom through no fault of their own are disabled. But those heroes tend not to be *representative* of Guinea-Bissauan immigrants, or of immigrants from, say, the Central African Republic, DR Congo, Burundi, Liberia, Niger, or Haiti.

People who bring little with them other than poverty and disease are nevertheless entitled to government services, even if they are here illegally. Under the Supreme Court's decision in *Plyler v. Doe*, which held that the plaintiffs (illegal aliens) could claim the benefit of the Equal Protection Clause of the Constitution, no State shall "deny to any person within its jurisdiction the equal protection of the laws."

Paying for those services won't affect everyone: only slightly more than half the country pays any income tax at all. But the people who pay no income tax are precisely the people most likely to be thrown out of work by low-skilled or no-skilled immigrants. And they might reasonably ask, "Whose country is this, anyway?"

Citizens not afflicted with Antitrumpomania might ask the same question. But a lot of them, perhaps some of the 83 percent married to someone of the same race, might also ask how many people who are seriously . . . *different* from us do we want to let into our country?

Is that racist?

In a 2006 paper, "Do We Prefer People Who Are Similar to Us?" two sociologists, Avner Ben-Ner and Amit Kramer at the University of Minnesota, came up with an astounding conclusion. In a series of experiments with approximately two hundred students, they found that the students favored "those who are similar to them on any of a wide range of categories of identity over those who are not like them. Whereas family and kinship are the most powerful source of identity in our sample, all 13 potential sources of identity in our experiments affect behavior."

The thirteen sources of identity were: family and kinship, gender, occupation, ethnicity, culture, nationality, race, religion, political philosophy, dress style, community type, interests, hobbies and leisure, knowledge, sentiment, generation and age, socio-economic status, musical preference, and sexual preference.

Identity, they say, has genetic, cultural, and neural bases grounded in an evolutionary process, which, translated into the political vernacular, reads: America First.

A preference for people like ourselves is as much a part of who we homines sapientes are as our gender is. And so the Left and friends are entirely consistent when they seek to delegitimize both the concept of gender and nationality.

The Left is crazy, of course, and probably evil. But that doesn't justify racism—properly understood: Western Civ, which the Left no longer subscribes to, commands us to do good unto all men. But Galatians 6:10 adds the qualification, "especially unto them who are of the household of faith."

What is now at stake in the Time of Trump is whether America will remain America. It is an epic struggle we have been losing. Until now.

Racism: The First and Final Insult of Losers
January 31, 2018

In the same fortnight that the Bureau of Labor Statistics reported that the unemployment rate for black workers was the lowest in the forty-five years that data has been collected, a great gaggle of congressmen called Donald Trump a racist for, among other things, the comment he made about Haiti and some African countries. Exactly what the president said is in doubt, but it's also irrelevant.

It is irrelevant because previous presidents have done much worse things, yet are still revered by the liberal so-called intelligentsia. Lyndon Johnson used the "n" word more than a Grand Wizard of the Ku Klux Klan, yet remains one of the stars in the liberal firmament. As does Franklin Roosevelt, who failed to press for an antilynching bill and who appointed an active member of the KKK to the Supreme Court. Liberal icon, and practically the inventor of progressivism, Woodrow Wilson was an ardent racist, and long after such an attitude had ceased being "acceptable." Yet today's liberals revere those men, showing that their objection to Trump is just posturing.

Rep. Tim Walz (D–MN) said of President Trump's reported comments: "This is racism, plain and simple, and we need to call it that."

House Minority Whip Steny Hoyer (D–MD) said Trump could be a "racist" for calling several nations "s—hole countries."

Democratic Rep. Jim McGovern of Massachusetts tweeted: "America's president is a racist and this is the proof."

Sen. Elizabeth Warren (FEATHERS–MA) called Trump a "racist bully" whose supporters are "white supremacists."

The Democrats have a problem. They've been losing elections for years, at the local, state, and federal levels. Now with the obvious success of Trump's economic program—deregulation and tax cuts—they are, truly, rebels without a cause. Not just a party without a cause, but rebels: rebels rebelling against what Americans, in large numbers, want. Yes, Donald Trump may have lost the popular vote, but Republicans have been winning the popular vote at the state and local levels for years.

The only card in the Democrats' deck is the identity politics card. They have relied on the black vote for decades. They extended that strategy by wooing other groups, whom they called "minorities," likening them to blacks: homosexuals, lesbians, bisexuals, transgendered, queer/questioning, and intersex—a whole bathhouse of sexual pathologies. But a bathhouse does not a majority make.

The squeamish—members of the snowflake generation and too many of their elders—may blanch at the description of the Democrats' most loyal members as abnormal or perverse. According to the Gallup organization, the American public estimates that 23 percent of Americans are homosexuals. Listening to Democrats, you'd think *they* think it's 55 percent. The actual figure is 3.8 percent. For Democrats and others who may have graduated from an American public school, 3.8 percent may seem like a majority. Actually, it isn't. It's 47.2 points shy of a majority, "shy" being a charitable term here.

Meanwhile back in reality land, according to the AP, President Yoweri Museveni of Uganda said, "I love Trump because . . . he talks to Africans frankly."

The five poorest countries in Africa are Malawi, Burundi, Central African Republic, The Gambia, and Niger (Uganda is only the sixteenth poorest). There may be some really bright and hardworking people in those countries; and that all of the people in those countries are God's children no one should doubt—except that the liberal progressives do doubt it because they don't believe in God, and thus can't believe that a single one of those Africans is a child of God, in which case why should we, or the liberals, or Trump, or anyone else give a good goddam about them (unless the goal is to import them into this country so they will vote Democrat)?

Here are some question to ask Democrats Walz, Hoyer, McGovern, and Warren: Have you ever been to Malawi, Burundi, Central African Republic, The Gambia, or Niger? If not, why not? Where did you go on your last junket? London? Paris? Rome? Perhaps some other lily-white country. Are you currently a racist?

A new Harvard-Harris poll tells us that 81 percent of voters want to reduce legal immigration from its current level of more than 1 million immigrants per year, and 63 percent want it cut by *at least half!* *Eighty-five* percent of blacks think people should not be allowed to immigrate to the US unless they bring skills or money.

That is why the Schumer Shutdown of the federal government collapsed. That is why Donald Trump won the election.

And that is why the president's remarks in the Oval Office will not be seen by most Americans as racist.

Russia Collusion Saga—Chapter 27
February 20, 2018

One problem with Special Counsel Robert Mueller's investigation is that we keep talking about it. That, of course, was the primary reason the Resistance wanted the investigation. It was a way of slowing down, if not absolutely paralyzing, the Trump administration. The Resistance's objections to the Trump administration are not primarily to President Trump; they are to his programs.

The lefties didn't want lower taxes. They don't want fewer regulations. And they don't seem to care that unemployment has already gone down—in the case of blacks and Hispanics, to the lowest levels since records have been kept. We know liberals don't care because when Trump mentioned the declining rates in his State of the Union address, Democrats sat on their left-wing fannies while Republicans jumped up and cheered.

The latest salvo in the Russia Collusion Saga comes not from Robert Mueller's indictment of thirteen Russians—who live in Russia and will never be brought to justice here, indicating that the indictments were primarily for (or only for) show; not that shows can't be important for making points.

No, the latest salvo comes from Obama-loyalist John Brennan, who was the director of the Central Intelligence Agency at the time of the 2016 election. He has put out on Twitter his take on the Russia collusion business and the recent Mueller indictments, making fun of Trump's claim that the Russia collusion narrative is a hoax. Brennan tweeted: "Claims of a 'hoax' in tatters. My take: Implausible that Russian actions did not influence the views and votes of at least some Americans."

Wow! And water has been discovered flowing downhill. If Brennan is to be understood as meaning anything serious, he must mean that *enough* votes may have been changed to affect the outcome of the election.

Now that is—or would be—interesting. It would be interesting because the January 6, 2017, report of the intelligence community, i.e., the CIA, NSA, and now-discredited FBI, says that although Russia interfered in the election: "We did not make an assessment of the impact that Russian activities had on the outcome of the 2016 election."

So when did Brennan make his assessment that Russian actions did influence the views and votes of at least some Americans? Brennan left the CIA on January 20, 2016. Did he make his assessment sometime in the fourteen days between January 6 when the report of the intelligence community was published and January 20 when he resigned?

If so, did he make his assessment all on his own, without any assistance from any of the CIA staff? He was sitting in his office late one night in the dark, nursing a sixteen-year-old single malt whisky when—bingo!—the light goes on (but it's only the charlady: she turns it off quickly) and he realizes that it's implausible that Russian actions did not influence the views and votes of "at least some Americans."

Or was he aided in his deliberations by CIA staff? If so, shouldn't the American people be informed of those deliberations? They were presumably not his own, or at least not solely his own—certainly not his own "property." They belong to the American people. Why weren't the American people informed by Mr. Brennan before now?

Or did Mr. Brennan come to his conclusion after he left the CIA? In which case, did he acquire new facts that were not available to the CIA when he was there? And if so, how on earth did he do that? Did he have the security clearance to see new information?

Or, a fourth possibility: Mr. Brennan is just pumping out a lot of hot air.

Meanwhile, back at the ranch, Democrats have been reduced to claiming that there was nothing wrong with using the Christopher Steele dossier (aka the Hillary Clinton–Democratic National Committee dossier) as the basis for the FISA warrant to spy on Carter Page, the sometime window-dressing "advisor" to the Trump campaign. There was nothing wrong, they say, because the "facts" in the Steele dossier may turn out to be true after all.

But of course that isn't the point. The point is that even if the facts in the dossier do turn out to be true, the FBI didn't know they were true at the time they presented the dossier to the FISA court. James Comey, the FBI director at the time, has described the dossier as "salacious and unverified." Basing an application for a FISA warrant on a document known to be unverified—and not just unverified but also from a highly partisan source, who would not be likely to present the whole truth—would seem to be . . . just what you'd expect from the Obama administration.

But, see? That's the problem. We're spending all this time on the Russia collusion story instead of on whether we should have a strong dollar, or cut the Department of Education budget by 5 percent (no!) or by 50 percent (yes!!), or make Colorado obey the national marijuana laws. That distraction is precisely what the Resistance wants.

And that's why Robert Mueller (an honorable man, as honorable as any man in Washington—and that includes women too) should be told to wrap up his investigation by, say, May 17, 2018, one year after he was appointed. There's a country to govern, and the Mueller investigation distracts us from that business and compels us to move on to: Russia Collusion Saga—Chapter 28.

Should the Pentagon Bend Over Backwards to Support Trans Military Personnel?

March 15, 2018

Any day now the Trump administration is expected to announce its policy on transgendered people serving in the military.

Can you imagine writing or reading that sentence twenty years ago?

On the morning of D-Day, Franklin Roosevelt asked the nation to join him in prayer for "our sons, pride of our nation" who had set upon a mighty endeavor, "a struggle to preserve our Republic, our religion, and our civilization."

That very civilization, which successfully repulsed the onslaught of the Boche, is under attack from top people in the American government. The Supreme Court has held, not just that prohibiting marriage between people of the same sex is unconstitutional, but that those who oppose the concept are bigots. Senator Bernie Sanders (honeymoon spot: Soviet Union) thought Russell Vought was unfit to be deputy director of the Office of Management and Budget because of his Christian belief that salvation is found through Jesus Christ alone. Sen. Diane Feinstein (D–CA) attacked Amy Barrett, a Trump nominee for the court of appeals who is a Catholic and a mother of seven, saying, "The dogma lives loudly in you, and that's of concern."

Is this a real concern or a media-created issue? How many transies really want to join the army? And, perhaps most important, do young people care? It is they, after all, who will have to share their foxholes. If they don't care, should we?

Perhaps. They may say they don't care. But what if military experience shows otherwise; shows that, when the incoming starts . . . coming in, the men in the foxholes care desperately?

And how many transies are there anyway? One estimate is that there is about one transgendered person in every 250 adults in the country. About 180,000 people join the military each year, which means there may be as many as 720 transies in that group. That is not a large number and the administration may simply not want to take on the fight that would be required to keep them out.

Why do transies want to join the military? One reason may be to have the government pay for their transgender surgery, the average cost of which is said to be at least $130,000.

Question: Why should taxpayers have to pay for that? Answer: They shouldn't.

What the administration may decide to do is allow transgendered people into the military provided they have already completed the transgender process, from soup to nuts, a process that could be administratively determined to be eighteen months. That will keep people from joining until they've settled into otherhood.

It's a reasonable guess that such a policy will discourage at least some, and perhaps many, transgendered people from trying to join the military. But will such a policy satisfy the LGBTQ political lobby and their frenetic—and Trump Resistance—allies, all of whom are probably less interested in gender travel than in trashing Western Civilization and the Trump administration while they're at it?

And who will make the decision? President Trump or Secretary of Defense James Mattis? It's not clear that the administration has the fortitude to take on the LGBTQ lobby. When the administration, at the urging of Secretary Mattis, nominated Mark Green, a former state senator of Tennessee and a physician who once served alongside Army Special Operations troops, to be secretary of the army, the LGBTQ lobby went berserk. Green has suggested that being transgendered is a disease. That shouldn't have been so shocking. It's binary: wanting to switch genders either is a disease or it isn't. Green's opinion probably reflects that of most Americans. Probably most doctors too.

Another question is how much influence Anthony Kurta will have on the decision. Kurta, an Obama holdover, has been nominated to be deputy under secretary of Defense for Personnel and Readiness, the office that is tasked, under a memo of Obama Defense Secretary Ash Carter, with creating, managing, and overseeing policies regarding transgender issues.

Last June, Kurta proclaimed that the US military would celebrate June as LGBT "pride" month (are Qs the new MIAs?) and he was a key speaker at the Pentagon's gay pride celebration—a speech probably not written by Phyllis Schlafly.

The question for the Trump administration is whether it needs to go to war with the LGBTQ lobby right now. Mark Green concluded it did not, or would not—or perhaps it was concluded for him—and withdrew his name from consideration, which means Green is out and Kurta is in: not the optimal situation for Western Civ.

Trump has a fair wind and following seas at the moment (tax cuts, deregulation, declining unemployment, Korea,) though there may be stormy weather ahead, but he may simply not care, or not care enough, about keeping a few oddballs out of the military—and yes, Virginia, one out of 250 is odd.

Probably, ordinary people, ordinary conservatives can live with letting the oddballs in, so long as the taxpayers don't have to pay the cost of their surgeries and consequent adaptations. Any policy more generous to the transies than that may produce blood in the streets in defense of Western Civ. But then, that's what blood is for.

Let the Word Go Forth: Chappaquiddick Invented the Cover-up

April 8, 2018

Chappaquiddick—a name that should live in infamy . . . as "Watergate" does. But as bumper stickers said during the Nixon scandal, nobody died at Watergate. And nobody's died at Mar-a-Lago either. You'd never know that the Kennedys' very own Chappaquiddick saga is the mother of all American scandals—and *that*, of course, is the real story.

The movie gives a more or less accurate picture of part of that story. Some say that Jason Clarke's portrayal of Edward M. Kennedy is perfect, including his voice. Different ears, perhaps those brought up near Boston, may think differently. Clarke makes Kennedy seem a bit listless—not the way most people remember him, but then Chappaquiddick took place only thirteen months after Kennedy's brother Robert was killed, and Kennedy probably was a bit listless.

In an early scene after the opening credits, Kennedy is talking to twenty-eight-year-old blond Mary Jo Kopechne on the beach (not by accident, probably, the director does not have them sitting close to each other) raising an obvious question: how did Kennedy get to the beach? Two methods leap immediately to mind: 1) He drove (the movie has him being driven down Dike Road and over the bridge—he's in the back seat reading the paper, presumably in English) and then walked to the beach; or 2) He rappelled down a seriously long rope from Apollo 11, then on its way to the moon.

The people of Massachusetts selected number 2 as the obviously correct answer because Kennedy said, later that week, that he was unfamiliar with that part of the Chappaquiddick Island, i.e., the road to Dike Bridge, the bridge itself, and the beach, and they believed him sufficiently to return him to the United States Senate.

Later the same evening, Kennedy and Kopechne go to the party at a rented house to be with others from Robert Kennedy's staff: nothing wrong with that. The group was described in some press accounts as six men and six women, imparting an almost certainly undeserved whiff of scandal—people expect one down-wind from the Kennedys. Kennedy and Kopechne leave the party in his Oldsmobile, park, and chat. After a few minutes, she says (this is a movie, of course), "We should get back." He replies, "No, we should go to the beach."

Kennedy overshoots the turn to Dike Road and stops on Willett Lane, a dirt road at the junction of the road to the ferry and to the bridge. Just then, about 12:45 a.m., Deputy Sheriff Christopher ("Huck") Look Jr. drives up, gets out of his vehicle, and asks if they are having car trouble, whereupon Kennedy backs up furiously, speeds down Dike Road, and careens off the bridge.

The rest, you might say, is history. But of course, it isn't, and neither are the opening scenes. A lot of it is conjecture because the Kennedy clan and its media mafia sought to sanitize the event in order to protect the sole remaining heir to the Kennedy throne—and bedrooms, where young staffers might be, uh, bedded.

Probably the two most damning facts in the movie, and in real life, are that when Kennedy walked from the bridge back to the house where the party was going on, he didn't stop at any of the four houses along the way to ask for help. Nor did he follow the advice of his two pals (Joe Gargan and Paul Markham) that he call the police as soon as he got back to his hotel in Edgartown. Why didn't he, or why didn't he stop at one of the four houses? Perhaps because he was drunk, and it would show. Nine or ten hours after the accident he did report it to the police, but by then Mary Jo Kopechne had drowned.

Only she probably didn't just drown. The diver, John Farrar, who extracted the body the next morning, said it was twisted in a way that suggested she was searching for pockets of air. Farrar said he could have gotten her out of the car in twenty-five minutes. That may be the crux of the scandal: Kopechne died because Kennedy dithered, probably thinking more about his political future (how he could beat up on Robert Bork by portraying his America as "a land in which women would be forced into back-alley abortions" and "blacks would sit at segregated lunch counters") than the girl in the car.

Kennedy is whisked back to the Kennedy compound in Hyannis Port, Massachusetts, and then the Kennedy spin doctors arrive to control the narrative: Theodore (Ask Not) Sorensen, Robert (even he himself conceded he was a failure) McNamara, Burke Marshall (head of the Justice Department's Civil Rights Division under President Kennedy) and family members, the Stephen Smiths and Sargent Shrivers. They plot and scheme how to lie, how to dissemble. Kennedy continues to screw up, wearing an obviously unneeded neck brace to Kopechne's funeral.

The story they concoct is that Kennedy left the party house around 11:30 p.m., in time to get the last ferry back to Edgartown (it stopped running at midnight). He said he was unfamiliar with the road, and instead of staying on the paved road which turned left, turned hard right onto the dirt road that led to Dike Bridge.*

In the end, there was a hearing. Kennedy pled guilty to leaving the scene of an accident and got a suspended two-month jail sentence—and may, or may not, have promised to say his prayers at night and eat only Grape-Nuts for three weeks.

Then there's a televised address to the people of Massachusetts. "I'm really sorry, and I was very confused." Yada, yada, yada. Then interviews with the voting public, followed by a recording of Kennedy's speech at the 2008 Democratic National Convention: "The work begins anew. The hope rises again." (And the nightmare lives on.) Fade to credits. End of movie.

But not end of scandal.

The rest of the scandal was detailed in pieces in the *Vineyard Gazette* and the *Washington Post* in 1989. The foreman of the grand jury that investigated the Chappaquiddick events told reporters that his jury was misled and blocked in its investigation. The judge at the inquest (which the Kennedy people had managed to have held behind closed doors) in his final report made it clear that the evidence was that Kennedy knew where he was headed.

The judge bullied the grand jurors and warned them repeatedly that they were bound to secrecy, and he even had a Roman Catholic priest in clerical garb sit beside him.

The grand jury foreman said that the judge so intimidated him that he didn't know that the panel didn't need the judge's permission to subpoena witnesses. The jury was also denied access to the

---

* For the implausibility of his account, see the video that I took about two weeks after the event: https://www.youtube.com/watch?time_continue=8&v=kaAdmY6lUts.

inquest report which said that Kennedy should have been charged with reckless driving.

"Yes, I think that we were manipulated," the foreman said, "and I think that we were blocked from doing our job, and if you want to use the term cover-up, then okay, that's what it was."

The grand jury foreman told the *Vineyard Gazette*, "There seem to be two sets of rules and justices that are doled out—one for the rich and powerful, and one for the regular people, for you and me." Exactly.

That's the real story, the story that should have been told to you and me, but for some reason that story doesn't make it into the movie. Instead of the roll at the film's end telling us what happened to some of the characters, the director could have just run the content of the five paragraphs that precede this one.

The Kennedy clan is said to be unhappy with the movie. Really? Then they couldn't have liked the best line in the movie: in the car going to Mary Jo's funeral, Teddy says, "Thanks for doing this, Joannie," and she gets to reply. The Kennedys should realize that it could have been worse. And should have been. What they should be is ashamed, at telling one small fib for the Kennedy clan, one giant fraud for the country.

Kids, Gun Control, and *Lord of the Flies*
April 25, 2018

"I'm not learning my subjects—I'm learning how to literally survive," said Marusya Airumian, a fourteen-year-old eighth grader at Takoma Park Middle School in Silver Spring, Maryland, cleverly splitting the infinitive in order to make her point.

She was one of thousands of students who walked out of their classrooms into schoolyards and streets to protest gun violence on April 20, the nineteenth anniversary of the school shooting at Columbine High School in Colorado.

Students by the dozens were interviewed by members of the press, but gun violence itself remained aloof, possibly ignoring the entire protest.

"We deserve to live without fear of violence," said Brianna Lee,

17, a junior at Walter Payton College Preparatory High School in Chicago, raising the question of what she or any of her classmates has done to *deserve* anything. They live in the United States of America, where most of the people on this planet would gladly give most or all of what they have to live. There are people who have struggled for a lifetime to support themselves, their children, and their communities who may deserve something, but surely none of them expected a life without struggle or suffering. How do adults define themselves if life is an unending downhill stroll?

It's part of American advertising culture that we all *deserve* a life without struggle or suffering—not to mention stomach upsets, or halitosis, or uncomfortable mattresses, or dishpan hands (ugh!), or psoriasis (whatever that is), or ugly handbags, or flat feet, and, if you're a college snowflake (especially at Yale), without safe spaces.

But what has a seventeen-year-old like Brianna Lee done to deserve anything? Get herself born, fed, inoculated, raised, dressed, and taken to school in the land of the free and home of the brave where 98 percent of the world's children would like to study; Walter Payton College Prep is a public four-year selective enrollment magnet high school—better make that 99 percent of the world's children who'd like to study there.

The *Washington Post* has determined that since the Columbine High shooting in 1999, 131 children, *educators, and other people* have been killed (and another 254 injured) in assaults at schools. Oddly— but not surprisingly?—the *Post* doesn't break down the number: lumping "educators and other people" into the count makes it larger. Now, 131 is not a large number in a country of 350 million people; even so, inserting "only" before it would be considered callous; and of course people have also been injured in the attacks as well as killed. Nevertheless, as perhaps a few students educated in America's public school system (which is run by and for the teachers unions), may be able determine, 131 is a far smaller number than 572; (Yale snowflake alert!) 572 is the average number of children (*not* including educators and other people) who are killed *each year* in automobile accidents, raising the question: Why isn't seventeen-year-old Brianna Lee skipping school to demand safer driving in America?

There are two answers to that question, one of which is that adults by the millions like driving too fast and under a bit of influence or on their cell phones and what do you know about driving anyway, kid, and besides it's my car, and I've been driving since before you were born, and you're damn lucky I don't make you walk to school the way Abe Lincoln did, and if you spend all day frolicking in the park with your greasy classmates you'll never amount to a hill of beans and get a job and be self-supporting so your mother and I can retire and have some fun.

Second: Cars are far more dangerous than guns, but car control is not chic—yet, so the kids are being used by their elders and the liberal media who, not having been able to win the intellectual argument for gun control, are shamelessly parading the kids around to make the emotional case for limiting the Second Amendment.

Marusya Airumian, of the split infinitive, was also quoted as saying, "Children shouldn't have to die because people in government are lazy." As a declarative sentence, that parses (e.g., a child shouldn't bleed to death because a government doctor wants to finish watching *The View*), but if that's Marusya's understanding of why her favorite piece of gun control legislation hasn't been enacted, she needs to repeat Government I, and learn also about disagreements, debates, and compromises . . . and other people's opinions.

And read *Lord of the Flies*, and try to understand why children, who aren't especially good at governing themselves, shouldn't—until they grow up—have a say in governing a republic whose founding documents were devised to filter and limit the power of the mob to rule the body politic.

Why President Trump Should Veto the Bill Prohibiting Him from Firing Robert Mueller

April 27, 2018

Last week a group of senators introduced a bill (the "Special Counsel Independence and Integrity Act") designed to protect special counsels like Robert Mueller from being fired by a president. Majority Leader Mitch McConnell has now said he will not bring it up for a vote, and that will deprive President Trump of a terrific opportunity to clean up a mess made by the Supreme Court in 1935. If Republicans were to vote for the bill, Democrats would too, presumably, in which case it would pass and go to President Trump for signature.

Or veto.

Not Jimmy the Greek, nor any of his ancestors going all the way back to Homer the Greek, would have seen such lopsided odds favoring a veto as there would be for this bill.

And the president would be on good constitutional ground, albeit a bit overgrown.

Once upon a time, the United States of America had a constitution that provided for three branches of government (stop me if you've heard this one before): a legislative branch, an executive branch, and a judicial branch.

The press, sometimes described as the Fourth Estate, is actually not mentioned in the US Constitution, an omission that continues to rankle to this day.

The branches share power, but only one is supreme: the legislative branch. It is supreme because (a) it makes the laws that the executive branch is supposed to execute; (b) it can remove jurisdiction from the judicial branch if it doesn't like the way it interprets the Constitution; and (c) it can remove the chief executive officer, the president, from office. And, not incidentally, the powers of the legislative branch are defined in the *first* Article of the Constitution.

The press also can remove a president from office, as it did in the case of Richard M. Nixon—but we digress, and will opine only that compared to the current occupant of that office, Mr. Nixon was a white-tie player, by the Marquis of Queensberry out of Emily Post.

Where in that constitutional scheme, the reader who has been paying attention might ask, does a special counsel who cannot be fired by the president fit? That of course is *the* question. *The* answer is: nowhere.

The Framers of the Constitution separated and diffused power in order to protect the liberty of the people. Checked power was dangerous enough; unchecked power more so. The more difficult it is to remove someone from his office, the more likely he is to abuse his power and the more likely it is that the people's freedom will be abridged.

That was, and is, the correct understanding of why power in our system of government was separated and diffused. But the Supreme

Court carved out an exception in a 1935 case involving a deceased member of the Federal Trade Commission.

William E. Humphrey was appointed by President Roosevelt to be a commissioner but was subsequently asked by President Roosevelt to resign because, essentially, he was a conservative. ("I do not feel that your mind and my mind go along together on either the policies or the administering of the Federal Trade Commission.")

Humphrey refused and Roosevelt fired him. Subsequently Humphrey sued for back pay, a suit that was carried on by his executor after he died and that eventually reached the Supreme Court—which got it wrong.

The Supreme Court deemed the Federal Trade Commission (and by extension the multitude of other so-called independent regulatory commissions like it—there are now at least fourteen such major commissions) to be a "quasi legislative and quasi judicial" body that "cannot in any proper sense be characterized as an arm or an eye of the executive."

But if those agencies cannot be characterized as arms or eyes of the executive, then they cannot be characterized as fitting into the constitutional scheme the Framers devised.

This could have been, and perhaps still could be, President Trump's finest hour. He could warn Congress that if it were to override his veto of the Special Counsel bill, he would, *that day*, fire not only the special counsel, but also all the commissioners on all of the so-called independent regulatory commissions that have not been appointed by him.

He could tell Congress and the nation that what Congress proposed is unconstitutional and that his sworn obligation is to support and defend the Constitution of the United States against all enemies, foreign *and domestic*, whatever the political consequences may be.

In the perfect storm that would follow, the special counsel, Robert Mueller, would become an insignificant datum—newspapers have only one front page. There are hundreds of lawyers in the country, perhaps thousands, who have a proper understanding of the constitutional structure of our government who would support the constitutionality of Trump's action even if they think it would be unwise of the president to exercise it by firing Mueller.

This could be Trump's finest hour. The briar patch awaits.

Make Congress Work Again
April 30, 2018

Will you love me in November as you did in . . . MAYDAY! MAYDAY! In a special election last Tuesday in Arizona's Eighth Congressional District, the Republican won but fell short of Trump's 2016 twenty-point margin by *fifteen* points—enough to spell "You've got trouble."

Now what? That's the question Donald Trump should be asking as the mid-term elections approach. Trump's a cagey fellow, and he certainly read America better than any of the other Republicans did in 2016. And better than Hillary too.

But if a week is a long time in politics, the 2016 election—and Trump's remarkable victory—takes us back to the Pleistocene epoch, back even before Al Gore was having global warming nightmares.

Now the ice age is back, at least in the Senate where Trump's nominees get the glacial treatment from the Democrats. At the current pace (two to three confirmations a week instead of ten or more), it will take nine years to fill the vacancies the president needs to fill in order to make sure *his* people are making the key managerial and policy decisions.

But there are other problems. One is the budget process. After the last fiasco—Congress sent a 2,232-page, $1.3 trillion omnibus spending bill to the president—the president said, "I will never sign another bill like this again." Really? Those are brave words. But what's he going to do to see that he doesn't have to sign such a bill again?

The Senate quite regularly works for only a few days a week— about three, actually, which affords them a four-day weekend. Not bad. But not good for the rest of the country that wants their government to work.

The gossip in Washington is that there is absolutely no chance Trump can avoid having to sign another humongous spending bill— "The Bad Government Spending Act of 2018," or perhaps "The Second Bad Government Spending Act of 2018." Congress will send it to the president; it will provide for, among other things, pay for the military; and Congress will dare the president not to sign it. What's he supposed to do, especially if it's right before the election? Not sign it? Stop paying the military? Shut down the government? Puh-lese.

Whatever he's going to do, he has to do *now*. He has to make Congress work, and especially the Senate. For purely partisan reasons, he should make the Senate work *at least* five days a week: that would keep vulnerable Democratic senators from going home to campaign for reelection.

But why not six days a week? Lots of Americans work six days a week. Why shouldn't congressmen? The country's debt is now gigantic—it's better to describe it adjectively rather than numerically because the number is so high it has become abstract. Any business or family facing a comparable debt would work seven days week.

Why not Congress?

Why doesn't President Trump plan a surprise visit to Capitol Hill on a Friday afternoon (or even a Thursday afternoon), with the appropriate film crews tagging along for fun. He could be seen going into the offices of senators and representatives and asking to see them and—stone the crows!—they're not there. Five or ten of those clips played on the evening news might send a message, to the politicians (maybe), but certainly to the voters: tell your representative or senator to get back to work, damn it!

Then the president should go on television and tell the American people how badly the system is working—he can replay the clips of the empty offices. He should ask the people to call their congressmen and tell them: no August recess unless you do your job and unless you can list five (ten?) actions that you'll take before skipping town.

That's just basic good governance. But there's a partisan kicker, if the Republicans will kick. It's Republicans, after all, who control Congress now, and if they want that to continue, they need to do something dramatic. The tax bill they passed, thought initially to be a magic carpet to reelection, has turned out, as even the Republican leadership now has realized, to be a low-end, already-frayed product. See: last Tuesday special election in Arizona.

Trump should tell the congressmen that he won't be campaigning for people who don't get with the program, *his* program, which includes immigration reform, the wall, defunding sanctuary cities, infrastructure, and defunding Planned Parenthood. He could even dip into his own fortune and mail out a hundred thousand "Make Congress Work Again" hats.

Otherwise, he, and we, may get to experience a new political Pleistocene epoch.

What's Next for Conservatism?

June 2, 2018

For God, For Country, and For Main Street

Conservatives tend to be skeptical of joining great political movements because they tend to be skeptical of both politics and movements that are great. They prefer the little platoon, the shire, which they know to be safe—or at least probably safer than what lies beyond. Not all politics may be local, but all politics that isn't local tends toward the totalitarian, however far short of it it may actually fall.

That sounds almost like a philosophy of government—though not a government that any American alive today has experienced. But times can change, and they have with the election of Donald Trump. Conservatives who have been asking, "Where do we go from here?" have discovered the answer may be, "Where Donald Trump is going."

Most conservatives and many Libertarians saw the conservatism of William F. Buckley Jr., the founder of modern American conservatism, as a compromise. (Today's Libertarians tend to see it as just compromised.) Buckley was a free marketeer who opposed radical social experimentation. But he accepted the superstate (even knowing it was a threat to freedom at home) because it was necessary to do battle with the threat to freedom from abroad: communism, the force of darkness that threatened the globe for almost half a century.

Today's young Libertarians, who came of age as Ronald Reagan was readying history's dust bin for the Evil Empire, think the previous age consistently overrated communism's threat. It didn't; and the youngsters should show more respect for the analytical ability and survivalist instincts of their freedom-loving forebears whose blood ran strong for so long—even as they should respect their fore-bears' desire to preserve a culture free from, and opposed to, radical social experimentation unmoored from the truths and traditions that sustained Western Civilization for centuries.

None of this is to say we must speak Latin or Old English, or write in Carolingian script, however prettier that is than the scrib-bly scrawly scratches of the computer era. In 1964—the year Barry Goldwater kicked off the modern *political* conservative movement (the intellectual movement having begun in 1955 when Buckley founded *National Review*)—Buckley said, "Modern formulations are necessary even in defense of very ancient truths. Not because of any alleged anachronism in the old ideas—the Beatitudes remain the es-sential statement of the Western code—but because the idiom of life is always changing, and we need to say things in such a way as to get inside the vibrations of modern life."

Billions and billions of vibrations later, Buckley said that conser-vatism was in need of repristination, a fancy WFB word perhaps for his "modern formulations" of 1964.

But even before "modern formulations" and "repristination," there was the dedication in Buckley's first book, his history-making and history-changing *God and Man at Yale*: "For God, for Country, and for Yale . . . *in that order*," wherein lies a guide, if not a roadmap, to a conservative polity.

Can we have a vibrant conservatism without God? Self-described "amiable, low-voltage atheist" George Will says yes, as did serious Roman Catholic Buckley. Russell (*The Conservative Mind*) Kirk said no.

History, and especially the decade since Buckley's death, would seem to support Kirk. America's Founding Fathers were religious. As was William Wilberforce who led the decades-long movement to stop the slave trade in England. As was Martin Luther King Jr., the great civil rights champion in America. Perhaps the jury is still out, but it's not clear that the admonition to love our neighbors as ourselves (and its modern statist equivalents) has any moral force if it comes only from, say, a Barack Obama who ridicules people who cling to their Bibles, or from Senator Dianne Feinstein (D–Cloud Cuckoo Land dba CA) who insinuated that a nominee to the court of appeals couldn't be a good judge because she was a Catholic. What is the authority of the state—other than the Glock 22 with its fifteen rounds of .40 S&W cartridges carried by most police officers—to command us to be *nice* to our fellow man? Equality and respect for blacks—and for *Jews*? Who says?

True conservatism must include love of country, which means not just love of this country but a *preference* for this country over all others—even as people in other countries should prefer theirs to ours. Why do we want people from Haiti or the Central African Republic to come to the US, or from Mexico or El Salvador or other less happier lands? We have our own problems: the structurally poor, the undereducated, legions of fatherless children, an opioid crisis, and a growing debt that could usher in economic conditions that would make the Great Recession look like the Promised Land.

A conservative prefers his patch, his little acre, his blessed plot; his town to his state; his state to all the others. That is the essence of federalism, a founding principle of the Founding Fathers, and one that mimics the Catholic tradition of subsidiarity.

So what should a conservative polity look like? It comes as a shock—like a Bob Mueller raid in the dark of the night—to realize that many of the policies promoted by President Trump are out of the conservative playbook.

Trump is no pious Christian, *but* he is proud of his role, synecdochically significant, in making it safe to say "Merry Christmas" again. He has wooed people who cling to their Bibles (and to their guns). And he may be the most anti-abortion president we've ever had.

Trump prefers America to other countries, a preference reported as scandalous because of his accurate, if . . . famously unusual, description of some of those other hell-hole countries.

Trump seems naturally federalist—e.g., in wanting to get rid of those "lines around the states" that restrict the health insurance companies from writing policies on people who don't live in their states. He seems instinctively opposed to the superstate: his deregulation efforts have already gotten America moving again, and he's making it easier to fire workers who work for the federal bureaucratic leviathan state.

He seems to care about communities that have had their middle class jobs shipped overseas. The free trade purists have their arguments: they tell us that free trade makes the world richer, and that may be true. But the US share of world GDP has gone down in the last fifteen years, while the share of the Industrializing Six countries has gone up.

Could it be that "Make America Great Again" qualifies as a modern formulation of an ancient truth, even if not written in Carolingian minuscule? Many Americans, perhaps excluding the editors of some national political journals, would agree.

Trump came to his positions, presumably, because of the work the conservative movement has been doing all these years since 1955, and he has been, surprisingly to many, remarkably successful in changing America's course. But there remains much to be done by conservatives to prepare and popularize a conservative polity.

Trump has not yet taken on the new-age cultural Marxists who are so calculatedly evil that they are trying to erase the difference between the sexes, shamelessly milking the sentiment that promoted equality for blacks. Even a foul-mouthed, pussy-grabbing rhetoric is preferable to the cultural vandals who seek to institutionalize, through the courts—hello totalitarianism!—their own bizarre sexual proclivities, vandals like Friend-of-Hillary Obergroppenführer* of the liberal intelligentsia Harvey Weinstein, and so many of their friends. Better a one-night stand with a porn star (if you choose to believe that story) than accepting homosexual marriage as normal or forcing women and girls to shower with males who are so confused they don't even know what sex they are. Alas, even national magazines that review the culture and should be thwarting history tend to take a pass on the cultural issues if they have sitting around their own table people you, er, wouldn't want your children playing with.

Nor has Trump tackled America's amazing debt growth. But that is not a battle a politician can win on his own. Politicians who promise to cut Social Security or welfare significantly, even if only in the far distant future, will not get elected, absent a prior and successful intellectual campaign to educate the voters.

So, the problems of culture and debt remain, each potent enough to do America in, as sobering a fact to contemplate as a Cold War battery of totalitarian missiles aimed at the land of the free. Conservatives do not lack for challenges!

Still, battles have been fought and won, which indicates that it is

---

* Note to reader: I know, I know: it should be Obergruppenführer, but let's enjoy the pun.

still possible to fight and win battles. No one would be likely to describe Donald Trump as the Repristinator-in-Chief. But the country is already better off than if Clinton, or even any of Donald Trump's Republican opponents, had been elected president.

True conservatism was never a rigid ideology and never a political program defined by a particular politician. Conservatism is a way of life, a practical program for keeping the people of this country (shaped by history, faith, and culture) safe and free, and if necessary, more safe and free than prosperous. There may be calamity ahead—but there is always calamity ahead. Today, conservatives and *conservatism*, and the nation, are better off, and headed in a better direction, than they have been for years.

Repristinated or not.

D-Day 2018
June 5, 2018

D-Day 2018. Ah, but who knows what D-Day is? Or when?

D-Day is June 6. On that day in 1944, some 160,000 Allied troops landed along a fifty-mile stretch of heavily fortified Normandy coastline to fight the forces of Nazi Germany. (Normandy is in France—for the 10 percent of college graduates who think D-Day happened at Pearl Harbor.)

The D-Day assault was the largest amphibious assault in history. Ever. Ever in the past. Ever in the future. More than nine thousand soldiers were killed or wounded *that day* (more than twice the number of US soldiers killed in Iraq *since 2003*), and it is unlikely that any government will ever allow that to happen again. The US dropped two atomic bombs on Japan so that thousands more soldiers, primarily American and Allied forces, but also Japanese, would not have to die—in a war that by then it was clear the Americans were going to win, eventually.

What was it all about? It's a fair question, given how little younger Americans know about history in general, or World War II in particular.

It was a war about *civilization*. On the eve of the Normandy invasion (by Allied troops, primarily American, British, and Canadian)

President Franklin Roosevelt spoke these words on the radio to anxious parents, wives, and children whose family members and loved ones were about to embark on the most extraordinary adventure the world had ever seen.

> Almighty God: Our sons, pride of our Nation, this day have set upon a mighty endeavor, a struggle to preserve our Republic, our religion, and our civilization, and to set free a suffering humanity. Some will never return. Embrace these, Father, and receive them, Thy heroic servants, into Thy kingdom.

In the multicultural and increasingly anti-Christian America of today, we can marvel at his formulation: "our Republic," "our religion," "our civilization."

What is "our civilization" for which so many died on that day in Normandy, and on so many other dying days during World War II?

Our civilization, our European civilization, was shaped by Christianity, from whence came chivalry, courtesy, constitutions, congresses, and courts. It is a life guided by traditions, which is to say, by the wisdom of our ancestors, who were every bit as bright as we are and who were also shaped and governed primarily by Christianity. Those rights and traditions can be enjoyed by non-believers, but it is not clear they can be sustained by non-believers.

In the US, the share of Americans who identify as Christians is dropping, as the number of US adults who do not identify with any organized religion is growing. In Britain the collapse of Christianity is unmistakable. The number of Britons who call themselves Anglicans decreased by 1.7 million between 2012 and 2014, while the number of Muslims grew by almost a million. Lord Carey, a former archbishop of Canterbury, has said that Christianity in England is "one generation away from extinction."

For this more than a million soldiers were killed or wounded in WWII? Something's wrong with this picture.

What to do? One action would be to re-invigorate the Christian tradition everywhere, failing which—if that is a bridge too far—at least to recognize the role it played in civilizing the . . . civilized countries.

For reasons that get lost in the fog of democracy, Roosevelt's prayer was not included on the WWII Memorial in Washington DC when it was completed in 2004. But in 2014, a bill introduced by Sen. Rob Portman (R–OH) was signed into law directing the secretary of the Interior to add FDR's D-Day Prayer to the WWII Memorial.

However, the legislation stipulates that no federal funds may be used to implement the directive. The cost of adding the prayer is estimated to be $3 million, funds that Friends of the National World War II Memorial is seeking to raise.

Wouldn't you think the government could find $3 million somewhere? Citizens Against Government Waste issues an annual report, *Prime Cuts*, of wasteful spending. The 2017 version contains 607 recommendations that would save taxpayers $336.2 *billion* in the first year. Somewhere in that gargantuan waste there must be the $3 million needed to add FDR's prayer to the WWII Memorial.

Questions: Is a nation that wastes $336 billion a year but can't find $3 million to add a prayer to the WWII Memorial worthy of the sacrifices of the men who died in that war? And will it be able to preserve the civilization they died for?

Donald Trump Is No Franklin Roosevelt—Thank Heavens

July 26, 2018

Trashing Donald Trump is the favorite indoor and outdoor sport of the liberal media, the deep state, the so-called intelligentsia, and all the people who still can't believe Hillary lost—including the Never Trumpers. Now they're all busy writing stories about what a disaster Trump's meeting with Vladimir Putin was.*

But why is the Left so unkind to Trump when they tend to be so nice about President Roosevelt's meeting with Joseph Stalin toward the end of World War II?

Here's what one high school American history textbook says about that meeting:

---

* For a different view, and the best report on that meeting, see Angelo Codevilla's piece at
https://amgreatness.com/2018/07/17/diplomacy-101-vs-politics-writ-small/.

The Soviets had never ceased their clamor for an all-out second front, and the time rapidly approached for Churchill, Roosevelt, and Stalin to meet in person to coordinate the promised effort. Marshal Joseph Stalin, with a careful eye on Soviet military operations, balked at leaving Moscow. President Roosevelt, who jauntily remarked in private, "I can handle that old buzzard," was eager to confer with him. The president seemed confident that Rooseveltian charm could woo the hardened conspirator of the Kremlin from his nasty communist ways.

That is balderdash, as is much of the rest of what appears in *The American Pageant* by David M. Kennedy, Lizabeth Cohen, and Thomas A. Bailey. *The American Pageant* is one of the most widely used high school textbooks in the country today—and that is what it teaches!

Puh-lese! The authors of *The American Pageant* portray Roosevelt as savvy in his handling of Stalin. That's ridiculous. Roosevelt was deluded and thought Stalin was a trustworthy ally. Of communist Russia, Roosevelt said, "They all seem really to want to do what is good for their society instead of wanting to do for themselves." Of Stalin in particular, Roosevelt said, "I think if I give him everything I possibly can, and ask nothing from him in return, *noblesse oblige*, he won't try to annex anything and will work with me for a world of peace and democracy."

Many Russian experts disagreed with FDR, and patiently explained to him that Stalin was a tyrant and a dangerous mass murderer. William Bullitt, ambassador to Russia, told FDR that Stalin was a "Caucasian bandit whose only thought when he got something for nothing was that the other fellow was an ass." But other Americans, and Churchill, too, could not get Roosevelt to abandon his faith in Stalin. When one of his advisors investigated the murder of thousands of Polish officers in the Katyn Forest, Roosevelt admitted Russia was probably guilty, but said that he "didn't want to believe it," and if he had to believe it, he would "pretend not to."

The textbook continues:

Teheran, the capital of Iran (Persia), was finally chosen as the meeting place [for a conference with Roosevelt, Churchill, and

Stalin]. To this ancient city Roosevelt riskily flew, after a stop-over conference in Cairo with Britain's Churchill and China's Jiang Jieshi regarding the war against Japan. At Teheran the discussion among Stalin, Roosevelt, and Churchill—from November 28 to December 1, 1943—progressed smoothly.

Smoothly for whom? For Stalin! He got a commitment from Roosevelt to establish a western front to take the German pressure off Russia.

Reading the account of the meeting in Teheran is pitiful. Yes, Roosevelt flew to Teheran, some six thousand miles total, and was exhausted when he got there. He was already ill, and would be dead less than a year and a half later. The Soviets bugged Roosevelt's room, and many of the "servants" at the conference were actually Soviet spies. Stalin secured a commitment from FDR that Russia would have hegemony in Poland after the war. Poland would be part of the corridor of countries whose people Russia would control for decades after the war. FDR was giving tacit approval, and even said at one point, he "was confident that the people [of Poland] would vote to join the Soviet Union."

Nothing Trump has ever said matches the delusional Franklin Roosevelt.

Fake news, fake *current* news is one thing. "Fake news" history books, like *The American Pageant*, is something else. What can be done about that?

What The Education and Research Institute of Washington DC (of which I am chairman) is doing is putting critiques of American history textbooks online, so students can learn true American history.

Much of the commentary above is taken from ERI's critique of *The American Pageant*. It is sobering—and frightening—to see what biased textbook writers have done in the past, and see that bias at work again today.

Unfortunately, it shows that trashing Donald Trump is likely to be the favorite indoor, and outdoor, sport of the liberal-progressive writers of American history textbooks for years to come.

History *Is* Bunk—If It's Not Taught Properly

August 6, 2018

Summertime and the livin' is easy—but school lurks. Its inevitability is the uninvited guest at every summer picnic and party. School days, and dear old golden rules days, threaten, even in July.

What is that Golden Rule in education? Presumably teaching children in the manner you would want your own children taught, a manner that sticks to the facts and omits the editorializing.

Alas, there are many American history textbooks that fail to meet that standard. The question is, does anyone care?

A conservative might want American history slanted toward his political opinions of American history, even as a political liberal-progressive might want it slanted toward hers. But a classroom is likely to have both kinds of students in it, and so wise parents will want their children to learn true American history. Any bias, er, emphasis, can be added later under parental guidance.

If the reader doubts there is bias in American history textbooks, he is urged to read one. But here, for parents and others to ponder, is an example of bias in one of the most widely used American history textbooks. The actual bias in the textbook in question is either conservative or liberal, but below are two versions of an offending paragraph: one of the versions is quoted from the textbook; the other is a construct, paralleling the real version, which presents the opposite point of view. The reader is asked whether he objects to one, both, or neither of the presentations.

Version A: The chapter begins with a quote from Henry Adams: "*Grant . . . had no right to exist. He should have been extinct for ages. . . . That, two thousand years after Alexander the Great and Julius Cæsar, a man like Grant should be called—and should actually and truly be—the highest product of the most advanced evolution, made evolution ludicrous. The progress of evolution from President Washington to President Grant, was alone evidence enough to upset Darwin. . . . Grant . . . should have lived in a cave and worn skins.*"

There is no mention in the textbook that Henry Adams' brother, Charles Francis Adams, had a different point of view.

Version B: The chapter begins with a quote from Charles Francis Adams: *"I do not think that any intelligent person could watch [Grant], even from such a distance as mine, without concluding that he is a remarkable man. He handles those around him so quietly and well, he so evidently has the faculty of disposing of work and managing men, he is cool and quiet, almost stolid. He is a man of the most exquisite judgment and tact."*

There is no mention in the textbook that Charles Francis Adams's brother, Henry Adams, had a different point of view.

Which version is preferable?

The answer, of course, is neither. If one Adams is to be quoted by the textbook authors, the other Adams, who had the opposite opinion, should be quoted also. Clearly, the authors of the textbook were stealing a base when they omitted the quote from the other Adams brother. Unfortunately, probably most American history textbooks are as biased as the one from which the quote above (whichever is the real one) was taken. What to do?

What The Education and Research Institute of Washington DC has done (full disclosure: I am the chairman of ERI) is put online a critique of one such biased textbook, the twelfth edition of *The American Pageant* by David M. Kennedy, Lizabeth Cohen, and Thomas A. Bailey. The book is riddled with biased statements (like whichever is the genuine quote above) that are meant to indoctrinate students into the authors' point of view—e.g., that President Grant was either a terrible president or a great one.

Maybe Grant was a terrible president. Or maybe he was a terrific president. Or perhaps he did some good things and some bad things. What Grant *did* is history. Whether it was good or bad is interpretation. In this #MeToo era, textbook writers, like movie moguls and others, should keep their hands, and their biases, off the students.

ERI's analysis critiques several hundred of *The American Pageant*'s comments at TrueAmericanHistory.us so that students can go online and learn, as the URL states, true American history, not the one-sided version that the textbook's authors want to inculcate in them. Readers of this column are also are invited to visit the website and examine the text and ERI's commentary for themselves.

Summertime, and the livin' may be easy, but writing an unbiased textbook on American history is hard, and takes both skill and humility—the humility to remember that there might just possibly be more than one point of view, and that the author's biases shouldn't be passed on to the nation's school children.

Martin Luther King, History, and Donald Trump
August 28, 2018

Martin Luther King Jr. would be pleased that we are celebrating the fifty-fourth anniversary of his "I Have a Dream" speech on August 28. We can expect not only the usual adulation for the speech from the keepers of America's conscience, but also the knee-jerk condemnation of President Trump, the cause of everything evil in this land—from fires in California and constipation in Florida to acid reflux at the *New York Times*.

If you think current accounts of what Donald Trump has done for blacks (unemployment at the lowest level ever since the Earth's surface cooled sufficiently to make life possible except for small babies [disproportionately black] disfavored by the Democratic Party) are vicious, think what the history books, at least those written by left-wing zealots (which is most of them) will say. If the past is any guide, it will not be pretty.

Here, for example, is what *The American Pageant* (twelfth edition), widely used in US high schools and especially in AP courses, has to say about President Eisenhower:

> President Eisenhower was little inclined toward promoting integration. He shied away from employing his vast popularity and the prestige of his office to educate white Americans about the need for racial justice. His personal attitudes may have helped to restrain him. He had grown up in an all-white town and spent his career in a segregated army.

That is very misleading. Eisenhower, in fact, was positive and forceful in promoting integration. He started his presidency with supportive words, and followed them with action. In his first State of the Union message, Eisenhower said, "Our civil and social rights form a central part of the heritage we are striving to defend on all fronts and with all our strength. I believe with all my heart that our vigilant guarding of these rights is a sacred obligation binding upon every citizen. . . . A cardinal ideal in this heritage we cherish is the equality of rights of all citizens of every race and color and creed."

He followed this address with a pledge to end segregation in Washington DC that was so heavily imposed by Woodrow Wilson (a Democrat, to whose virulent racism the textbook authors devote *only three sentences*). Ike ordered an end to segregation in schools run by the federal government in military posts. He further appointed Frederic Morrow as the first black to serve on a president's staff; Eisenhower also created the Civil Rights Division within the Justice Department.

Eisenhower's policies impressed leaders in the black community with the president's seriousness of purpose. The NAACP praised Ike's "strong and constructive" leadership on race, and Congressman Adam Clayton Powell of New York, probably the leading black spokesman in America, endorsed Eisenhower for reelection in 1956. No wonder. Eisenhower's Republican Party platform in 1956 proclaimed, "The Republican Party accepts the decision of the US Supreme Court that racial discrimination in publicly supported schools must be progressively eliminated."

The Democrats in their 1956 platform stated, to the contrary: "We reject all proposals for the use of force to interfere with the orderly determination of these matters [of racial integration] by the courts." The conflicting views of the two parties on racial integration resulted in the strongest black vote for a Republican presidential candidate—Eisenhower—in the preceding eighty-five years. He received almost 40 percent of the black vote, which helped him win reelection by a landslide. Ike was leading Americans where they wanted to go—but he was Republican, so the textbook authors don't give him any credit.

The Education and Research Institute of Washington DC (of which I am the chairman) has put online a critique of *The American Pageant* from which the comments above are taken. ERI's goal is to give students a chance to learn real history, *true* American history, not the left-wing biased version.

MLK Jr. began his speech by saying, "I am happy to join with you today in what will go down in history as the greatest demonstration for freedom in the history of our nation." But how does a speech "go down in history" if historians and textbook writers distort the truth?

Which is what they are doing with the story of Donald Trump. Trump hasn't a chance in the history books, as he has no chance in the daily news.

Even so, back at the ranch, blacks have jobs, and more jobs than the left-wing Black Lives Matter-type politicians have been able to provide—*ever*!

Martin Luther King Jr. would be pleased.

But Who Will Investigate the Mueller Investigation?

September 4, 2018

Donald Trump says Robert Mueller's investigation is a witch hunt, and many others have now reached the same conclusion. The Russia connection seems tenuous and the provenance—a Deep State FBI hostile to Donald Trump's presidency—is sketchy.

Today the administration—which is to say the administration of the Government of the United States of America—is hobbled by the possible findings of a special counsel who, after more than a year of searching has found, so far as we know, nothing that would disqualify Trump from being president.

It's true that if there were illegal campaign activities or even, perhaps, if there were legal but unseemly (whatever that might mean, and unseemly to whom?) activities connecting the campaign to the Russians, the American people should know about them.

But at what cost should that knowledge be obtained? Any cost? Should Mueller's investigation continue for ten years? Eight years? Four years? At some point shouldn't the American people be left to judge Trump on his performance as president, not as candidate?

We have an election coming up and a country to govern. We need some assurance that the "Russia" investigation is proper and still necessary.

Trump could demand that Mueller, who technically works for the president, brief him and the American people on the status of the investigation. But that would probably produce a firestorm, albeit only from the usual no-credibility suspects. Even so, a firestorm going into a congressional election is something to be avoided.

But something needs to be done. The mere continuing presence of the investigation is likely to influence the congressional elections in November, even as it hampers the administration day after day. It's a reasonably good bet that President Trump will fire Mueller the day after the November elections no matter which party takes the House of Representatives—wouldn't you?—and he should prepare for that action now.

There are two issues here: the people are entitled to know the propriety and the status of the investigation; and the responsibility of continuing an investigation with the import of the Mueller investigation should not be left to one person. That is more power than any one individual, except perhaps the president, should have.

What to do? President Trump should appoint a committee of three to investigate the provenance and scope of the special counsel's mandate and his progress.

The committee members can determine whether the provenance of the investigation was proper (or was it just a setup by the Deep State FBI?) as well as if it should be allowed to continue, that is, if there is credible evidence of "any links and/or coordination between the Russian government and individuals associated with the Trump campaign"—the language is taken from deputy attorney general Rod Rosenstein's letter appointing Mueller.

If the committee determines that the provenance was proper and that the investigation should continue, they can so inform the president and the American people. If they determine otherwise, they can so state—and at that point Trump could ask Mueller to resign.

Who should be on the committee? People like former Senator, Under Secretary of State, and Circuit Court Judge James L. Buckley. And Judge Laurence H. Silberman. And former Senator Joe Lieberman. (Not, alas, former FBI head Judge William H. Webster; he's too close to the FBI.) People like Buckley, Silberman, and Lieberman are statesmen. They have standing. Gravitas. They can be trusted. And it would be difficult for the liberal-progressive anti-Trump media complex or denizens of the Deep State—or anyone else—to second guess them.

Would Trump appoint such a committee? There's a risk for him—but only if there is in fact "credible evidence" of a Russia connection. Trump should know, although it's possible, if any connection was only with lower level munchkins, that he does not—but then why would we care?

How long would it take the committee to do its work? Two weeks: three days for each member to find one person to work with as staff; three days for Mueller to make his case (if he can't make it in three days he doesn't have a case;) three days for the committee and staff to review all the evidence; three days to write a report; two days for unexpected events. Easy.

That may sound fast for Washington, but it's how Trump gets things done.

If there is no credible evidence of any improper links or co-ordination, Trump can end the investigation and get on with presidential business. If there is reason to continue the investigation, the American people should know it, and know that the administration's cry of "witch hunt" is, at best, ignorant, at worst, smoke screen.

Either way, the American people are entitled to that knowledge. It's their country, after all, and Mueller really works for them.

Next Case: The Judge vs. The Vigilante
October 1, 2018

It is clear that Democrats have no concern for Christine Blasey Ford's welfare. She is just a tool, like a basin wrench, for doing a particular job. That job is to prevent President Trump from ever appointing *anyone* to the Supreme Court again. *Ever.*

There may be a few people who don't understand that, as there may be a few Japanese soldiers who haven't yet heard that World War II has been concluded—and, as the emperor of Japan told his people, "not entirely to Japan's advantage." (That was then.)

Ford has been presented as a sympathetic figure, even by some who favor Judge Kavanaugh's confirmation. They need to take another look, keeping our longstanding jurisprudential rules in mind, especially the presumption of innocence.

Suppose—as the law school professors say—suppose a case similar to, but not identical with, the one Ford has described. Suppose that the bedroom door had not been closed, and that the staircase had been just outside the door. Suppose that during the struggle the young girl had managed to get her knees up to her chest—or the perpetrator had pushed them up there for nefarious purposes—and suppose that with a herculean effort, driven by terror and adrenalin, the girl had managed to catapult the perp into the air (more or less) so that he staggered, dazed, and then fell down the stairs, breaking his neck. The result being that he had to be hospitalized for six months, recovering only after many months of therapy, but never sufficiently to play sports or coach Little League.

Would we shed a tear? And if so, for whom? For the young girl who thought she was about to be raped by a drunken seventeen-year-old? Or for the young boy, a drunken adolescent? Or both?

Now—as the law professors continue—suppose our young woman was not able to catapult the young perp down the stairs. Suppose that, instead, thirty-six years later she runs into him at a party. He has been nominated to serve on the Supreme Court. She knows that if she tells the truth about him, no one will believe her. She remembers what happened back in 2018 when a Christine Blasey Ford accused a Supreme Court nominee of sexually molesting her thirty-six years earlier. Some people believed her, but many did not, primarily because she couldn't find a *single* person to corroborate her story.

When our woman, no longer young, comes upon her assailant of thirty-six years before, he is standing at the top of some cellar stairs, and the door is open. She crashes into him, deliberately, and down the stairs he goes, breaking his neck. He is hospitalized for six months, only recovering after many months of therapy, but never sufficiently to play sports again or coach Little League—or sit on the Supreme Court.

As the law school professors ask, What crime if any?

What's the difference between what our hypothetical woman did and what Ford did?

With the best of intentions she did what she could to save the country from the man who thirty-six years earlier had behaved like a monster, albeit a seventeen-year-old monster. She stopped his political ascension and perhaps ruined his life. And she did all that even though there did not exist a single person who would corroborate her story.

Question: Which woman is the antecedent for the pronoun "she" in the preceding paragraph: our hypothetical woman or Christine Blasey Ford?

A normal person would be horrified at what our hypothetical woman did. She took the law into her own hands: she needed no trial because *she* knew the man was guilty; and *she* meted out the punishment that effectively ruined his life.

How does that differ from what Ford has done?

In the real world, a man who was pushed down the stairs could sue the woman for damages. It's a simple case of battery.

How would she defend? By saying she acted from high motives: to save the country from his serving on the Supreme Court? Please. She would be found guilty in a trice and have to pay damages. Her high motives wouldn't begin to justify her conduct.

And neither do Christine Blasey Ford's "high" motives justify her conduct. She has damaged her victim, Judge Kavanaugh, by, *inter alia*, telling her story to the *Washington Post*, and he is entitled to redress. Normally, a public figure who sues for libel or slander must show actual malice. But accusing someone of a crime thirty-six years after it allegedly happened without a shred of corroborating evidence, and not even verified by people *the victim* named as witnesses, should be deemed constructive malice. As if she'd pushed him down the stairs.

Vigilante justice is not justice.

Judgment for the plaintiff.

Next case.

Brett Kavanaugh Should Sue Ford and *The WaPo* for Defamation

October 6, 2018

Republicans have to realize that henceforth for all their nominees to the Supreme Court, there's a Ford in their future.

The battle over Brett Kavanaugh's confirmation was the Second Battle of Tours. At the first battle, just 1,286 years ago (around October 10–11), Christian Europe decisively defeated a massive invasion that would have destroyed Europe's civilization and changed the course of history.

Now the Democrats are the invaders, come years ago to spoil our culture. That's what their opposition to Kavanaugh is all about. They are willing—no, eager—to discard the presumption of innocence, a hallmark of Anglo–American jurisprudence and of Western Civilization. "Off with his head," said these modern-day zealots wielding their high-tech media scimitars—and who cares about rules of procedure?

Sen. Richard Blumenthal (D–CT), who famously (but not famously enough) lied about serving in Vietnam, was quite explicit in an interview during a break in the Ford–Kavanaugh hearings. He outright said the issue was actually about abortion, and he was right. That's the major cultural issue of our time.

Kavanaugh's confrontation with Ford was an extension of the Me Too movement. It is now enough, or almost enough, just to make a charge of inappropriate behavior against a man to get him convicted in the left-wing fever swamps. Men, especially white men, are presumed guilty—at least, by Democrat senators and their allies in the press.

But perhaps this is not yet so in the law courts of this country. Our law provides a remedy for the nightmare Judge Kavanaugh has been through. Sue!

Kavanaugh has been libeled and slandered. For that the law offers redress. He should sue Ford and the *Washington Post*. For $20 million. Each.

If he thinks it unseemly for a judge to sue, he can donate his cause of action to a trust. The beneficiary of the trust could be his favorite charity—perhaps the Catholic Church, perhaps a group of Western Civ charities. But they would be beneficiaries only; they would not have the right to manage the suit, because they might decide to cave under pressure from the usual scimitar-wielding lefties.

Ford has clearly libeled Kavanaugh. Libel is a published false statement that is damaging to a person's reputation. Ford gave uncorroborated information to the *Washington Post*, which published it and damaged Kavanaugh's reputation.

In a court of law, unlike in a court of Democrat senators, the burden of proving the truth of a derogatory statement is on the defendant. Ford would have to prove that her charges were true. We know now that she can't.

Of course, Ford may not have $20 million handy, or even the few hundred thousand she'd need to defend herself (libel suits are cheap to bring, expensive to defend). But perhaps her supporters in liberal land can run a crowd-funding operation for her.

The *Washington Post* would rest its defense on *New York Times Company v. Sullivan*, a 1964 case which held that for a public figure to be successful in a libel suit he must show actual malice on the part of the defendant, i.e., that the defendant acted in reckless disregard of the truth of the published claim.

New York Times Company v. Sullivan is ripe for being overruled. Yes, the Supreme Court can overturn prior cases. See *Plessy vs. Ferguson*.

Justice Antonin Scalia said he abhorred the *New York Times* case: "You can libel public figures at will so long as somebody told you something, some reliable person told you the lie that you then publicized to the whole world—that's what *New York Times v. Sullivan* says."

A court should hold that Ford, dredging up a thirty-six-year-old uncorroborated claim, is guilty of constructive malice—reckless disregard of the truth. She is, at best, a vigilante. But we have to remember that vigilante justice works in the movies only because we know the bad guy did it.

It would be poetic justice if Justice Kavanaugh could be the deciding vote—on his own case! Well, okay, maybe not. Poetic justice is no more just than vigilante justice is. He, and we, will have to wait for

President Trump's next Supreme Court justice. If you wonder why you should have voted for Donald Trump in 2016, now you know.

Could the next Senate confirmation hearing of a Supreme Court nominee be worse than the Kavanaugh–Ford hearing? Who would have thought that a hearing could be worse than Chappaquiddick Teddy Kennedy's attack on Judge Bork, or the "high-tech lynching" of Clarence Thomas?

Here is what ordinary Americans have to understand: it can always get worse, and it will, until we change the culture. Until then, there's a Ford in all our futures.

Banging the Diversity Drum
October 28, 2018

We should cut Carly Fiorina a lot of slack for her courageous stand on abortion during the last presidential campaign. She values life, and kudos to her for that.

But she has fallen into the diversity trap: in a recent op-ed in the *Washington Post* she gives a predictable left-wing cheer for diversity. Fiorina writes: "There simply is not a representative number of women or people of color in positions of influence, impact and leadership in business, politics, religion or the social sector" and then trots out a number of statistics.

Here's one: "Nearly 90 percent of all executive directors or presidents of nonprofits or foundations are white." Are we shocked?

What percent of those executives or presidents does Ms. Fiorina think should be white? In 2014, whites were 77.35 percent of the population. Is Ms. Fiorina saying that no more than 77 percent of those executive directors or presidents should be white? And no fewer? But why? Perhaps blacks or women or members of other diversity groups don't want to be in the nonprofit or foundation world. Perhaps, if they're good enough to be in that world, they prefer to work in different worlds were they can make more money. Or perhaps they think teaching is a more public-spirited occupation. Does Fiorina know?

Then she references data from a McKinsey & Co. study which says: "Ethnically diverse organizations are 35 percent more likely to outperform their competitors. . . . In the United States, for every 10 percent increase in racial and ethnic diversity on the senior-executive team, earnings rise 0.8 percent."

Even readers who skipped Statistics 101 may know enough to distinguish between correlation and causality. It's possible, of course, that the more successful companies studied by McKinsey did better because their workforces were diverse. But it's also possible that because those companies were doing well they could afford to hire underperforming diversity candidates—which is not (let us not get distracted, please) to assume that all minorities (women, blacks, immigrants, whoever) are likely to underperform.

Probably we should look at the McKinsey study ourselves to see if they know the difference between causality and correlation. It turns out that there's a number of McKinsey studies, the later ones referencing the earlier ones. But here's the key sentence from McKinsey's February 2, 2015, Executive Summary of "Diversity Matters":

> The relationship between diversity and performance highlighted in the research is a correlation, not a causal link. This is an important distinction, but the findings nonetheless permit reasonable hypotheses on what is driving improved performance by companies with diverse executive teams and boards.

We all love a reasonable hypothesis, but there's only so much you can squeeze out of one.

And who counts as "diverse" anyway? Blacks? Of course. (Is that a racist statement?) Women? Presumably. Asian Americans? Hmm. That's tougher. Here's McKinsey on Asian Americans:

> For example, if one company had 8 white and 2 Asian executives and another company had 8 white, 1 Asian, and 1 black executive, using the HHI formula allowed us to credit the second company as having a more diverse executive team.

Okay?

How would McKinsey rank a company all of whose executives were black? Would McKinsey and Fiorina predict that a company run by (in the late Interior Secretary James Watt's immortal phrase) a black, a woman, two Jews, and a cripple would outperform a company run by five Asian Americans who had been lucky enough to get into Harvard?

About 77 percent of Americans are white. And about 77 percent of blacks born in the US today are illegitimate. How many of *them* are likely to be able to join the ranks of executive directors or presidents? Fiorina doesn't say.

For Democrats, banging the diversity drum ("Diversity is our strength!!") means primarily letting lots of illegal immigrants into the country to replace the blacks who used to vote monolithically for Democrats but who are now taking the very visible aboveground railway off the Democrats' plantation to jobs created by Donald Trump's economic policies, which have resulted in the lowest black unemployment numbers *ever*.

This means the country, and especially minorities, are lucky Donald Trump beat Carly Fiorina in 2016.

On the same day Fiorina's piece appeared in the *Washington Post*, the *Wall Street Journal* ran a piece by Ted Van Dyk, a man involved in Democratic politics for forty years. He wrote:

> Democratic seniors look back to their roots in the Civil Rights Act and wonder why we so relentlessly attack Republicans as racist when Democrats, the party of civil rights, have no apparent agenda to address daunting school-dropout and incarceration rates, drug trafficking and use, unemployment, violent crime, and broken or nonexistent family structures in afflicted urban neighborhoods.

Van Dyk is onto something, and kudos to him for it.

Explosive Politics? You Ain't Seen Nothing Yet
November 10, 2018

Before Election Day we were urged to "defuse our explosive politics." Okay, maybe—but they were explosive for a reason. Now that the Democrats have won the House of Representatives, politics is likely to get even more explosive. So now what do we do?

For many decades American politics was essentially a one-party affair.

From 1933 to 1981 the Democrats controlled both houses of congress except for two periods, 1947–1949 and 1953–1955. Republicans were junior partners in the firm and showed respect to their betters.

With the election in 1980 of Ronald Reagan, a serious conservative who wanted to bring serious change to Washington (unlike two previous Republican presidents, Eisenhower and Nixon), politics began to get nasty. They got nastier still after Republicans won the House in 1994. It's never been the same since. And it isn't going back.

During all that time, the culture was changing. The sixties' civil rights movement was a great moral crusade, but it didn't by itself change what might be described as the moral tenor of the country, though it may have sown the seeds for some of our present discontent. Bussing and affirmative action took the bloom off the movement, even as the counterculture warriors were changing . . . the culture.

Exactly why, how, and to what extent is up for debate. The rich got richer, family life declined, divorce became common, illegitimacy became so common it became un-PC to call it illegitimacy, and the culture became coarser (foul popular music and pornography went mainstream). And then what might be called the second sexual revolution hit: the tsunami of identity politics, involving—among other positions—a veritable alphabet of bizarre sexual practices.

Blacks, for reasons yet to be determined, allowed liberal-progressives to hijack their civil rights movement and fly it to Sodom and Gomorrah.

All the while, Hollywood, academia, and the media were pushing left-wing nostrums. Prominent lefties called half of the country "deplorables" and "the dregs of society."

If you think the penance you are doing now for your sins is not adequate, try reading the *New York Times*. Article after article, editorial after editorial, op-ed after op-ed, show unrelieved hostility to President Trump, or bizarre pieces on sex, or pieces on bizarre sex (e.g., "Why Sex is not Binary") that you wouldn't want your children to read.

In the face of all that, we are to "defuse our explosive politics"?

Well, perhaps we should. But we are not likely to. Ideas matter. They have consequences. And the consequences, when they are negative, are visited on the most vulnerable of our citizens, who are not the people who live in the super zip code gated communities described by Charles Murray and who write for the *New York Times*.

Charles M. Blow, a columnist for the *Times*, wrote a column just before the election titled "Liberals, This is War." In it he claimed that "the founders, a bunch of rich, powerful white men, didn't want true democracy in this country, and in fact were dreadfully afraid of it. Now, a bunch of rich, powerful white men want to return us to this sensibility, wrapped in a populist 'follow the Constitution' rallying cry and disguised as the ultimate form of patriotism."

Even though the Democrats now have a majority in the House of Representatives, much of what happens politically in the next two years is likely to be managed by the same "bunch of rich, powerful white men" so feared by Blow, suggesting that politics is not likely to get less explosive.

Perhaps the most optimistic scenario for the coming two to four years is the awakening, finally, of individually powerless men and women in the black community to the realization that they've been had for decades, by Democrats, the party of segregation for so many years.

It's easy to hurry past the salient statistic: that black unemployment is the lowest ever. But the meaning is as significant as the results of the civil rights movement. It would be celebrated from New York to San Francisco—if it had occurred under Democratic leadership. But it didn't.

Yes, the Democrats have won back the House of Representatives, but the music of increasing prosperity in minority communities will be the dirge of the Democratic Party. Our politics is likely to become even more explosive, not less, the fuse having been lighted by Democrats in reaction to Donald Trump's victory in 2016. The conflagration will be great, and the smoke of the Democrats will go up as the smoke of a furnace.

Explosive politics? You ain't seen nothing yet.

How Reagan Defeated Gorbachev: The Story Public Schools Never Taught

November 14, 2018

Mikhail Gorbachev, head of The Mikhail Gorbachev School of American History, has called President Trump's decision to have the United States withdraw from the Intermediate-Range Nuclear Forces Treaty reckless and not the work of "a great mind." The laugh bubbles up from the toe bone, past the ankle bone, all the way up to the neck bone and then *back down* to the funny bone, finally exploding in a huge GUFFAW!

Gorbachev, the final leader of the Soviet Union, had such a great mind himself that he was a confirmed believer in all that communist–socialist nonsense and insisted that the state-directed Soviet economy was "fundamentally sound." He even argued, as late as 1987, that "the works of Lenin and his ideals of socialism [were] . . . an inexhaustible source of . . . creative thought, theoretical wealth, and moral sagacity."

That is nonsense of a kind only a fool—or twenty-eight-year-old Democrat somethings like Alexandria Ocasio-Cortez (Democrat candidate for Congress in New York's 14th congressional district)—could believe.

But the Left loves Gorbachev, even as it disparages President Reagan who forced Gorbachev's hand. You see it in history books.

In *The American Pageant*, for example, a textbook widely used in American high schools, Reagan is described as a bumbler, and Gorbachev as more or less a "great mind." Here's how the authors introduce Reagan: "Though Reagan was no intellectual, he drew on the ideas of a small but influential group of thinkers known as 'neoconservatives.'"

Reagan no intellectual? What bias! What about FDR? He had a

"C" average in college, but the authors of *The American Pageant* treat him as the wisest of men.

Their description of Reagan tells only a small part of the story. Reagan paid much more attention to classical liberal thinkers from Adam Smith to Friedrich Hayek and to the founding magazines of modern conservatism, William F. Buckley Jr.'s *National Review*, as well as *Human Events* and *The Freeman*, but *The American Pageant* doesn't mention those widely influential sources of conservative thought. The textbook says:

> An actor-turned-politician, Reagan enjoyed enormous popularity with his crooked grin and aw-shucks manner. The son of a ne'er-do-well, impoverished Irish-American father with a fondness for the bottle, he had grown up in a small Illinois town. . . . Good looks and a way with words landed him acting jobs in Hollywood, where he became a B-grade star in the 1940s. . . . In 1954 he became a spokesman for the General Electric Corporation at a salary of some $150,000 per year. In that position he began to abandon his New Dealish political views and increasingly to preach a conservative, antigovernment line.

Get it? Reagan was "no intellectual" and he listened to neoconservatives. The textbook authors say Reagan's father was a drunk and he became merely a "B-grade" actor. But when he started making money with General Electric, well, then he "began to abandon his New Dealish political views" deciding instead "to preach a conservative, antigovernment line."

Here's what the textbook authors have to say about Gorbachev:

> Gorbachev was personable, energetic, imaginative, and committed to radical reforms. . . . He announced two policies with remarkable, even revolutionary, implications. Glasnost, or 'openness,' aimed to ventilate the secretive, repressive stuffiness of Soviet society by introducing free speech and a measure of political liberty. Perestroika, or 'restructuring,' was intended to revive the moribund Soviet economy by adopting many of the free-market practices—such as the profit motive and an end

to subsidized prices—of the capitalist West. Both glasnost and perestroika required that the Soviet Union shrink the size of its enormous military machine and redirect its energies to the dismal civilian economy. That requirement, in turn, necessitated an end to the Cold War.

Those comments are a work of almost pure fiction. They give no credit to Reagan. And they suggest that "personable, energetic, and imaginative" Gorbachev, a lover of freedom, changed the Soviet Union and ended the Cold War because he wanted to do so. That's ridiculous. Probably the beginning of the end of the evil empire was Reagan's liberation of Grenada in 1983. Then, by proposing the Strategic Defense Initiative (which came to be called "Star Wars") Reagan forced Gorbachev, who knew the USSR could never win a competition with the United States, to restructure the Soviet Union.

And the rest is history—but not history you will find in a typical high school American history textbook.

The Education and Research Institute (of which I am chairman) has put online a critique of *The American Pageant*. It is an attempt to ensure that students have an understanding of true American history—not one from biased American journalists and other liberal writers, most of whom could qualify as adjunct professors at The Mikhail Gorbachev School of American History.

Whose Side Are You On, Anyway: Alexandria Ocasio-Cortez's or Amazon's?

November 23, 2018

Here are three rules for better living: (1) keep matches out of the hands of small children; (2) if you agree with an editorial in the *New York Times* you may want to reconsider your opinion; and (3)—we'll get to that one in a minute.

After much public angst and media hype, Amazon has finally decided where to locate its second, and as it turned out, third headquarters. The winning cities are (drum roll) New York City and Arlington, Virginia.

That is one of the greatest letdowns since Bill Clinton said, "I did not have sex with that woman, Ms. Lewinsky."

In a political season rent by dissent and disagreement, Amazon's announced deal produced a sense of unity in the country not seen since President Kennedy pardoned the 1963 White House Thanksgiving Turkey: everyone, except some politicians, is against the Amazon deal.

Jeff Bezos is Amazon's founder, chairman, and CEO and, at a net worth of $122 billion, doubles as the richest man on the planet. His fortune makes Donald Trump (net worth: $3 billion) look like a welfare recipient. According to the usual well-informed sources, Bezos spends $3 billion on aftershave lotion, each week.

Bezos drove a hard bargain with the luminaries of New York and Virginia politics.

The deal requires New York State to give Amazon $1.85 billion and allows Amazon to apply for tax credits that could be worth $1 billion. Because Amazon's new "campus" will be located in a federal development area, the company will qualify for additional corporate tax breaks. All in all, a $3 billion package.

Virginia offered to spend, sort of, about $1.495 billion, over a number of years.

Both New York City Mayor Bill de Blasio and New York Governor Andrew Cuomo are said to be pleased with the deal—finally a report that doesn't sound like fake news. Gov. Cuomo had offered to change his name to "Amazon Cuomo" in order to get the deal, an offer that has proved, so far, to be unnecessary. Mayor de Blasio, whose winter came early this year, might have been willing to make the same offer, but it would have been less convincing, the mayor having already changed his name twice, first from Warren Wilhelm Jr. to Warren de Blasio-Wilhelm, and subsequently to the current Bill de Blasio.

Meanwhile, the outrage spreads, from far-left Alexandria ("three chambers of government") Ocasio-Cortez, the newly elected Democratic representative from New York's 14th Congressional District, to the aforesaid *New York Times*, all the way over to *National Review*, Mark Levin and Tucker Carlson on the right.

Ocasio-Cortez tweeted, "The idea that [Amazon] will receive hundreds of millions of dollars in tax breaks at a time when our subway is crumbling and our communities need MORE investment, not less, is extremely concerning to residents here."

But the subway has been a disaster for years, and for years the politicians have been unable to fix it. Does Ms. Ocasio-Cortez think that her arrival on the scene will change that? Mark Levin thinks Amazon should have gone somewhere else. But that's not a principled argument against selecting the places Amazon selected, just a detail, because that somewhere else would have been picked by Amazon because of the deal it was offering.

Here's another way to look at it.

Milton Friedman said you should be glad you don't get all the government you pay for. Politicians and governments waste money. They waste huge, gargantuan, brobdingnagian, mountain-size amounts of money. As a pretty reliable rule of thumb, the less spending they control, the better off you will be.

Successful companies, on the other hand, tend to spend money wisely—that's why they're successful.

Basically, what's at stake in the two Amazon deals is about $4.5 billion. Here's the question: Who would you rather have control the spending of that money? Jeff Bezos, arguably the most successful businessman on the aforementioned planet? Or some politicians, at least one of whom can't decide what his name should be or even get the snow ploughed in his own city?

The lawyers will tell you that that question falls into the *nolo contendere* realm, a fancy-pantsy term for "C'mon, stop arguing about it."

The money that New York State and City and Virginia are not going to get to spend will be spent (invested) either by Amazon, its employees, or its stockholders. Who can doubt that they will spend it more wisely than the politicians?

So the third rule for better living is similar to the first: keep money out of the hands of politicians. They can probably do more damage with it than even small children can do with matches.

Would the Democrats Really Pack the Supreme Court?

November 26, 2018

Extra! Extra!
Chief Justice Roberts Shocked to Find Gambling Going On in Court

"I can resist everything except temptation," Lord Darlington says in Oscar Wilde's *Lady Windermere's Fan*. Two characters not on stage when the lord's remark entered the quotation books in 1892 were President Donald Trump and Chief Justice John Roberts. They missed opening night by more than half a century. Even so, Darlington might have been speaking for them.

In a now-typical fit of frustration, President Trump couldn't resist lashing out at a federal judge who blocked his new refugee asylum rules, calling him "an Obama judge."

Chief Justice Roberts, unable to resist the temptation to criticize President Trump, promptly replied: "We do not have Obama judges or Trump judges, Bush judges or Clinton judges."

Whereupon Senator Charles Grassley (R–IA), chairman of the Senate Judiciary Committee, couldn't resist the temptation to point out that Chief Justice Roberts had failed to criticize President Obama for rebuking Justice Alito during a State of the Union address. Obama had complained about the Court's ruling in *Citizens United v. Federal Elections Commission*, a major campaign finance case.

Who—except, perhaps, a chief justice who could find Obamacare constitutional—would be shocked, shocked to find politics going on at the Supreme Court?

If federal judges are not political judges, what on earth was all that fuss about at Justice Kavanaugh's confirmation hearing—the noisiest confirmation hearing *ever*? Topping even Judge Bork's hearing and Justice Thomas's.

Of course we have Obama judges and Trump judges; and before them we had Franklin Delano Roosevelt judges and judges nominated by FDR's predecessors. When the Supreme Court refused to validate some of FDR's New Deal economic programs, he announced he was going to "pack" the court by expanding it from nine justices to as many as fifteen. The public outcry was swift, negative, and conclusive. FDR demurred. Within months, however, the Court started upholding Roosevelt's programs.

The number of justices is not prescribed in the Constitution. The first judiciary act, passed in 1789 when the Supreme Court was set up, established six as the number of justices, two for each of the judicial circuits.

Then, as the country grew, the court grew: in 1807, the number of justices was raised to seven, in 1837 to nine, and in 1863 to ten.

But then, dreaded politics intervened: in 1866, the Republican Congress reduced the number of justices from ten to seven in order to thwart President Johnson's ability to appoint justices. Republicans thought Johnson's plan for the restoration of the seceded states to the Union did not give adequate protection to the former slaves.

Finally, in 1869, Congress increased the number of justices from seven to the current number of nine. But there is no constitutional proscription on the number's being increased again.

Trump has already established a more-or-less conservative majority on the Court by appointing two justices. And whether or not he gets a second term, he may add one or two more. That means the court could have a conservative majority for the next forty years or so. What are Progressive-Socialist-Identity Politics-New Age-Sexual Morality-Gender-Fluid Democrats to do?

If they were to win the presidency and both the House and the Senate (where they could, and surely would, eliminate the filibuster), what would stop them from increasing the number of justices again—to whatever number would give them a majority?

Impossible, you say? Democrats are already talking about packing the Court.

A quick review of Andrew Johnson's unexpected presidency is instructive. Johnson, who became president when Lincoln was assassinated, was far more accepting of southern state politics than were the Republicans who wanted to deal harshly with them. Johnson viewed the Republicans' actions as not supported by a majority of the country, and so he vetoed an extension of the Freedman's Bureau bill as well as the Civil Rights Act of 1866, both of which were aimed at protecting blacks.

In other words, Johnson opposed issues that all the "proper" people supported—and so Congress took the highly political step of ensuring that he couldn't appoint any Supreme Court justices.

Today, in the view of all the "proper" people—Hollywood, academia, and the media, that is, keepers (at least in their own minds) of the country's morality—Donald Trump is a modern Andrew Johnson. Or worse.

In the future, some of those keepers may look back and be shocked, shocked at the idea that the Democrats might *not* have packed the Court.

And after the packing? What will the people who cling to their Bibles and guns and traditional Western Civ morality do? Will they be able to resist the temptation to fan the flames of violence against the constitutional and cultural vandals of the Left, violence so recently counseled by the Left? And then will we be shocked all over again to find the country coming apart?

December 7, Pearl Harbor, and Franklin Delano Infamy

December 7, 2018

On December 7, 1941, the Empire of Japan bombed the US Pacific Fleet which was stationed in Pearl Harbor on the Hawaiian island of Oahu. In addressing Congress the next day, President Roosevelt called December 7 "a date which will live in infamy."

But Roosevelt's reputation should live in infamy too. The line that Roosevelt enthusiasts and left-wing historians have peddled for so many years is that the attack was a complete surprise.

Here's a sample from *The American Pageant*, a typical left-wing American history textbook widely used in American high schools:

Officials in Washington, having "cracked" the top-secret code of the Japanese, knew that Tokyo's decision was for war. . . . Roosevelt, misled by Japanese ship movements in the Far East, evidently expected the blow to fall on British Malaya or on the Philippines. No one in high authority in Washington seems to have believed that the Japanese were either strong enough or foolhardy enough to strike Hawaii.

That's the Left's version, and it's in line with the rest of the "fake history" they want American high school students to learn. The Education and Research Institute (ERI—of which I am chairman) has written a critique of *The American Pageant*, which tells a more accurate story about Pearl Harbor and scores of other events in American history.

The American Pageant gives almost no blame to FDR for the Pearl Harbor disaster—even though the United States had broken the Japanese secret code and knew an attack was imminent. The textbook authors assure us that "no one in high authority in Washington seems to have believed that the Japanese" had the ability to launch such an attack.

But that is simply wrong. Some people high up in the US Navy did believe a surprise attack at Pearl Harbor was a possibility, but FDR disagreed with them and he removed those contrary voices from positions of power.

The commander of the US Pacific Fleet in Pearl Harbor was Admiral J. O. (Joe) Richardson. Unlike Roosevelt, Richardson did not underestimate the Japanese—and he had studied them and the dangerous Pearl Harbor location thoroughly.

Richardson said that a simulated aerial attack that the US had conducted at Pearl Harbor in 1932 proved that torpedo planes could cripple any fleet stationed there.

Even before Roosevelt ordered the Pacific Fleet to stay at Pearl Harbor indefinitely, Richardson had protested that keeping the fleet there posed a danger to every ship. He had been attempting to monitor the military movements of the Japanese to give the United States time to evacuate Pearl Harbor in case of danger.

Richardson, after writing many letters warning of danger at Pearl Harbor, was ordered to Washington to meet with the president. At the meeting, Richardson strongly recommended moving the Pacific Fleet back to San Francisco immediately.

When Roosevelt dismissed his concerns, the frustrated Richardson said, "Mr. President, I feel that I must tell you that the senior officers of the navy do not have the trust and confidence in the civilian leadership of this country that is essential for the successful prosecution of a war in the Pacific."

FDR replied, "Joe, you just don't understand that this is an election year [1940] and there are certain things that can't be done, no matter what, until the election is over and won."

Then, when the election was over and FDR reelected to his third term, he fired Richardson from command of the Pacific Fleet and installed a lackey, Admiral Kimmel, to take his place. Kimmel agreed with FDR that Pearl Harbor was safe.

But of course it wasn't safe, and actions Roosevelt took before and after the election made it even less safe. In January 1940, Roosevelt had terminated the United States–Japan trade treaty. In July 1940 he had restricted exports to Japan. In September 1940 he had sent $25 million to the Chinese resistance against Japanese incursions, and he had also embargoed shipments of scrap iron to Japan. In July 1941, Roosevelt had frozen all Japanese assets in the United States and expanded the embargo.

The official State Department history concludes: "Faced with serious shortages as a result of the embargo, unable to retreat, and convinced that the US officials opposed further negotiations, Japan's leaders came to the conclusion that they had to act swiftly." That seems to have been what Roosevelt wanted.

On Monday, November 24, 1941, only thirteen days before the Pearl Harbor attack, Henry L. Stimson, Roosevelt's Secretary of War, recorded in his diary a meeting with Roosevelt:

He brought up the event that we were likely to be attacked perhaps (as soon as) next Monday [December 1], for the Japanese are notorious for making an attack without warning, and the question was what we should do. The question was how we should maneuver them into the position of firing the first shot without allowing too much danger to ourselves.

On November 25, Secretary of State Cordell Hull demanded that Japan withdraw from China. The following day Hull wrote this: "The matter is now in the hands of the Army and the Navy."

A few days later, on December 7, 1941, the Japanese attacked: 2,403 people died, eight battleships were sunk or damaged, and 188 airplanes were destroyed.

The United States took a long time to recover.

But FDR escaped blame. Today we should remember that it's not just December 7, 1941, that should live in infamy, but Roosevelt's reputation as well.

China, Trade, Donald Trump—and the Long Game
December 13, 2018

Can Donald Trump play a long game against China? Can any US president play a long game against China? China—the commentators relentlessly tell us—has been around for four thousand years, which puts the United States, now in only its third century, at a disadvantage. So the answer to the question is maybe . . . maybe not.

The Chinese economy—*pace* those who told us that trade with the outside world would convert the Chinese into westernized free marketeers—is still a command-and-control economy. And, as the wags say, if command-and-control economies worked, we'd all be speaking Russian.

China has several problems. One of them is named Donald Trump. Robert Lighthizer is the point man for the negotiations with the Chinese, but it's his boss who will call the shots.

Who is the better negotiator: President Trump or China's "President" Xi Jinping? (His title is in quotes because Americans are used to thinking of presidents as leaders who get elected by the people. Just when was the last Chinese president elected?)

Trump honed his negotiating skills in a free-market economy—though calling the New York City political environment "free market" guarantees a snicker from the back of the room. Still, that rough-and-tumble world was where Donald Trump learned his trade.

"President" Xi learned his skills in a controlled economy, where power comes from a barrel—and not a barrel of laughs. Xi reminds us of the quote attributed to Al Capone: "Things go great with a smile and a gun. But I find they go pretty well with just a gun." The Chinese may be building big weapons, but they're not ready for a shoot-out with the US military just yet.

China has other problems too. It's more dependent on exports than the United States is. The total tariffs on $505 billion of Chinese goods that the US has proposed would reduce China's GDP by 1.2 percent while reducing US GDP by only 0.2 percent. It's true that in a democracy, economic pain can be transmitted to the top quickly through the electoral process. But having half a billion or so very unhappy formerly middle-class Chinese bicycling around looking for dried rice can present . . . problems—even if you are good with a smile and a gun.

At the recent meeting between Trump and Xi in Buenos Aires, the United States agreed to suspend for ninety days the tariff increase on $200 billion worth of goods from 10 percent to 25 percent slated for January 1. Trump indicated that ninety didn't mean ninety-one days.

While Trump and Xi were having dinner, the Canadians, at the Americans' request, detained Meng Wanzhou, the forty-six-year-old chief financial officer of (and daughter of the founder of) Huawei Technologies. Huawei, the world's largest maker of telecom equipment, is suspected of exporting American technology to Iran at Meng's direction.

The Chinese Foreign Ministry put out a statement that was pure Harvard Lampoon. It accused Canada of "severely violating the legal, legitimate rights of a Chinese citizen." Don't miss the "severely." And also don't miss the recent increased persecution of Christians in China, said to be the most intense since the "Cultural Revolution."

The big question at the dinner in BA was: Did Trump know about Meng's apprehension in advance? The White House claims no. The Chinese probably can't believe that (can you?) and that's just fine. We want them to see Trump as an American cowboy who just might—what the Hell—hike the tariffs up to 25 percent a few days early because he wanted to go golfing at Mar-a-Lago. That's the art of the deal.

Another of China's problems is that economics is not Trump's only concern, and probably not even his top concern, which is jobs. Creating jobs for out-of-work Americans is more important to him than the country's bottom line, e.g., the size of the GDP, the Dow Jones Industrial Average, or the fortunes of the Wall Street "bankster"—most of whom are friends of Hillary anyway.

It's true that unemployment is as low as it's ever been, at least for blacks (how those numbers must sting former President Obama!), but those numbers only take you so far.

As Oren Cass—the author of a brilliant new book, *The Once and Future Worker*—pointed out in a recent op-ed, although the unemployment figures are low, millions of working age men are no longer looking for jobs. Cass says that by "the pre-2007 standard, today's labor market would be the worst on record." Those unemployed people who weren't on opioids on November 8, 2016, voted for Donald Trump. He hasn't forgotten that. And neither should "President" Xi.

Given Donald Trump's negotiating advantages, when the deal is finally done, "President" Xi is likely to be jinping up and down in frustration. But even he—or Xi—can't do that for all of Donald Trump's remaining two, or maybe six, years, much less four thousand years.

The Diabolically Clever Mr. Trump: An Alternative View

January 16, 2019

Richard Nixon is often said to have been the trickiest president the United States has ever had. "Tricky Dick" was his nickname, although in the end, he wasn't tricky enough to escape from the snares laid for him by the hard-left Democrats who never forgave him—and haven't yet—for nailing the commie spy Alger Hiss, the toast of the Georgetown set. Or for getting the Vietnam War won—which then required them to lose it by failing (after Nixon resigned) to honor the US commitments to the South Vietnamese.

But President Trump makes Richard Nixon look like junior high.

Among Trump's many and signal accomplishments is one he achieved even before being elected; indeed it was at least partly *because* he accomplished it that he got elected. And that, of course, was neutralizing the mainstream (i.e., hard-left) media. They have lost all credibility, except among their own hard-left readers. Even a former editor of the *New York Times* has said the grey lady has lost her soul—always assuming she had one to lose.

For the first two years of the Trump presidency the Democrats were obsessed with Russia. The whining, moaning, and gloating were non-stop and unrelenting, not just bordering on, but going well beyond, the deranged.

Russia has been a single obsession—like Andy Warhol's silent movie "Empire," an epic eight-hour black-and-white shot of the Empire State Building. The Empire State Building for eight solid hours in black and white. One single eight-hour scene only: the Empire State Building. Eight whole hours of a single shot of the Empire State building. Eight hours. The Empire State Building.

Russia. Russia. Russia. Russia.

Meanwhile, back at the ranch, Donald Trump was getting his pro-middle class, "Make America Great Again" program rolling, getting GDP growth up to 3 percent. (The Obama people having assured us that 2 percent growth was the new normal.)

Taxes cut / Russia, Russia, Russia. Regulations eliminated, including, especially Dodd–Frank regulations / Russia, Russia, Russia. Unemployment low, and at record lows for blacks and Hispanics / Russia, Russia, Russia. Federal judges appointed, including two to the Supreme Court / Russia, Russia, Russia. The US withdrawn from the Paris Climate Accord, and NAFTA renegotiated / Russia, Russia, Russia.

What have the Democrats got to show for their 2017 and 2018 paychecks? Nothing. Nothing. Nothing. Of course, they had no legislative power then, being in the minority in both houses of Congress. But they had the power of honest discourse, which remained totally unused.

Now that they have a majority in the House of Representatives, what's the plan? You have to see it not to believe it. The game plan is to investigate in order to prove: Russia, Russia, Russia.

As long as Robert Mueller keeps his investigation going, the Democrats can hope and pray—well, not *actually* pray; they're Democrats—that something dastardly done by Donald Trump will come to light, making all the Democrats' efforts worthwhile. But it's a little like a grade school kid's hoping, hoping, hoping that it snows on the day of the test because he hasn't opened a book since September.

What are the Democrats, and most especially their presidential candidate, going to run on in 2020?

It is always possible that Mueller has discovered, or will, something that will sink the Trump ship, but as time goes by that seems less likely even as Democrats, now the majority in the House, crank up their rhetoric.

The folly of having oversold and overpromised will be clear. It's already clear enough now that it's inexplicable Democrats continue to invest so much in their "dream" outcome of the Mueller investigation. They'll do their own investigating (and hold hearings) in the House, but what are they likely to find that Mueller will not have been able to find?

Will Trump fire Mueller? *Of course not.* That's another dream scenario for the Democrats. It's a Washington truism that what gets you is not the crime (often because there isn't one) but the cover-up. Trump knows that. But, as if dragging a hundred-dollar bill through a trailer park, he rails against Mueller on a regular basis, deliberately taunting the Democrats by saying that of course he has the power to fire Mueller—which of course he has.

Trump is just playing the Democrats for fools: which they seem to be, investing their whole portfolio in Mueller's report and the Russia canard. It's tulips from Amsterdam all over again.

And when the Mueller investigation ends and it's election time again, and the tulips haven't been delivered again, what will the Democrats run on?

Meanwhile, back at the great ranch in the sky, looking down with admiration on Donald Trump is the ghost of Richard Nixon.

The PC Enforcers Ride Again
January 18, 2019

You don't have to be Jewish to love Levy's Real Jewish Rye Bread, and you don't have to like Representative Steve King (R–IA), or what he has said, to know that he was scalped by the identity-politics-driven hypocritical posturing Left.

Earlier this month, King remarked: "White nationalist, white supremacist, Western civilization—how did that language become offensive?" That was not his first foray into dangerous territory. In its January 16, 2019, issue, the *New York Times* has a long list of what they consider to be other offensive statements or actions. Some are, some are not, but even those that are not could be described as unwise, given the current power of the PC police, the posturing self-appointed guardians of our—or more accurately "their"—culture.

Why King would conflate white nationalists and white supremacists with Western civilization is worth remarking on—some other time.

But you don't have to be a political genius to suspect that endorsing, as King did, a Toronto mayoral candidate who had recited the "14 words" spoken by a neo-Nazi ("We must secure the existence of our people and a future for white children") is stupid at best.

But whatever happened to the doctrine of "clean hands"? How can the Left criticize anyone?

Where were they when Charles M. Blow, columnist for the *New York Times*, wrote, "The founders, a bunch of rich, powerful white men, didn't want true democracy in this country, and in fact were dreadfully afraid of it. Now, a bunch of rich, powerful white men want to return us to this sensibility, wrapped in a populist 'follow the Constitution' rallying cry and disguised as the ultimate form of patriotism." That's a few more than fourteen words, but how is it significantly different from what Rep. King has said?

How much criticism of Blow's column have you seen?

Rep. Hank Johnson (D–CA) compared Jewish Israeli settlers to termites in 2016 while speaking at an event sponsored by an anti-Israel organization that supports boycotts of the Jewish state. How much criticism of that speech have you read in the *New York Times*?

Recently hired *New York Times* technology writer Sarah Jeong was discovered to have tweeted such edifying comments as: "White men are bull—"; "#CancelWhitePeople"; "oh man it's kind of sick how much joy I get out of being cruel to old white men" and "f— white women lol."

But the *Times* covered for her: she was, after all, young, foreign-born (Korean), and a woman. Bliss it is to be alive, Ms. Jeong must think. But to be young, foreign-born, *and* a woman is very heaven.

In the rap "singer" Jay-Z's latest album there are these lyrics: "You wanna know what's more important than throwin' away money at a strip club? Credit / You ever wonder why Jewish people own all the property in America? This how they did it."

Ah, well, the self-appointed guardians of "our" culture might say, he's just a rap singer who doesn't like Jews. What's new?

This is what's new: a nominee to a position in the US government has been grilled about her religion. Sen. Diane Feinstein (D–Cloud Cuckoo Land) stated to a nominee to the federal bench, a faithful Catholic: "When you read your speeches, the conclusion one draws is that the dogma lives loudly within you, and that's of concern when you come to big issues that large numbers of people have fought for for years in this country." And fought against, Sen. Feinstein might have added but didn't.

And US Senators Mazie Hirono (D–HI) and Kamala Harris (D–CA) have questioned nominees about their membership in major Catholic organizations causing the Senate, remarkably, to pass, unanimously, a resolution disavowing opposition to federal appointees on the basis of membership in the Catholic organization Knights of Columbus.

What we have here, and have had for many years, is a culture war. That is made very clear by other quotes from Rep. King which the *Times* headlines as "Incendiary Remarks and Divisive Actions." *Inter alia*, King introduced a bill to make English the official language of the United States. (How incendiary can you get?) And he referred to multiculturalism as, "a tool for the Left to subdivide a culture and civilization . . . and pit us again each other."

And King asked where did any subgroup of people other than whites contribute more to civilization? If by civilization he meant, as he probably did, the constitutional republic we live in, the answer is pretty clear: nowhere. The genius of the Founding Fathers has been extolled for decades across continents. It is true they were white, which is not to say people of other races couldn't have accomplished what the Founding Fathers accomplished: but none of them did. That is a consequence of historical developments, not racial genetics. King is focused on the consequences; the Left on the genetics. King's statement is certainly no more objectionable than the widely unremarked column of *New York Times* columnist Charles Blow quoted above.

There's a culture war going on in the United States and for years the Left has been winning. Now, finally, the traditional American culture has a champion. Donald Trump, with all his faults—and let him who is without faults write the first editorial—seems to understand what's at stake. That gives Western Civ a chance—Western Civ, from whence come all our rights, including the right not to like Levy's Real Jewish Rye Bread, as well as the right not even to like Levy.

BuzzFeed's Flub Reveals Mueller May Not Have a Lot on the President—and Never Will

January 21, 2019

On Thursday, BuzzFeed, a more-than-slightly-disreputable news outlet that first published the now-infamous Steele dossier implicating President Trump in serious misbehavior, appeared on the screen with a story claiming that Trump ordered his lawyer, Michael Cohen, to lie to Congress about his hotel business operation in Moscow.

For most of Friday, the country's news media—overwhelmingly hostile to Trump—ran the story editorializing that "if true" Donald Trump's impeachment was all but inevitable.

That was not a far-fetched conclusion. The BuzzFeed story quite clearly implicated the president in obstructing justice: telling people to lie is obstruction of justice. Few people doubt that, which is why the BuzzFeed story got so much coverage. The story was all the more powerful because it had nothing to do with Trump's colluding with Russia, which had been, until Thursday, the linchpin of the anti-Trump forces' case for impeachment, but for which evidence is scant.

But late on Friday, Special Counsel Robert Mueller's office issued an unprecedented statement saying: "BuzzFeed's description of specific statements to the special counsel's office, and characterization of documents and testimony obtained by this office, regarding Michael Cohen's congressional testimony are not accurate."

Later on Friday, BuzzFeed was still standing by its story, nitpicking at the special counsel's statement.

It is simply inconceivable, however, that the BuzzFeed story is essentially correct, and that the special counsel's statement was only a clarification, however badly worded, of minor details.

There are two significant points in this story. The first is that the special counsel thought it necessary to do something to counter the BuzzFeed report. Even that is extraordinary, given the tight-lipped practice of Robert Mueller's operation.

What was the point of the special counsel's statement? Presumably to negate a report that would hobble the president from carrying out his presidential duties.

But the real significance of the special counsel's unprecedented statement is what it tells us about Robert Mueller. If Mueller thought it necessary, in the interest of allowing the president to carry out his constitutional responsibilities, to scotch the BuzzFeed report, it suggests that he would not pursue his investigation into the Russia collusion business past the point where he had found sufficient, convincing evidence of impeachable behavior by President Trump.

If, say, five months ago, Mueller had found sufficient evidence to lead to the cashiering of the president, his action today suggests he would have made that evidence public at that time.

Some people had doubted Mueller's probity. His action this week suggests that he is concerned about the ability of the government—which means most especially the president—to function unimpeded by rumors of impeachable behavior.

As a result of Mueller's actions now, it seems most unlikely that he has already uncovered evidence of impeachable offenses committed by the president. And given the length of time he has been looking, it seems unlikely now that he will.

And, given the thoroughness of the Mueller investigation, it also seems unlikely that any congressional investigating committee will find evidence of presidential misbehavior.

This movie may not be over yet. But it looks as if we're coming to the end of the final reel.

Is It Un-American to be Super-Super Rich?
January 29, 2019

Alexandria Ocasio-Cortez, the twenty-nine-year-old Democrat recently elected to Congress from New York, has famously suggested (but not yet proposed) that a federal tax of 70 percent be imposed on the portion of a person's income that exceeds $10 million.

Backward reels the mind to the pages of yesteryear when President Roosevelt's top tax rate was 94 percent. He had proposed a rate of 100 percent, saying that at a time of grave national danger (i.e., World War II) no American should have a net after-tax income of more than what today would be $400,000.

Ocasio-Cortez and her ilk see another "emergency," and one far more threatening than a simple world war. Their emergency is climate change, to the reduction of which, via a Green New Deal (which would end fossil fuel use in twelve years), Ocasio-Cortez's tax funds would be devoted.

One is tempted to howl with derision at the proposal of AOC (as she is now known), but a part of what she says is worth listening to—for the same reason some voters in 2016 had trouble deciding between Bernie Sanders and Donald Trump. Between Bernie Sanders and Donald Trump? Holy cow! What's the similarity?

This is the similarity: both Sanders and Trump were "for" the middle class, and recognized that that class had been essentially abandoned by both political parties. The party of the rich (Republicans) had abandoned them in the quest for corporate profits (however acquired) often by transferring middle-class jobs to China. The other party of the rich (Democrats) had abandoned the middle class in its quests for corporate profits, a pre-industrial-era environment, and identity politics warfare.

There are several problems with AOC's proposal. First, as always, is the uneasy case for taxing people differently. Why should A pay a larger percentage of his income than B? Whatever happened to the idea of equal treatment?

Second is the problem with giving money to government, an act that can be as dangerous as giving matches to small children.

What would government do with the extra money collected by AOC's tax? It would likely do what it is currently doing: give it to the maker of Tesla electric cars, Elon Musk—whose take-home pay in 2016 was $99,744,920, paid for in part by the $7,500 tax rebate the federal government gives each purchaser of a Tesla car (priced from $68,000 to $138,800, while supplies last).

Still . . . sky-high salaries *are* a problem, and seem un-American. The Blackstone Group's Stephen Schwarzman's 2018 take home pay of $786.5 million may make the compensation of Apple's Tim Cook

($150 million), Google's Sundar Pichai ($106 million) and IBM's Ginni Rometty ($96 million) look paltry, but they all set bad examples.

Milton Friedman, asked about sky-high salaries, said they were a problem, but that any attempt by government to deal with the problem was likely to be worse than the problem itself.

In the opening of F. Scott Fitzgerald's short story "The Rich Boy" (1926), the narrator says, "Let me tell you about the very rich. They are different from you and me."

Perhaps, but for at least some of America's history the rich weren't all that different, if only because there wasn't that much to spend money on. Really rich people could buy big estates and have liveried servants weeding the vegetable garden and they could have private railway cars. But there wasn't any television or treatment for cancer, and traveling by private railway car was far more challenging than rolling out the G5.

The rich may have been different but, in the pre-tabloid, pre-television age they and their excesses were far less visible.

As recently as 1963, Charles Murray writes in *Coming Apart*, "America didn't have a lower class or an upper class." Many poor people refused to identify themselves as lower class, and many affluent people refused to call themselves upper class.

"Those refusals," Murray writes, "reflected a national conceit that had prevailed from the beginning of the nation: America didn't have classes, or, to the extent that it did, Americans should act as if we didn't."

Today we have a hollowed-out middle class, and especially hollowed-out middle class men: unemployed, unmarried, childless, and plagued by opioids.

Ocasio-Cortez's Green New Deal is malarkey of course, but she's young and new at this game, which is why she proposed a ho-hum rate of only 70 percent. But when—if?—she grows up, she'll be proposing FDR's 100 percent rate on people who've gotten uber-rich at the expense of the middle class, the funds to be devoted to assisting that middle class, not some fatuous green dream. *That* proposal may get serious attention.

Where Has All the Culture Gone?

February 8, 2019

From the New York island to the Redwood forest, Western Civilization continues to collapse, gradually now, but soon, maybe, suddenly. For now, only a relatively small band of traditionalists are manning the gates against the cultural nihilists. And, of course, manning is the right word. Once upon a time, hand-to-hand combat was not thought to be women's work: if the women were killed in battle, who would take care of the children?

Assuming there are any children. About eight hundred thousand babies are aborted each year in the United States. Given that about 39 percent of those babies are black but that blacks are only 12 percent of the population, why isn't abortion seen as racist? Whatever happened to disparate impact?

How can Democrats, who are the primary advocates for abortion, say with a straight face that their pro-abortion stance isn't a dog whistle for racists? Can Democrats say they know no one who favors abortion who has not also at least once said, or perhaps "opined," that a complementary effect of abortion is that it helps keep down the poor black population?

If Ralph (not his real name) were to beat a black man to death in the forest while yelling racial insults, but the *New York Times* didn't cover the attack, would it be a racist act?

Just recently the governor of Virginia, Ralph Northam, indicated that he would not oppose an "abortion" even *after* a baby was born. Most people were scandalized by his remarks, but the only remarkable aspect of them was that he said them out loud, not that he had thought them. That he, and thousands of others, had thought them is really unremarkable, because of Burnham's Second law: "Who says A must say B." (James Burnham was a philosopher and a founding editor of *National Review*; he wrote many books, including his seminal work, *The Managerial Revolution.*)

Burnham's Second Law makes the point that taking one position can require taking a subsequent position. If you murder Duncan, you must also kill Banquo.

A baby in the womb either is or is not a person. The abortionists say "it" is not (they have to say that because it is still not quite acceptable to kill "people"—unless perhaps they are really old or sick and, you know, like, really not enjoying life), but the abortionists refuse to say when "it" does become a person. In theory they might say "when it is born," but that is now transparently only terminological. Even a fool can tell that there's no substantive difference between the personhood of a "baby" in the womb on December 24 and that same baby born on December 25. But where are the fools when we need them?

The pro-abortion crowd was able to avoid addressing that issue as long as people weren't having abortions in the last days of a pregnancy. Now Governor Northam has spoiled the game by conceding that in the minds of the pro-abortion crowd there really is no difference between babies not born and babies just born: and that a baby fully born can be terminated, as Banquo was.

In New York state, the legislature has just passed legislation that allows non-doctors to perform abortions, and right up to the point of birth—if the life or health of the mother is deemed at risk or the baby is not viable, which is legislative bureaucratese for "Whenever, dude."

Meanwhile, back in the US Senate, Senators Kamala Harris (D–CA) and Mazie Hirono (D–HA) questioned a judicial nominee on his membership in the Knights of Columbus, a Catholic organization opposed to abortion, a member of which might be inclined to overturn *Roe v. Wade*. It is true that subsequently the US Senate unanimously passed a resolution that said disqualifying a nominee on the basis of membership in the Knights of Columbus would be unconstitutional, but what's important is that the senators felt safe playing to their constituencies in attacking the religion, Catholicism, of the nominees. Whatever happened to diversity?

Well, it's alive and well at Hedge Fund Academy, a tony New England prep school (tuition for boarders: $59,560), which last week sent out an email touting its commitment to diversity.

Our commitment to expanding diversity education and programming is vital to preparing our students for the next stages of their lives. Diversity, equity and inclusion work at Hedge is an intrinsic part of the strength and success of our community, woven into the full range of our daily academic, social and professional lives.

In the Hedge community, we have people who identify as transgender and gender non-binary. Our responsibility to support their health and well-being stands clear. As part of an evaluation of our practices with regard to gender inclusivity, we modified restroom facilities to provide additional single-stall, all-gender restrooms across campus.

Aren't you glad your last year's contribution to Hedge went to adding single-stall, all-gender restrooms?

HFA's list is singularly deficient, of course, omitting as it does most of the diversity menu: LGGBDTTTIQQAAPP, which stands for lesbian, gay, genderqueer, bisexual, demisexual, transgender, transsexual, two-spirit, intersex, queer, questioning, asexual, allies, pansexual, and polyamorous. But you knew that.

Despite Hedge's "diversity" a good bet is that the curriculum isn't diverse enough to include this writing from the fifth-century Christian writer Salvian, who contrasted the chastity of the Vandals with the complete corruption of the Romans.

> More grave and criminal was the fact that those vices, about which the blessed Apostle Paul complained with the greatest lament of his soul, were almost all practiced in Africa. That is, men, having put aside the natural use of women, burned in their desires for one another; men doing base things with men, and receiving to themselves the reward of their error which they should receive. . . . Did the blessed Apostle say this about barbarians and wild peoples? No indeed. But about us, that is, the Romans in particular.

About 1,590 years after Salvian wrote those words (i.e., last week), the House of Representatives in Colorado passed a bill that would require the state's public school sex-education curriculum to include instructions on LGBT relationships. The bill also prohibits teachers "from explicitly or implicitly teaching or endorsing religious ideology or sectarian tenets or doctrines, using shame-based or stigmatizing language or instructional tools, employing gender norms or gender stereotypes, or excluding the relational or sexual experiences of lesbian, gay, bisexual, or transgender individuals."

Fools, the Knights of Columbus, and others may object. But will that matter?

From New York to Virginia to Colorado to California, the lamps are going out all over America: and we shall not see them lit again in our lifetime, unless we make a more serious effort than we have been making to preserve our precious Western Civilization heritage.

A Quiz: How Should Neomi Rao Have Answered Cory Booker?

February 21, 2019

"Are gay relationships, in your opinion, immoral?"

That was the question Senator Cory "Spartacus" Booker (D–NJ) asked DC Circuit Court nominee Neomi Rao at her recent confirmation hearing.

In this quiz you are asked to determine three items: (A) the correct answer to the above question, (B) the answer actually given by the witness, and (C) the staircase wit answer. "Staircase wit" is the remark, often a repartee, you think of *after* the event, probably on your way up the staircase to bed. For example, in October 1988, after vice presidential candidate Dan Quayle mentioned President Kennedy in a debate with vice presidential candidate Sen. Lloyd Benson, Benson said famously, "Senator, I served with Jack Kennedy. I knew Jack Kennedy. Jack Kennedy was a friend of mine. Senator, you're no Jack Kennedy," to which Quayle might have replied, but didn't, "If you knew him that well, Lloyd, you'd know Michael Dukakis is no Jack Kennedy either."

Please choose A, B, and C from the following possibilities:

1. "Um, senator, I'm not sure the relevance of that to—"

2. "Senator, that could depend on the nature of the relationship. Many relationships could seem to be one thing, but actually be something else. Or they could seem to be another kind of relationship,

but actually be something entirely different. Without knowing all the facts, it can be difficult to say with certainty. A senator and a page would be one kind of relationship but two senators might be something different."

3. "Senator, do these relationships of which you speak involve sex? And if so, could you please graphically describe the sexual acts, including naming the interacting body parts?"

4. "Senator, that is actually a very interesting question. I would answer by noting that homosexuals comprise only about 4.5 percent of this country, according to a new estimate by the Gallup Organization. And while that amounts to more than 11 million people, it is still a small percentage. That figure of 4.5 percent is up from the 3.5 percent figure Gallup found in 2012, the first year Gallup started asking the question. The new, higher figure is driven, it is thought, by the millennials (people born between 1980 and 1999), but is suspect because they are probably to some extent simply experimenting with lifestyles, based on popular culture, and not yet committed to any one set of rules."

5. "Yes."

6. "Senator, are you asking me if I'm gay?"

7. "Senator, that question is most interesting because it posits the existence of right and wrong, of moral behavior and immoral behavior. You might ask, 'Is discrimination against blacks wrong?' I think we would all, or at least most of us, answer 'yes.' But why would we answer that? How would we get to that conclusion? Where do we look for the answer? Our parents? Our grandparents? Our schools and teachers? The news media? The Supreme Court?

"And does it depend on when you ask the question? If the answer today is that discrimination against blacks is immoral, can it be that it was not immoral yesterday? Is discrimination inherently immoral, today, tomorrow, yesterday, and always?

"And—and this is the important part—how do we tell? Do we vote on it? Is this a case of majority rule? What if a majority votes to discriminate against blacks? Does that make racial discrimination moral too? What if the Supreme Court says discrimination is okay: does that make it okay?

"I think it is fair to say that homosexual relationships either are immoral or they are not. I think you would agree that there cannot be any question that in our parents' day, homosexual relationships were immoral. If they are not immoral today, then the two key questions are, when and how did they become *not* immoral?"

The answers to the quiz: (A) #5 is the correct answer to Booker's question. (B) #1 was the answer given. (C) The staircase wit answer is #7 if you live in a five-story building and #6 if you live in a one-story walk-up.

Note to reader: After you hand in your bluebook, please phone Sen. Booker's office and ask when homosexual relationships became not immoral.

Max Boot, Bye-Bye
March 8, 2019

Max Boot has announced he is no longer a conservative. In cosmic time, the shocking announcement came at the *exact* moment in RACIST, RUSSIA-COLLUSIONIST Donald Trump's administration that black unemployment reached its lowest level *ever*. Like famed boxer Cassius Clay, Trump may be The Greatest, at everything, ever—but he sure makes a lousy racist.

Mr. Boot explains in a *Washington Post* op-ed:

It would be nice to think that Donald Trump is an anomaly who came out of nowhere to take over an otherwise sane and sober movement. . . .

Upon closer examination, it's obvious that the history of modern conservatism is permeated with racism, extremism, conspiracy-mongering, isolationism and know-nothingism. . . . There has always been a dark underside to conservatism that I chose for most of my life to ignore.

Oh, please. Even a fifty-year-old should have more perspective.

That there were some racists active in the early days of modern conservatism, and now too, should not surprise—Trump having been no more successful than William F. Buckley Jr. at abolishing original sin. However, Buckley, widely considered to be the founder of modern conservatism, did succeed in hiving off the anti-Semites and the fanatical John Birchers.

But the long story is complicated. It is true, as Boot says, that Buckley's *National Review* railed against President Dwight Eisenhower for being insufficiently anticommunist and insufficiently anti-New Deal. Why was that wrong?

Basking now in post-Cold War comfort, it is easy—and a cheap trick—to criticize the policies of an earlier period. We cannot know, now, what a more robust policy (Goldwater's?) of resistance to the communists might have delivered: perhaps a savings of billions of taxpayer dollars (is there any other kind?) which could have been spent . . . elsewhere? In retrospect, US policy (Reagan's building up the military, especially the navy) turned out pretty well, certainly for the United States if not for the millions of people starved, gulaged, and killed behind the Iron Curtain.

But probably it was wholly proper for us to be concerned only about ourselves, not about the millions subjected to communist rule from the 1950s to the 1990s. Raise your hand if that reminds you of America First? Or of isolationism?

Buckley and *National Review* also railed against Eisenhower's disinterest in rolling back the New Deal—indeed, Buckley essentially defined conservatives as people who had not made their peace with the New Deal. But he was overly optimistic, in 1955, noting that "the [liberal] Establishment has failed in its efforts to ease over to the federal government the primary responsibility for education, or health, or even housing."

There's been a lot of easing over since 1955. Now our primary and high school education system is a mess wholly run by the Democratic Party's teachers' unions; and our colleges teach almost nothing while miring students in debt that now exceeds the cost of Mr. Boot's beloved Iraq war.

It is often said that President Reagan was a convert to the New Deal. That's not entirely true. He recognized the obligation of Social Security to pay the people who had paid into the system, but knew also that there was a better way: to "privatize" it, at least for people who had the discipline to build their own retirement funds. And Reagan was an early deregulator.

The Civil Rights period is more complex. Buckley's position has been explored extensively by William Voegeli in *The Claremont Review*. The worst that can be said about Buckley is that he was late coming to the realization that some federal involvement was necessary to secure equality for blacks.

But his remark in 1961, that he hoped that "when the Negroes have finally realized their long dream of attaining to the status of the white man, the white man will still be free . . ." was prescient. Lincoln thought preserving the Union, even with slavery, would eventually be better for blacks. Buckley thought limited, constitutional government (what Goldwater had in mind when he voted against Title IV of the Civil Rights Act of 1964) would be better for everyone, including blacks.

You want racism? Try this, from *New York Times* columnist Charles Blow: "The founders, a bunch of rich, powerful white men, didn't want true democracy in this country, and in fact were dreadfully afraid of it. Now, a bunch of rich, powerful white men want to return us to this sensibility, wrapped in a populist 'follow the Constitution' rallying cry and disguised as the ultimate form of patriotism."

In any political movement there will be misfits and misanthropes, but it is immature to judge the whole by the part. Mr. Boot may be leaving the conservative side, but where is he going? The alternative is a socialist gulag, diminished First and Second Amendments, Orwellian speech codes, gender fluidity, and physical discomfort enforced by the climate police.

Have a good time, Mr. Boot.

Rand Paul's Republicans Should Really Restrict Executive Power Instead of Playing Democratic Games

March 11, 2019

Republicans in Congress are about to lose a game by avoiding an obvious triple play.

Left-wingers are gloating over the prospect that a majority of both Houses of Congress may pass a resolution disapproving President Trump's border wall national emergency declaration. It is tempting, especially for Conservatives, to cheer the assertion by Congress of its power—long dormant because of politicians' hardwired fear of doing *anything* that *someone*, even someone living on the moon, might not like.

Even after successful passage, however, the resolution is not likely to become law: Trump will surely veto it. Eventually the Supreme Court may get a chance to opine: the smart money is, like it or not, on Trump's winning.

Almost certainly, every Democrat who votes for the resolution is simply casting an anti-Trump vote. When was the last time you heard a Democrat complain about excessive power in the executive (or even excessive power in any part of government, except perhaps the police)? Certainly not during the Age of Obama. This resolution is just another swipe at the democratically elected president, as well as part of the Democrats' continuing attempt to flood the country with illegal aliens who, they assume (and probably correctly) will then vote Democrat to express their thanks. Wouldn't you under those circumstances?

Support by Republicans of this resolution curtailing the president's power is more difficult to understand, and demonstrates their inherent clumsiness when it comes to governing. Yes, of course, in theory, Republicans should be opposed to the massive ongoing abdication of congressional power to the executive branch, whether to the president or the departments or the so-called independent regulatory agencies.

But for decades, Congress, with Republican connivance, has essentially directed the executive branch to manage *everything*—and call us in the morning (not too early please) if (actually "when") you run out of money.

Now there are stirrings. Sen. Rand Paul (R–KY) said: "I support President Trump. I supported his fight to get funding for the wall from Republicans and Democrats alike, and I share his view that we need more and better border security.

"However, I cannot support the use of emergency powers to get more funding, so I will be voting to disapprove of his declaration when it comes before the Senate.

"Every single Republican I know decried President Obama's use of executive power to legislate. We were right then. But the only way to be an honest officeholder is to stand up for the same principles no matter who is in power."

That's noble, but voting to support this measure allows the Democrats to dress up as enthusiasts of limited executive power—and it's not even Halloween. We should applaud Republican efforts to take back congressional power, but at the same time, we should urge them to be a bit cleverer in the way they do it.

There is a way to (1) achieve a good goal (retrieve congressional power); (2) not diss the president; and (3) expose the hypocrisy of the Democrats—a triple play.

Republicans should amend the bill to have it take effect January 20, 2021, i.e., when the president who is elected in 2020 takes office. That president may be Donald Trump. But it might be Joe Biden. That would make the bill strictly non-partisan. Every Republican could vote for that bill. But would the Democrats? And if they did not, it would be plain that their support for this current resolution is only about thwarting Trump, not about recalibrating the distribution of power in Washington.

This country can survive one more excessive use of executive power. What will be more difficult to survive is campaigning by neo-socialist Democrats masquerading as limited government enthusiasts.

So yes, vote for this bill, but have it take effect in 2021.

Play ball.

Sex, Sin, and the Infield Fly Rule
March 23, 2019

David von Drehle, a columnist for the *Washington Post*, started his career as a sports writer. His most recent column proves he should have stuck with sports, and reminds of the sixteen-year-old who was asked by her teacher why she always wrote about sex. "Well," she replied, "you told me to write about what I know."

And von Drehle should write about what he knows, which, apparently, is not religion, as his column makes the reader blush at his ignorance.

"Jesus . . .," he begins—and you know that a column in the *Washington Post* that begins with "Jesus" is not likely to turn out well. It doesn't.

"Jesus invited disciples to put down their fishing nets and start hauling in believers. The catch was a motley crew of outcasts and sinners: tax collectors, prostitutes, cowards and doubters. Yet he was willing to die for them."

That lesson, he says, "is lost on many of today's Christian churches."

The person the lesson is lost on is von Drehle himself, even though his opening paragraph contains the word that's a key to understanding what's going on.

What kind of people were in the crowd? Sinners and prostitutes, *inter alia*. We'll come back to them.

Von Drehle's column is really about two separate events: the turmoil in the United Methodist Church, which recently passed a "Traditional Plan" that calls for enforcement of the denomination's ban against same-sex marriage and gay clergy; and the Archdiocese of Kansas which has blocked a "same-sex couple" from enrolling "their" child (whom we'll call Heather) at St. Ann's School in Prairie Village, Kansas. Von Drehle doesn't agree with either decision.

Von Drehle paraphrases the pastor of the Church of the Resurrection, which he tells us is the world's largest United Methodist congregation, a church that may have, he says, as many as a hundred same-sex couples: "To single out monogamous, loving homosexual couples for condemnation is cruel," said the pastor.

And von Drehle mocks the archdiocese's statement that "same-sex parents cannot model behaviors and attitudes regarding marriage and sexual morality consistent with essential components of the Church's teaching."

Von Drehle's problem, obviously, is that he doesn't agree that homosexual behavior is wrong, even a sin. (If he did, he wouldn't be a columnist for the *Washington Post*.)

Even so, as a sports writer he might understand that—to put it in layman's terms—organizations have rules. A basketball player cannot double dribble. A tennis player must keep his feet behind the base line when he serves. Players who break those rules are . . . "sinners," and if they persist in their behavior they will be removed from the group (i.e., not allowed to play the game).

Are such people evil? Not for committing those acts, though of course they may be for other acts they have committed.

Is it customary to make a rule-breaker the team captain? No. That sends the wrong message to the team, and to the society (sports players) they live in.

And so it is with homosexual acts. In traditional churches—and throughout most of American history (and Western civilization)—homosexual acts are like double dribbling: they are bad behavior and are therefore frowned upon. People who engage in such acts are not made leaders of a group, and if they persist they will be ostracized from their group.

You'd think even a *Washington Post* writer could figure that out.

It never occurs to von Drehle that the archdiocese may have been thinking of the loneliness the poor child of the "same-sex couple" might have had to endure at St. Ann's School. What "normal" parents at that school would let their child go home to play with Heather who has two mommies—both of whom are male?

Von Drehle knows, because he says so, that among Jesus's catch were sinners (i.e., people who do things that are wrong), but he seems to have no concept of how sinners should be treated. He's stealing a base: he calls them sinners, but he doesn't want them to suffer any consequences for their sins.

Von Drehle's problem is called the fallacy of the undistributed middle. A faulty syllogism would be: (major premise) half a loaf is better than nothing; (minor premise) nothing is better than Heaven; (conclusion) therefore, half a loaf is better than Heaven. The problem is with the word "nothing": it's the term that links the two premises—but it doesn't really link them because it means something different in each of the premises.

So with von Drehle. In the beginning he makes a big deal out of the *sinners* being forgiven (presumably because they are guilty of doing something wrong). Then he praises the pastor who welcomes the homosexuals, who, certainly in von Drehle's eyes, are *not* sinners. The word "sinners" is the undistributed middle term in von Drehle's piece.

He should stick to baseball—but what's he going to say about players who persistently violate the infield fly rule?

China Disconnect: What's Wrong with a Great Trade War?

April 22, 2019

In his new budget for 2020, President Trump has asked for $750 billion for defense. Ah, remember the days when the Cold War ended and—the peace dividend—we could go back to maximizing GDP?

We need the $750 billion, according to the administration, to counter the threats posed primarily by the Chinese, but also by the Russians—which is puzzling.

Russia, when it is not colluding with the president to subvert our democracy/utterly confounding the *Washington Post* and the *New York Times* and the rest of the mainstream Trump-resistance media (pick one) has, it would seem, devolved into a second rate power (it was never as strong as we thought it was, certainly not at the end of the Cold War): it is now said to be only a gas station run by alcoholics.

Not so China. The days of making cheap party-favor paper umbrellas has long passed. It has now gained, or is about to gain, military parity with the United States. *That* is a problem.

But it's not the only problem caused by China. Through its "One Belt, One Road" policy China is sucking other countries into its economic orbit. (China is already big in Venezuela.) This week China's President Xi Jinping is visiting Italy on a tour that China hopes will lock other G7 nations into its economic embrace. That is just what Russia has done with Germany: made it dependent on Russian natural gas piped in under the Baltic Sea to northern Germany through the 700-mile Nord Stream 2 pipeline.

Germany's agreement with Russia has been criticized for years, by US administrations as well as European countries. Trump originally blasted the Germans (who have just announced that again they will fall significantly short of NATO's defense spending goals) for becoming dependent on Russian gas at the same time they, and the rest of Europe, wanted the US to continue its major support of NATO, which was designed *specifically* to counter threats *from Russia*. Recently, however, and strangely, Trump has softened his position on

Germany's linking up to Nord Stream 2.

China presents a similar danger with its One Belt, One Road policy, but China goes the alcoholic Russian gas station attendants one better, much better, with its selling of technology (probably stolen from the US) to various countries.

The Chinese company Huawei ("hwha-way") has become a leader in G5, the next wave of information technology. It is busy selling its technology to any country that will buy it. The US concern is that the technology may pose a national security risk: the Chinese may have built back doors into the software that would give them the ability to spy on any country using it, and especially on that country's military. But some of those countries don't take that threat seriously: they think the US is just pushing for its own economic advantage.

What to do? Or more precisely, what to do in a democracy, and one that worships GDP?

What would happen if we simply pulled up the trade drawbridge and let the Chinese . . . dump their products into the China Sea? This is what would happen: the multitudinous purveyors of cheap plastic goods from China would have a cow (bad for the environment).

In 2018 the US trade deficit in goods with China was $419 billion: imports from China were $540 billion; exports to China were only $120 billion. That means that a trade war hurts the Chinese far more than it hurts the US, and parents and taxpayers (at least those who could take time out from buying more plastic) might ask, Why are we spending gazillions of dollars on military hardware to counter a military threat from the Chinese at the same time we're trading with them and making them rich?

We didn't make the Russians rich during the Cold War, partly, of course, because the Cold War generation of Russians, also alcoholic gas station attendants (but without the gas) didn't make anything we wanted—not even cheap party-favor paper umbrellas. But we also didn't build factories there and give them access to our technology.

Which is to say, during the Cold War we took the Russian threat seriously. Now we seem ambivalent about the Chinese.

There's probably a Chinese proverb that covers this situation, something like, "The greatest victory is the battle not fought."

Or maybe, "Country that worships GDP will get deserved punishment."

Free the Students. Sink the Colleges.
May 7, 2019

Senator Elizabeth Warren has called for forgiving student loans (a proposal first made here back in 2014*). But Warren would eliminate only $50,000 of student debt, and only for students whose income was less than $100,000, approximately 42 million people.

Of course, being Sen. Warren, she has also proposed that the government cover all tuition at all two-year and four-year colleges, and—well it goes on and on, essentially socializing the cost of everything, probably including toothpaste, chewing gum, and wampum belts.

The cost of the debt-forgiveness part of her proposal is said to be $640 billion. (Total student debt is estimated at $1.56 trillion.)

Just because Warren has latched onto the idea doesn't make it kooky—though we are right to suspect anything that the first faculty member of color at Harvard Law School says.

Donald Trump should steal this idea, feathers and all, for the 2020 campaign.

Part Two of this column's original proposal was that the federal government would pay for the loan cancellations by eliminating most of its grants to higher education institutions. Today total federal support of education is about $102.5 billion a year.

People who are skeptical of Part Two need to understand something about "higher" education: for most people it is worthless, as education. *Completely worthless.* And actually, worse than worthless because it corals young people into institutions for two or four of their most formative years where they learn *absolutely nothing*! And wind up in debt up to their keisters.

In his book, *The Case Against Education*, Bryan Caplan makes, inter alia, two important points. The first is that students learn nothing: "Barely half of American adults," he writes, "know the Earth goes around the sun." Read that again, slowly, and contemplate the usefulness of a college education.

We should not be surprised. Richard Arum and Josipa Roksa in their book, *Academically Adrift*, agree with Caplan ("American

---

* http://tiny.cc/r6ojfx

education is characterized by limited or no learning for a large proportion of students") and suggest why. "On average, [students] report spending only 12 hours per week studying." Arum and Roksa also tell us that "fifty percent of the students in our sample reported that they had not taken a single course during the prior semester that required more than twenty pages of writing, and one third had not taken one that required even forty pages of reading per week."

Bryan Caplan's second point is that education is all about credentialing. "The labor market doesn't pay you for the useless subjects you master," he writes, "it pays you for the preexisting traits you reveal by mastering them."

The education racket is all about the "sheepskin" effect. Graduates of the twelfth grade in high school earn more than graduates of only the ninth, tenth, and eleventh grades *combined*. In college the sheepskin effect is even more pronounced: graduates earn *more than twice as much* as students who complete only one, two, or three years *combined!*

One theory—only a congressman could believe it—is that the teachers or professors save all the really important information for the last year. Horse feathers!

If college is all about credentialing, why not find another way to credential the nation's young people? Why not make tasks available that would allow Johnny to show that he has the grit to stick with a difficult job?

Why not create service opportunities for young people to engage in, in addition to military service? They could work at senior citizen institutions, hospitals, high schools, or any number of other charitable institutions that serve the public. The work could be demanding: show up on time; learn specific skills; take responsibility. "Undergraduates in Service to America—USA all the way." William F. Buckley Jr. wrote a whole book about it in 1990 called *Gratitude*.

Service would not be mandatory, of course—no indentured servitude. It would simply be an opportunity for young people to show what four years of college shows prospective employers now: that the "student" has the fortitude to persevere.

The feds could even "subsidize" part of the program by not taxing the income of people under the age of twenty-two in such a program.

Young people with good jobs and without huge loans could move out of their parents' basements (or teepees), get married, have children, and lead normal, productive lives—the way Americans used to.

If a few big corporations started accepting as evidence of maturity and perseverance a work substitute for a sheepskin, the change could happen like a California wildfire.

By stopping support to higher education, the federal government could pay for the debt cancellation in less than a decade—much, much less if the government forgave only the first $10,000 of debt, which would eliminate the debt of about a third of borrowers.

But note that a key part of the proposal is stopping payments to the nation's colleges. Those institutions, bloated with high-paid administrators and grievance counselors, are the fever swamps of the Left, inculcating young people in big government, socialist, and often anti-American nostrums. Stopping that is worth twice the price.

This is a win-win-win proposition for Republicans: get the students to vote Republican; save a generation or several generations of young people from wasting four important years in colleges where they will learn almost nothing; and defund the Left's higher ed propaganda machine.

Thanks, Feathers, for reminding us of the opportunity.

The Contest between Diversity and Merit
May 8, 2019

The *New York Times* began its story on Stuyvesant High School in New York City with this paragraph, meant to be heart-wrenching:

> Sarai Pridgen had just gotten home from debate practice on Monday evening when she opened her laptop to find her Facebook feed flooded with stories about a staggering statistic: only seven black students had been admitted into Stuyvesant High School, out of 895 spots. The number was causing a wrenching citywide discussion about race and inequality in America's largest school system.

What to do? What to do when the irresistible force (mandatory integration) meets the immovable object (low black test scores)? Who should win in the great contest between diversity and merit?

This should be fun to watch—it's always fun to watch the lefties fighting each other. But there's tragedy here, and it's largely of the Left's making.

William Lohier, 17, is one of just 29 black students out of about 3,300 teenagers at Stuyvesant. Lohier, whose father is black and whose mother is Korean American, said the numbers had made him feel both angry and committed to improving the school culture.

Sarai Pridgen, whose father is black and grew up in New York City and whose mother is from Spain, said, "I've been told that the only reason I got into Stuyvesant is because I'm black, even though the test doesn't even factor that in."

Last year, the mayor of New York, whose current name (his third) is Bill de Blasio, proposed scrapping Stuyvesant's entrance exam and instead taking the top performers at every city middle school. Many were not amused.

Even a graduate of a New York City high school—well, that may be a stretch—could tell that de Blasio's plan would greatly reduce the intellectual level at Stuyvesant. His plan is opposed by Stuyvesant graduates and by Asian American groups. Hmm. Why Asian American groups?

Because 73 percent of Stuyvesant's students are Asians, that's why. Only 20 percent are white, only 3 percent are Hispanic, and just under 1 percent are black.

New York City's school system as a whole, however, is nearly 70 percent black and Hispanic, and only 15 percent white and Asian.

Asians, as a group, are hardworking, and going to Stuyvesant or one of the other NYC select schools is their big chance—as it would be for any black or white or Hispanic student as well.

Just why do Asians do better? Are they genetically different? It is surely okay (or is it?) to say that Bob is brighter than Sam (i.e., his genes make him more intelligent). But is it okay to say that Asians are brighter than . . . other people?

And is that not what the statistics at Stuyvesant are telling us? Not all people are equal in their abilities. Black children in New York City are not equal in their abilities to other New York City children, especially Asians. Of course, blacks have, or at least have had, an obvious excuse: centuries of discrimination that deprived them of, inter alia, educational opportunities.

But that excuse is wearing thin: we've had affirmative action now for decades.

Obviously, there are factors beyond genetics and historical discrimination. Here are some other statistics worth considering. In 2016, 66.5 percent of black children born in New York City were illegitimate. The rate for Asian children isn't recorded: they are included in "other," for which the rate was 19.5 percent. For the United States as a whole, however, the rate of illegitimacy for Asians is only 11.8 percent, and it's a reasonable guess that the figure for New York City is comparable.

Does anyone doubt that family structure is a major determinant in how well a child does? Illegitimacy is a structural problem for blacks and a political problem for liberals. What's the likelihood of a *New York Times* reporter telling us whether the few blacks at Stuyvesant live with both parents? Or making the point that living with both parents gives a child a better chance in life?

Liberals have spent decades trashing the cultural inheritance of Western Civilization—who needs marriage?—even while sneakily observing it themselves. If they really cared about blacks, they would speak up for marriage. They don't.

And so for most black children, in New York City and elsewhere, the tragedy goes on: life will continue to be one of poverty: financial poverty, intellectual poverty, and probably spiritual poverty as well.

Except for the few lucky ones, probably living with both parents, who can escape to the Stuyvesant highs.

The China Problem—Or Is It the Joe Biden Problem?
May 19, 2019

Joe Biden's a nice guy, they say, but his statement on China should alarm not just his campaign staff but the rest of us as well. After all, he *might* (if the gods are snoozing) become president.

Last week, the former vice president said this: "China is going to eat our lunch? Come on, man. They can't even figure out how to deal with the fact that they have this great division between the China Sea and the mountains in the east, I mean in the west. [Those pesky directions.] They can't figure out how they are going to deal with the corruption that exists within the system. I mean, you know, they're not bad folks, folks. But guess what, they're not competition for us."

That's dumb, man.

Or maybe devious. Readers of Peter Schweizer book, *Secret Empires: How the American Political Class Hides Corruption and Enriches Family and Friends*, may remember the account of Joe Biden's son, Hunter, flying to China with his then vice president father and ten days later signing an exclusive mega-deal with the Bank of China, the most powerful financial institution in the country. No wonder Joe Biden doesn't want folks focusing on China.

It is true that Biden's comments may reflect the received wisdom on China of twenty years ago (when he was fifty-six), but not now—raising the question, is Biden simply out to lunch, covering for his son, or is he perhaps . . . a *Chinese agent?*!

Bob Mueller, call your office.

While Biden has been snoozing, China has been developing cutting-edge military technology. As a Defense Intelligence Analysis makes clear, although China's double-digit economic growth may have slowed recently, it has served to fund several successive defense modernization Five-Year Plans. In addition, China has sought to acquire technology by any means available.

As has been repeatedly reported in the US press, China has required foreign partners of Chinese-based joint ventures to "share" their technology in exchange for the right to do business in China's lucrative market. China has also used other means (e.g., theft) to secure technology and expertise useful to its military buildup.

The result: China is on the verge of fielding some of the most modern weapon systems in the world. In some areas, it already leads the world.

China also has a fast-growing economy (which has supported its military efforts), aided often by theft of intellectual property. The Chinese are investing heavily in tech talent. China has eight times as many STEM graduates as the US has. Three of the top eight internet companies are Chinese, including Tencent, Ali Baba, and Baidu (which most Americans have never even heard of). The four largest banks in the world are Chinese. Last year the Chinese bought twice as many German luxury automobiles as we did.

During the Cold War there was a saying: if command economies worked, we'd all be speaking Russian. We're not speaking Chinese, yet, partially because we still have freedom and the rule of law. And we live in a system that makes decisions democratically. But democracy has its own built-in . . . challenges.

Ivory tower economists tell us continually that trading with China isn't dangerous because trade deficits don't matter. Trade deficits, they say, are an accounting concept. In markets with transparency and without tariffs or tariff-like requirements, a deficit doesn't matter. Most discussions of "trade deficits" focus on the deficit in goods, where economists point out that there may be a surplus in payments for services (the "other ledger"). The usual "offset" is that when the US purchases more from one country than that country purchases from the US, the mirror image of that deficit in goods is a surplus of payments to foreigners.

Question: What are the foreigners going to do with the money (i.e., the claim on US resources)? Often, *but not always*, they invest it in the US, and often in real estate. No problem, here, folks. Keep moving.

The real takeaway, however, is this: trade is making the Chinese rich. It's rather odd to hear economists tell us that trading with China isn't dangerous, when the economists have told us for years, and are still telling us, that trade makes nations rich.

Exactly! Trading with China has made them rich and will make them richer in the future, raising the question: Why do we want to make China rich? Trade may not be the only way the Chinese are becoming rich: abandoning collectivism and the communist economic system has assisted them dramatically, of course.

But the central question remains: Why should the US trade with China if China is our enemy? Would the US be poorer if it stopped trading with China? Of course. But we are so much richer than the Chinese that we could take that hit to our economy far more easily than the Chinese could. They may start discovering that *this week*.

The lesson here is *at least* that President Trump should drive a hard bargain in our trade negotiations with the Chinese.

Our democratic system may be far superior to theirs, both for encouraging production and for living free. But our system makes it vastly more difficult to have (i.e., to get Congress to pass) a defense budget that is adequate to meet the threat from our enemies; a governance problem China doesn't have.

And it still won't have even if Joe Biden gets elected president. Everyone says Biden is a nice fellow. That may be, but that's not enough.

Rudy Giuliani, asked about a potential Biden–Trump match-up in 2020, said, "Joe Biden is a moron. I'm calling Joe Biden a mentally deficient idiot."

Asked by CNN's Chris Cuomo why he had said that, Giuliani asked, "You mean that he's dumb?"

"No," said Cuomo, "that would have been a compliment."

Giuliani explained: "I didn't mean [that he was mentally deficient]. I meant he's dumb. . . . Joe was last in his law school class."

Cuomo attempted to rehabilitate: "He wasn't last in his class. He *was* low."

Giuliani: "Actually, he was second to last, and then the other guy died."

Guess Biden's not a Chinese agent after all, just a guy (and devoted father) who finished last, or second to last, in his law school class.

Whatever. Biden, and our economist friends who are still promoting "free" trade with China, need to wake up and smell the rice paddies—before we have to fight in them.

D-Day, 2019

June 9, 2019

June 6, 1944, is D-Day, the date of the beginning of the greatest invasion—and the greatest liberation—in history, the date Allied forces landed in Europe, in Normandy, France, to finally start the beginning of the end of World War II. June 6 is half a calendar year away from December 6, the date that lives in infamy, the date of the bombing of the US Pacific Fleet in Pearl Harbor by the forces of imperial Japan that brought the US into World War II in 1941.

But this year, the 75th anniversary of the Normandy invasion, the celebration at the American Cemetery in Colleville-sur-Mer was particularly poignant: most of the veterans of World War II are in their nineties now, and at least one, Sidney Walton, is a hundred. Many—no, most—will not be at the next great remembrance of the D-Day landing.

The weather in Normandy is uncertain, always, as General Eisenhower discovered in 1944 (the landing had been postponed from June 5), and as the crowd that attended the ceremony at the American Cemetery this year discovered. Rain was predicted for the entire week. The prediction was almost accurate: it was cold, rainy, and bleak on the morning of June 5 and cold, rainy, and bleak again on the morning of June 7.

But on June 6, there was no rain: the day was sunny, though cool.

What a lucky break for the fifteen thousand attendees at the ceremony, including most especially the 170 veterans of World War II, for whom six hours of inclement weather would likely have been more than an inconvenience.

Not that they are the kind of people who would have minded a mere inconvenience or two. People whose lives are shaped by the inconveniences the soldiers who landed on the Normandy beaches encountered that day tend not to be bothered by trials and tribulations that so upset members of subsequent generations. Attendees at the ceremony were told of some of those inconveniences by President Trump, who gave one of the best speeches of his presidency that day.

Perhaps it was easy. Trump didn't write it, of course. Most presidents can't write the kind of prose that is appropriate for a D-Day ceremony—Ronald Reagan was an exception. But Trump delivered his remarks well, and all the more impressively because he is not a polished orator. The stories he told almost tell themselves—stories of brave boys doing brave deeds on a bloody beach, but now old men molded by time into old heroes, legendary heroes even, but not just heroes in the history books of legends, but old heroes actually sitting behind the president as he spoke.

Trump told the story of, among other heroes, Ray Lambert, a mere twenty-three years old that June. Only Ray and five others from their Higgins landing craft made it to the beach that morning. The fire was intense. "Again and again," as the president told the story, "Ray ran back into the water. He dragged out one man after another. He was shot through the arm. His leg was ripped open by shrapnel. His back was broken. He nearly drowned. He had been on the beach for hours, bleeding and saving lives, when he finally lost consciousness." At the age of twenty-three.

Now, seventy-five years later, ninety-eight-year-old Ray Lambert was seated, in real life, behind the president, with a number of his D-Day comrades, five of whom, only minutes before, had been awarded the Legion of Honor by President Macron who had spoken just before President Trump.

Not all the veterans in attendance at the ceremony had fought in Normandy. Some were in the Pacific theater, including the now hundred-year-old Sidney Walton, and former Senator–Undersecretary–Judge James L. Buckley, age ninety-six. Buckley had spoken the night before the ceremony of being in a fleet of LSTs (landing ship tanks, known as "long slow targets") while a kamikaze pilot flew over the fleet so low the men on the ships could see his face. Why had Buckley, and doubtless tens or hundreds of thousands of others, enlisted? That's what men did in those days.

After D-Day, Buckley and tens of thousands of other naval troops were slated to go to the Pacific on impossible missions (they were considered expendable) but were spared, along with millions of Japanese soldiers and civilians, when President Truman authorized the dropping of the atomic bombs on Hiroshima and Nagasaki—a decision still contested by a few today, though less so by those Americans and Japanese who didn't perish in battle, and their progeny.

Yes, war *is* Hell—though it is perhaps easy for civilians, and maybe soldiers too, to forget that fact in the pageantry of the D-Day remembrance: the military bands playing, presidents Macron and Trump flying in on their helicopters, the singing of national anthems, huge television screens, military men in handsome uniforms, and fly-overs by amazing aircraft.

But the many stories of glorious heroism that President Trump told were sobering nevertheless, despite the pageantry: stark reminders of courage, and death, like the 9,388 grave markers, crosses, and stars of David, spread out across the cemetery at Colleville-sur-Mer.

Grave markers spread out across a field with a to-die-for view of the sea.

Lest we forget.

D-Day Soldiers Died to Save Western Values; That's a Legacy Worth Preserving

July 3, 2019

It's quiet here at the American Cemetery in Colleville-sur-Mer, France, where the 75th anniversary commemorating D-Day was held last month. It's cold and drizzly, typical weather for Normandy. The chairs, the bleachers, the tents have been taken down. Most of the workmen are gone. Yet, weather be damned, two million visitors are expected to come this year to pay their respects, or just to take a tour.

The cemetery is, simply, the eighth wonder of the modern world—a modern world shaped by the United States. And the 9,387 graves serve as a reminder to us all, in Kipling's phrase, "Lest we forget."

Lest we forget what?

Lest we forget what we, or perhaps more accurately what *they*, fought for. Here's what President Roosevelt, in his prayer as Operation Overlord began, said they were fighting for:

> Almighty God: Our sons, pride of our nation, this day have set upon a mighty endeavor, a struggle to preserve our Republic, our religion, and our civilization, and to set free a suffering humanity.

Interesting. Our "Republic," not our democracy. Our "religion," not anyone else's religion and not the separation of church and state either. And our "civilization," by which he meant Western Civilization, the great heritage of Athens, Rome, Jerusalem, and Runnymede (the foundation of limited government and the juridical traditions of the Anglo-American system), not an Islamic state, not a multicultural state, undefined by any known or commonly held set of beliefs.

Listen to the Democrats running for their party's nomination for president and you will hear no talk of "our civilization."

Even to allude to FDR's "civilization" would these days be

described by the left-wing deophobic, babysidic, climaticimaniacal, genderdenying progressives as privileged white-supremacist, racist, homophobic speech.

Bret Stephens, writing in the *New York Times*, stated the problem: "Nor do we believe any longer in the ideals for which they fought."

One question for Mr. Stephens, and for us, is, who are the "we" Roosevelt was talking about when he said "our" religion and "our" civilization? Did it include those people who might be described as, or who in previous eras might have been described as, the "upper classes"? People who read newspapers, grew up in the super zips with the benefits of wealth and privilege, went to tony colleges, and do indoor work, often on Wall Street? People who are meant to be natural leaders? In other words, those who now call themselves Democrats? They certainly don't believe in the civilization Roosevelt was talking about.

Democrats—at least the noisy ones—are now consumed with guilt (or pretend to be) for all the sins committed against blacks, Indians, women, and any other group now described as "oppressed" or "marginalized," not to mention the birds and the bees and other creepy crawly things; but through the magic of political prestidigitation the Democrats have transferred that guilt to *you*! Democrats, all those Rhodes Scholars (time out to contemplate the irony of two Democrats' running for their party's nomination having accepted scholarships named for Cecil Rhodes!)—Democrats, as Americans, may have *inherited* that guilt, but they are now busy atoning for their guilt by telling *you* how awful *you* are.

Democrats emphasize "democracy" now because they want to give the vote to sixteen-year-olds (i.e., ignoramuses), felons (even those still in prison), and illegal (and mostly non-English speaking) aliens. Democrats are the party of stamping out religion and religious practices. They want to compel bakers to make cakes for people who transgress their religious principles. Democrats want to keep abortion legal, the third most horrific systematic killing of innocents in history—third after Mao and Stalin. Nice company.

Those are the ideals of modern Democrats. Stephens is right: "we," at least, the prominent Democrats among us, certainly do not believe anymore in the ideals Roosevelt contemplated in his D-Day prayer.

Was it all in vain? Did the 9,387 soldiers buried in the cemetery at Colleville-sur-Mer—and the tens of thousands of others around the world—die for nothing permanent?

How do you tell when you're entering a dark age? Where do we, the "we" who still believe in the civilization Roosevelt was talking about, go from here?

It's a good question. It is, in fact, *the* question, the defining question, for this age, perhaps for all ages. Where do we go from here?

Things can look bleak. Things *do* look bleak. But as William F. Buckley Jr. remarked many years ago—practically in a different civilization (it was in 1959): "The wells of regeneration are infinitely deep."

And so we must hope—remembering always that hope is not a strategy, certainly not one for a people whose forebears fought and died for our republic, our religion, and our civilization, some of whom are buried in the serenely beautiful American Cemetery in Colleville-sur-Mer.

America Isn't Quebec, Mexico, or Brazil—And That's Worth Celebrating

July 4, 2019

What does the Fourth of July mean? Does the answer depend on who you are? And what you believe? How long will we be "allowed" to celebrate the Fourth of July?

In a society that increasingly judges the actions of the past by the standards of the present, how long can we celebrate the accomplishments of imperfect men who did their remarkable deeds almost two and a half centuries ago? Have we, like Europe, lost faith in our beliefs, traditions, and legitimacy?

The writing and signing of the Declaration of Independence can be viewed as an exercise in imperfection, or worse, hypocrisy: grand pronouncements about equality in a land where slaves were held and would be for almost another century; followed, we should take time to note, by the Democratic Party's own policy of Jim Crow, which was outlawed finally by the votes of Republicans in Congress.

Thomas Jefferson, the prized author of the Declaration was himself a slaveholder, as was George Washington, the Father of our country. All the signers were white European men of privilege. Eight of the fifty-six signers were born in Britain, a fact that reminds us where our laws and customs came from.

Remembering that our forbears, like those eight, came from somewhere else, too many people (certainly too many politicians who should know better) say we are a nation of immigrants. Not so. About half the US population is descended from settlers: people who carved a nation out of a wilderness and built a civilization. People who came before there were welfare programs were settlers. The immigrants came later.

And for decades those immigrants adopted the traditions they found in their new country. But that has changed: immigrants now come in such numbers that they are able to preserve their old culture in their new land, aided by the liberal-progressive elite who seeks to destroy the traditional American culture.

Which raises the question, Will the country (and its customs) last? Could America fall apart?

How you tell if you're entering a dark age (religion is disparaged, rampant sexual perversions meet approval, babies are killed by the millions) is related to the issue of how you tell when your country starts ceasing to be your country.

Which leads to the next question, What is it that makes a country a country? Probably at least such aspects as a common language, a common or at least dominant religion, a common culture, common traditions, and geographical boundaries.

Suppose the Nazis had captured France and required German to be taught in schools and used in all government activities and radio and television broadcasts, and—you knew this was coming—required all cooking to be German (while humming Wagner), what would France have been like, say, seventy-five years later, i.e., today? (We have just finished celebrating the seventy-fifth anniversary of D-Day.)

French territory would have become part of Germany (as Alsace-Lorraine did in 1871), the language would have become German, the culture would have become Wagnerian, and after seventy-five years many historic French traditions would probably have just . . . disappeared.

You don't think so? How many of the French would have remained *really* French if following German rules had been required for economic success or survival?

The answer is, probably the same number of big American law firms that resist the cultural demands of their corporate clients, which, these days, won't allow a whiff of disapproval of modern cultural depravity from partners.

Is the United Sates similar to our imaginary (Deo gratias) France? No. Or certainly not yet.

But our traditional religion, Christianity, is under assault. Our mores have not just declined; they have been driven down by progressive-liberals. Our language, English, the pride of the civilized world, is still dominant but no longer exclusive (about 27 percent of people in the country speak Spanish). Our culture is under assault, especially by the media, and by our universities, which are meant to be guardians and transmitters of culture, i.e., *traditional* culture.

About all that is unchallenged is our geographical integrity, but then the geographical integrity of our imaginary France was also still intact. And what is the meaning of geographical integrity other than keeping out people you don't want in?

And is our geographical integrity truly unchallenged? The invasions by 22 million illegal Spanish-speaking immigrants is a threat not to be taken lightly, as it is by 99 percent of our media and other supposed "guardians" of our culture. (Some 63 percent of non-citizen households access welfare programs compared to 35 percent of native households.)

So, again, the question: When does the America that came into being on July 4, 1776, cease being *that* America?

Given all that's happened, what *are* we to celebrate this Fourth of July? Samuel P. Huntington, in his book *Who Are We?* provides one answer: "Would America be the America it is today if in the seventeenth and eighteenth centuries it had been settled not by British Protestants but by French, Spanish, or Portuguese Catholics? The answer is no. It would not be America; it would be Quebec, Mexico, or Brazil."

There's one thing to celebrate: We're not Quebeckers, Mexicans, or Brazilians.

What is our nationality? American, if we can keep it.

Have a blast.

Are the Four "Housewomen" of the Apocalypse better for Democrats or for Trump?

July 28, 2019

Donald Trump got himself back in the soup (though "back" may be superfluous) with his comment about the "Four Housewomen of the Apocalypse." He suggested they go back to the "places from which they came." Not even not ending his jibe with a preposition could save him.

But to some—some racists, of course—his insult seemed more like a football cheer ("Push 'em back, push 'em back, waaaaay back!") than a racist slur.

The Four Housewomen are New York Rep. Alexandria Ocasio-Cortez ("AOC"), Minnesota Rep. Ilhan Omar of the doubtful spouses, Michigan Rep. Rashida ("We're going to impeach the motherf—er") Tlaib, and Massachusetts Rep. Ayanna ("We don't need black faces that don't want to be a black voice") Pressley.

Trump critics have duly noted that only one of the Four Housewomen was, in fact, born abroad, but surely it's a bit too technical to demand that an insult be exactly correct.

Perhaps Trump was just channeling a memorable line from the late '60s Broadway comedy "There's a Girl in My Soup." It went (more or less): "If you don't like the country that gave you your birth, why don't you go back to where you came from."

Racism as a term is wearing thin these days. If everyone is a racist, then no one is, or at least being a racist is a pretty ho-hum thing. As an epithet it lacks most of its former punch.

One of the Four Housewomen, Omar, came to the US as a refugee. Without the generosity of the people of the United States she would be leading a miserable life in hell-hole Somalia (GDP per capita: $478) or perhaps just dead. That could be better than living in her native land, which, it's a good bet, is not even one of the top twenty destinations for congressional junkets.

Unfortunately for them, when the four gals saddled up, their bags of marbles tore, allowing them to ride on unencumbered,

Sufficiently unencumbered to call Nancy Pelosi, the speaker of the House of Representatives of the United States of America, a racist.

Bear baiting and cockfighting are illegal in most states these days. Those "sports" are thought to be inappropriate for a civilized people. (Boxing is exempt from the proscription, probably because it's easier to fix—how do you teach a cock to take a dive?)

However, the Four Housewomen's calling Pelosi a racist provides much of the same pleasure as a good cockfight.

Pelosi chastised the four of them (now known as "The Squad") for attacking other Democrats personally, warning them that the party infighting was jeopardizing its majority—by which she meant primarily it's chance of unseating Donald Trump.

That got AOC sufficiently riled that she charged Pelosi with targeting "newly elected women of color." You see why this is as entertaining as cockfighting.

The crowd is going wild. In comes Maureen Dowd, to rescue poor feathers-flying Pelosi:

[AOC] slimed the speaker, who has spent her life fighting for the downtrodden and who was instrumental in getting the first African-American president elected and passing his agenda against all odds, as a sexist and a racist.

Not a stylish sentence: the phrase "as a sexist and a racist" is too far away from the noun, "speaker," that it modifies; and "passing his agenda" should get a good guffaw given what's happened to ObamaCare.

Dowd continues: "AOC should consider the possibility that people who disagree with her do not disagree with her color"—whatever "disagree with her color" means.

Ooooh! Did you ever think you'd see that sentence in the *New York Times*? Where are the refs when you need them?

But there you have it—and hometown papers, and South Bend Mayor Peter Buttigieg, please copy—it's possible to disagree with a person of color without objecting to that person's color.

Buttigieg said on National Public Radio last week that "white America" needs to come to grips with the "systemic racism all around us. It's in the air we breathe." He says that explains all today's racial inequalities. Yeah. Sure.

Hmmm. Black unemployment, in the time of Trump, is at its lowest *ever*, and the black illegitimacy rate (from whence flow so many of the blacks' problems) is sky-high, the gift, over decades, of trendy Western Civ-trashing liberals, the kind of people who write for the *New York Times* and of people like AOC who call everyone who disagrees with them a racist.

But Liberation Day may be coming, the day when blacks vote, again, for Trump, but in even larger numbers than before, terrifying, one has to suppose, every good progressive liberal, and most especially the Four Housewomen of the Apocalypse.

What Did We Really Learn from the Mueller Investigation?

July 29, 2019

That the world ends with a whimper we have on the authority of T. S. Eliot. But that the Mueller "RUSSIA!" probe ends with a whimper we have on the authority of our own eyes—or at least the eyes of those who watched the Mueller hearing on July 24.

It was, in its own way, sad when the great Robert Mueller went down—though no husband or wives or little children lost their lives. But it was still sad.

Several points should be made. The first point is that Robert Mueller is a good man. Not, perhaps, a great man, but a good man. That's a lot. Most good people are only good people, not great people. Mueller served his country, both in war (wounded in Vietnam, received a Bronze Star) and in peace, as a US attorney, US assistant attorney general, and US deputy attorney general, and as head of the FBI, where he did two stints, a first. After a single stint, Mueller could have gone to a prestigious law firm and made, literally, millions. Instead, he chose to serve his country. Quick: name three people who have not cashed in the way Mueller could have.

The second point is that even good people make mistakes. Mueller made six in his capacity as the Special Counsel:

1. He accepted the assignment. We know, more or less but sufficiently, that former FBI head James Comey was a snake in the grass
of the Russia probe, perhaps *the* snake. The Russia probe business
was a set-up by the deep state folks who wanted to unhorse Donald
Trump who out-jousted St. Hillary in the 2016 contest. Comey was a
central player in that setup, perhaps because his actions as FBI head
during the 2016 campaign (reopening with great publicity the investigation into Hillary's email scandal) may have caused Hillary to lose
the election. There's nothing wrong with Mueller and Comey being
friends, but because of that friendship Mueller should not have taken
the assignment.

2. Mueller hired a bunch of hardcore liberals to help him investigate
the president. At the very least, that gave the whole investigation the
patina of a witch hunt. We pause to note that there's nothing wrong
with hunting witches and burning them when you find them, so long
as the burnees are actual witches. (Question to reader: Can we say
this or are witches now a protected class?)

There is one, theoretical, excuse for Mueller's having hired a
bunch of lefties for his team: it might have made any finding of no
collusion more definitive—and perhaps acceptable to the Left, to
the left-wing crazies, to the deep state never-Trump left-wing crazy
zealots.

It didn't. Which means it simply tainted Mueller's whole investigation.

3. Mueller apparently didn't investigate the Fusion GPS operation,
which was the genesis of the Russia collusion theory. If A says B
murdered C, an investigation into whether B actually did murder C
should take a look at A. Did A have any evidence for his claim that
B murdered C? And what was A's motivation for making the charge?
Mueller failed to pursue that line.

4. Mueller seems not to have been actively in charge of writing
the report—and perhaps not in charge of the investigation either.
Asked at the hearing about the firm that produced that Steele report (Fusion GPS), Mueller responded, "I'm not familiar with that."
If you've read the book and still don't know it was the Grinch who

stole Christmas, something's wrong with you.

It's not clear who did write the report. It looks now as if Andrew Weissmann, described by the *New York Times* as Mueller's legal pit bull, and a friend of Hillary's (he attended her "victory" night party in 2016), was in charge. We don't know that, but Mueller's extraordinary unfamiliarity with the report at the hearing (he was once known for his sharpness) suggests that someone else was actually in charge. Weissmann is the obvious suspect. Weissmann is anti-Trump.

5. Mueller (almost certainly) didn't end the investigation when he should have. The question is, when did Mueller determine that Trump had not colluded with the Russians? We don't know, but a good guess is, a long time ago, even before the 2016 midterm election. In which case, Mueller's not shutting down the investigation before that election may have influenced the election's outcome. That is bad, *verrry bad*. And Mueller bears responsibility for that—as much responsibility, ironically, as has been foisted off on the Russians for their attempts to disrupt the 2016 election.

6. Mueller's arrests of Paul Manafort and Roger Stone were scenes out of Communist Russia or Nazi Germany. Probably Weissmann was in charge of those operations, but the buck stops at Mueller's desk. Shameful.

7. Mueller's report said it could not exonerate the president. But that is true of all investigations. How do you ever prove a negative? You don't. You just say that there is not sufficient evidence to make the positive claim. But the Mueller report (which may not be the same as Mueller himself) didn't say that. It said Mueller and his investigator couldn't prove that Trump had not colluded with the Russians. That was a gratuitous smear of the president, and Mueller bears responsibility for that.

The third point to be made is that Mueller's performance at the hearing seemed odd; oddly incompetent. One news account after another reported that Mueller wasn't the sharp lawyer he used to be. Some people thought he'd had a minor stroke. So we are required (by Western Civ standards) to be charitably disposed to Bob

Mueller, a good man, a good family man, and to his family—even as the whole sordid (anti-Trump, anti-democracy) business winds down to nothing.

And so it ends, not with the bang of impeachment but with Democrats whimpering that the only way to dispose of President Trump is by an election. What finally, are we likely to learn from this whole sordid business?

The smart money is on: nothing.

Fifteen Questions to Peel the Skin Off the Democrats
July 29, 2019

Here are fifteen questions for contestants in the coming debate among the Democrat presidential hopefuls, a debate that should be more entertaining than seeing gladiators fight lions—with the advantage that no animals will be harmed during the performance.

1. As you know, the major television networks—CNN, MSNBC, and almost all the rest except FOX News—got the Russia collusion story wrong. They told their viewers that it was all but certain that Donald Trump had colluded with Russia to "steal" the 2016 election. In view of the findings of the Mueller investigative team—most of whom it turns out were Democrats—are you willing to say that the major networks were wrong to push that story for so long?

2. Do you think Donald Trump colluded with Russia to steal the 2016 election?

3. Do you think it is sane or insane to believe that Vladimir Putin has personal, political, or financial information about Donald Trump which would enable Russia to get Trump to do Russia's bidding?

4. Do you think Russia is controlling Robert Mueller?

5. The Mueller investigation lasted almost two years, cost $31 million, and produced a 448-page report. Do you think there is anything

Congress can now discover that the Mueller investigative team did not discover?

6. In view of Russia's attempt to hack our electoral process, do you think we should have more stringent voter ID laws? Do you think we should move to internet voting or go back to universal paper ballots?

7. As you know, during the Mueller investigation, both Paul Manafort and Roger Stone were arrested by the FBI in a manner ordinarily used for criminals who are likely to be armed and dangerous, although there was no indication whatsoever that either one of those men presented that threat. Do you think the manner of their arrests was proper—in the United States of America?

8. Do you think Russia is the most dangerous foreign threat to America?

9. Do you think it is a good idea to have district court judges continually block President Trump's initiatives? And what will you do if district court judges block initiatives of the next Democratic president the way they have blocked Trump's initiatives?

10. There seems to be evidence that Democratic Representative Ilhan Omar from Minnesota entered into a sham marriage with her brother in order for him to gain US citizenship. Do you think that's wrong? And given her prominence, as a member of Congress who should be setting an example for the rest of the country, do you think she should be investigated?

11. Under the First Step Act, enacted by Congress last year, thousands of prisoners have been released from federal prisons. The First Step Act was sold to the American people as an act that would release only non-violent offenders from jail—people who had been incarcerated for, for example, possessing only small amounts of marijuana. It turns out, however, that thousands of those released were violent offenders, people who were convicted of sex crimes, robbery, aggravated assault, and homicide. Did you vote for the First Step Act, and

if so, and given the recidivism rate of serious criminals, do you now think you made a mistake?

12. Under the Head Start Program, the US government spends approximately $10 billion a year. Research shows, and has shown for years, that Head Start has little to no lasting positive effect on the children who participate in it. Moreover, the Department of Health and Human Services' *own* research has found that Head Start participants performed lower than their peers in kindergarten math and "by third grade, Head Start had little to no effect on cognitive, social-emotional, health, or parenting outcomes of participating children." Given that record, are you in favor of canceling the Head Start program?

13. Foreign Aid spending is approximately $50 billion. Afghanistan was the largest recipient in 2017, receiving about $4.7 billion, which went toward the building of a national education system, reproductive health, and basic infrastructure, such as schools and hospitals. Do you think that money from US taxpayers would be better spent here in the United States?

14. In April 1933, President Franklin Roosevelt signed Executive Order 6102 which forbad "the hoarding of gold coin, gold bullion, and gold certificates within the continental United States." The order was made under the authority of the Trading with the Enemy Act of 1917, as amended by the Emergency Banking Act the previous month.

In effect, as we know, Roosevelt simply confiscated all the gold owned by the people of this country, paying them only a fraction of what gold was valued on the open market. Do you think the president of the United States should have that power? And is that something you would ever do as president?

15. Do you think the decision to terminate the life of a newborn baby should be between only the mother and her doctor?

What are the odds that a single one of these questions will be asked?

Slim to none.

Smearing at the Rhodes Scholar Level
August 5, 2019

Democratic presidential candidate and South Bend, Indiana, mayor, and Rhodes Scholar Pete Buttigieg sure knows how to smear. He was quick off the mark on a Sunday morning talk show to blame President Trump for the killing of twenty people in El Paso, Texas. The killer appears to have been a white nationalist (whatever exactly that is), and Rhodes Scholar Buttigieg said white nationalism is "condoned at the highest level of our government."

Rhodes Scholar Buttigieg said, "And then when you have an actual incident of white nationalist terrorism [as distinguished from the El Paso incident, which he has just blamed on Trump?] like the killing in Charlottesville related to people saying, 'Jews will not replace us' and the president saying you've got very fine people there . . ." Buttigieg's quote appears to drift off.

Actually, that's not quite what the president said after Charlottesville, but when you're polling at 0 percent among African Americans, you're facing desperate times, and we all know what kind of measures desperate times call for—not, probably that Rhodes Scholar Buttigieg needs a special occasion to smear.

What Trump actually said was: "You also had people that were very fine people, on both sides."

That, we can admit, was not the politic thing to say after Charlottesville (as Rush said), but it was surely accurate. The Charlottesville incident took place at a rally at which many people were protesting the taking down of a statue of Robert E. Lee. (The president asked, "Is Washington next?" reminding reporters that Washington held slaves).

Trump said: "And you had people—and I'm not talking about the neo-Nazis and the white nationalists—because they should be condemned totally. But you had many people in that group other than neo-Nazis and white nationalists. Okay? And the press has treated them absolutely unfairly."

"Now, in the other group also, you had some fine people. But you also had troublemakers, and you see them come with the black outfits and with the helmets, and with the baseball bats. You had a lot of bad people in the other group."

Trump's whole exchange with the media is worth reading* because it shows what a smear job the press were attempting (largely successfully) to do on Trump. If you're into smearing at the Rhodes Scholar level like Mayor Pete, you just leave out the good parts of what Trump said and show only the parts of the quote that make your point.

Buttigieg knows, or can fairly be charged with knowing, what Trump actually said about Charlottesville—but of course Rhodes Scholar Buttigieg has no interest in truth. The smear's the thing.

Of course, there were other Democrat presidential contenders who were quick to blame Trump for the shootings. Robert Francis (dba "Beto") O'Rourke (most polls show him now in the single digits, one of which digits is 0) also attacked Trump when an ABC News reporter set up the opportunity by asking him if Trump had any responsibility for the shootings. "Yes," replied the skateboarding contender.

Skateboarder Beto went on to say: "We've had a rise in hate crimes every single one of the last three years, during an administration where you have a president who's called Mexicans rapists and criminals."

But, of course, that's not what Trump said. What he said was: "When Mexico sends its people, they're not sending their best. They're not sending you. They're not sending you. They're sending people that have lots of problems, and they're bringing those problems with us. They're bringing drugs. They're bringing crime. They're rapists. And some, I assume, are good people."

Now it's true that that's a long paragraph for a Columbia University graduate to remember verbatim (Beto was not a Rhodes Scholar), but even a non-Rhodes Scholar Columbia graduate might be expected to remember the *sense* of what Trump said.

But, of course, Beto doesn't care. He'd distort anything for political gain. Single digits is more than he deserves, and assuredly—as assuredly as the sun rises in the East and sets in the West, as assuredly as the *Washington Post* will try to best the *New York Times* in art of smearing—more than Beto will eventually get. Bye-bye, Beto.

But the smearing goes on, and will go on, the Democrats having

* You can see it at https://www.politifact.com/truth-o-meter/article/2019/apr/26/context-trumps-very-fine-people-both-sides-remarks.

nothing else to run on except identity politics—the politics of hate and division, precisely the politics they so assiduously ascribe to Donald Trump. The press can and will continue to smear, and at the Rhodes Scholar level. Will democracy see us through?

What Happens If America Goes Bilingual?
August 14, 2019

A scholarly retired senior European diplomat who read my Fourth of July column wrote:

> Regarding your definition of what makes a country a country: does Switzerland (4 official languages), or, for that matter, Belgium (3 official languages and as many official religions), qualify as a country? Or, indeed, Spain, where both Catalan and Basque are officially spoken? Or France, where Breton has been spoken since the 4th century, as well as Catalan and Basque? Or Ireland, where both English and Gaelic have an official status? Or the UK which has Welsh, Scottish Gaelic, Cornish and a plethora of hardly mutually understandable dialects?

I had written: "What is it that makes a country a country? Probably at least such aspects as a common language, a common or at least dominant religion, a common culture, common traditions, and geographical boundaries."

The diplomat's question prompts two observations.

First: There's a sense in which Switzerland (population 8.5 million) isn't really a country at all: it's a federation. It isn't very big, it isn't very powerful, and it has only a small, means-tested welfare program (which therefore engenders little dissent). It's not a city on a hill, and it doesn't win World Wars or Cold Wars. It can get away with having several languages.

Belgium (population 11 million) is also a small operation. Spain (population 47 million) has several languages, but Spanish is the first language of at least 72 percent of the population and probably the other 28 percent speak it fluently. In Ireland, 94 percent of the people speak English. In the UK, 98 percent of the people speak English.

So a general rule might be that a powerful country (which because of its power has lots of contentious political issues) has to have a dominant language.

Language may be important in important countries. In the US, English is spoken by about 230 million people, Spanish by 40 million. But there's a problem in the US—actually there are three.

The first is that many of the Spanish-speaking people are illegal immigrants. The count of illegals varies, but a recent Yale study, which apparently surprised the authors themselves, estimated that there are 22.1 million illegal aliens ("undocumented immigrants" in snowflakeese) in the United States. It's a good bet that most of those illegals are poor and not proficient in English, and not likely to become proficient, and most of them probably live in the shadows. That is a problem.

A second problem is that many Mexicans in the US, whether citizens or not, remain Mexican enough to send billions of dollars in "remittances" back to their relatives in Mexico—about $25 billion in 2016. That is money not invested in *their* US communities. The French speakers in Switzerland aren't sending money back to relatives in France.

A third problem is that many Mexicans don't even think of themselves as Americans: they remain Mexicans—they even vote in Mexican elections. And some of them even have dreams of reuniting with Mexico the territories lost in the Mexican–American war (1846–1848)! They don't call it Mexifornia for nothing.

So, yes, a common language is important. Currently, America seems to be coming apart: the Left is doing its best to drive a wedge between regular Americans and the immigrant (and illegal immigrant) communities. The Left promotes open borders (if they're open, are they really borders?), amnesty for illegals, and even voting by illegals.

That's a recipe for unrest—unrest that will redefine the country. Masses of non-English speaking people (many of them shadow dwellers) are unlikely to know, understand, appreciate, and internalize our customs—the Anglophone customs and rules for civilization that have built the best and freest society the earth has ever known—rules that didn't just fall from the sky.

Another correspondent wrote:

And so, we here on the Southern tip of the dark continent of Africa, who put our blood and sweat into transforming jungles into cities, see our civilised ideals whittling away under the pressure of the majority voters who pretend to yearn for tribalism to the uninformed masses in the name of "decolonialisation," but who simultaneously and shamelessly enjoy the benefits of a Westernised, free market society, as if those just fell from the sky. . . .

Without getting into the politics of South Africa's past, it seems fair to say that some customs are better than others, and that law and order, of the kind the Anglophone countries vouchsafe to their citizens, are a *sine qua non* for the kind of civilized living we in America are used to, precisely the kind of living that attracts immigrants to America. But if they are poor, non-English speaking, and uneducated, they will not understand the magic that produces our way of life. And then the socialist Democrats—the party of Alexandria Ocasio-Cortez—will tempt them with the black magic of redistribution. Redistribution works—once. But what do you do for an encore? What the rich will do is hightail it to Switzerland where English will displace Italian as the third language.

It may be possible for America to become a bilingual country and still preserve the Anglophone way of life. But we don't know. And the more the other language is Spanish, and the more its speakers are tied, emotionally and financially, to a different country, which they consider their home country, and the more they consider the United States to be a hostile power occupying "their" land, the less likely it seems that bilingualism will serve America well.

Suicide Watch at the NRA
August 26, 2019

Most gun deaths in the US are by suicide, an activity the NRA seems to be currently attempting. The organization appears to be imploding, and at a time (after two mass shootings and at the start of another presidential campaign) when it is badly needed to help preserve the Second Amendment.

The trouble—the visible trouble—began last April when Oliver North announced that he would not serve a second term as NRA president. His stunning announcement came at about the same time that New York State Attorney General Letitia James, who has called the NRA "a terrorist organization," started an investigation into NRA finances. The NRA is incorporated in New York State, while the NRA Foundation, its affiliated charity, is incorporated in the District of Columbia.

North's resignation as president followed a power struggle which North, having unsuccessfully called for the resignation of NRA Chief Executive Wayne LaPierre, lost. North said the NRA had "a clear crisis" and needed to investigate financial improprieties. Uh-oh.

Then the flak began to fly. North was accused of having a sweetheart deal with the NRA's publicity firm, Ackerman McQueen, which, according to LaPierre, paid North "millions of dollars." The amount may seem high, especially to NRA's small donors, people who give only tens of dollars, but without knowing what North—a high profile individual—did, doesn't seem like a lethal charge. The NRA had sued Ackerman and North had taken Ackerman's side.

Then in June, the NRA suspended its second-in-command and top lobbyist, Christopher W. Cox, one of the public faces of the NRA, who subsequently resigned.

A good rule of thumb, certainly in Washington but probably everywhere, is that when there's a lot of money sloshing around, you can be almost certain someone is pinching part of it. The NRA is huge: in 2017, its total revenue was $378 million; in 2018 it was $412 million.

Where all that money went is a good question, of course. We don't know. What we do know is that Wayne LaPierre sure knows how to spend it. He billed the NRA $39,000 for a single day of shopping at a Beverly Hills clothing boutique. He spent $18,300 for a car and driver in Europe, and spent tens of thousands of dollars on his wife's makeup. And he almost succeeded in getting the NRA to buy him a $6 million mansion in Texas, for, er, security reasons.

Mr. LaPierre is married but has no children. The NRA is his life: he *is* the NRA (or at least may think he is), in which case what's wrong with spending its money as if it were his own? Answer: a lot.

According to *Pro Publica*, William A. Brewer III, one of the NRA's outside counsels, billed the NRA $24 million for a thirteen-month period; and in the first quarter of 2019 was billing at the rate of $97,000 *per day*. Ouch!

Clearly the NRA has problems, exacerbated by its corporate structure: it has approximately seventy-six board members. It's a reasonable bet that any organization that has a board of seventy-six members isn't being run by the board. Who is running the NRA? Wayne LaPierre apparently, and, it seems, without the supervision that a board is supposed to provide.

Bad as that all sounds, it has just gotten worse, much, much worse: just this week the NRA announced that it will no longer retain the law firm of Cooper & Kirk, one of Washington's leading law firms, to represent it. (Full disclosure: I have known and admired Charles Cooper for over three decades.) Cooper is a pro—the kind of person who belongs on, and who has been on, the short list for attorney general of the United States.

In a statement following the NRA's action, Mr. Cooper said, "Throughout the over three decades in which I have represented the NRA, I have adhered to the highest standards of professionalism." He said he owed an "ethical duty of loyalty to the NRA itself" and not to "any individual officers or directors." Exactly. That must have stung LaPierre, as, it's a good bet, it should have.

Too much money and too little board supervision is a recipe for trouble. To the outsider, the NRA looks rotten on the inside. If the NRA board members, who probably have power if they choose to exercise it, won't take appropriate action, the NRA will commit suicide—with a likely assist from the New York attorney general, proving, once again, that guns don't kill; people do.

That will not be beneficial for the good people of the United States or their freedom.

Counting Your Blessings—In the Age of Mass Shootings

August 28, 2019

There was a joke in the Reagan years: a *Washington Post* headline that was supposed to have read, "World to End. Reagan to Blame."

Reagan was said by liberals and the media—the same people or their forebears who ascribe all modern evil to Donald Trump (and all ancient evil to white males)—to be responsible for all bad things that happen.

Liberals tend not to believe in original sin, at the same time that they also believe in the perfectibility of man. Therefore, if something goes wrong, someone must be to blame. Someone's got to pay.

We saw that on Jack-and-the-beanstalks hormones this week when there were mass shootings in Dayton and El Paso. It was all Trump's fault—his hateful and racist rhetoric. Progressive Democrats of America were quick to weigh in: "We blame President Trump for feeding into the anti-immigrating frenzy and white supremacist violence. Yes, you, Mr. President, had your finger on the AK-47."

But the prize for liberal gobbledygook goes to Charles M. Blow, a columnist for the *New York Times*, whom, I fear, one criticizes at the risk of being called either a racist or white supremacist or both. (Mr. Blow is black.) Blow blamed the shooting on the lack of gun control, of course. ("Are these shootings a gun control issue? Of course.")

We pause to note that it's a pretty good bet that these mass shootings are fed by publicity—crazy or evil people copycatting other crazy or evil people. Wouldn't it make more sense to outlaw media coverage of the shootings rather than to outlaw guns, Mr. Blow?

Blow also blamed the shootings on opposition to open borders and unlimited illegal immigration. ("There is no doubt that Trump and Republicans are making poisonous anti-immigrant rhetoric part of their platforms.")

That's pretty standard fare for the *New York Times* and the others. But here's where it gets, well, interesting, yes, but also *absurd*. Blow wrote—this is true; you're not being had: "The policymakers believe they can accomplish with legislation in the legal system what the terrorists are trying to underscore with lead. In the minds of the policymakers, border walls, anti-immigrant laws, voter suppression and packing the courts are more prudent and permanent than bodies in the streets."

As in: "Extra! Extra! World to End! Trump's Nomination of Two Supreme Court Justices to Blame." *That* is weird! Sufficiently weird that it's not clear that even a ten-step ObamaCare-funded program would be enough to cure Mr. Blow.

Meanwhile, in the same issue of the *Times*, the editors chastised those who are opposed to mass illegal immigration, writing:

> Discussions of Americans being "replaced" by immigrants, for instance, are a recurring feature on some programs on Fox News. Fox hosts Tucker Carlson and Laura Ingraham, for example, return to these themes frequently. Democrats, Ms. Ingraham told viewers last year, "want to replace you, the American voters, with newly amnestied citizens and an ever-increasing number of chain migrants."

Well, yes, that's true: that's exactly what Democrats want. But not all people like that policy and the *Times,* if it were an honest paper, would recognize the policy issue instead of calling everyone who disagrees with them a white supremacist.

It is worth noting that the people who are most likely to be replaced by immigrants are those on the bottom rungs of the economic ladder, and that they tend to be disproportionally black—yet vote, to their disadvantage, if not their shame, almost 90 percent for Democrat candidates for president. A question for Donald Trump is, can you connect with those people whose interests you, but not Charles Blow and the *New York Times,* are looking out for? Trump's words are factually correct. But when 99 percent of the media is willing to distort everything you say, being factually correct may not be enough—even though you've gotten black unemployment to its lowest level *ever.*

The Wall Street Journal, to its credit, and not surprisingly, noted that these shooters are nut cases—people who have mental health issues—people who used to be locked up in nut houses (mental health institutions). Sequestering mentally ill people used to be standard policy, and then liberals and libertarians came along and said those mentally disturbed people all had civil rights to wander around making a mess of things, which they have done with abandon.

We live in a country of about 328 million people. Some of them, even those who don't write for the *New York Times,* are crazy, and some are evil. There is a difference. But no amount of gun control, Trump control, or appointments-to-the-Supreme-Court control is going to eliminate the horrible things they sometimes do.

A generation or two ago more people died of routine diseases than currently die in mass shootings. Life in the media publicity age, and the internet age, may not be perfect. But there's a lot to be thankful for.

Why Kirsten Gillibrand Dropped Out
August 31, 2019

Sen. Kirsten Gillibrand, Democrat of New York, whose politics are, er, flexible has dropped out of the presidential sweepstakes, and not a moment too soon. Her politics were so "flexible" she didn't get traction even with women voters, who were her primary target. She was a giant hypocrite among hypocrites. And she played the race card shamelessly.

It's too bad the moderator of the recent debate didn't list the other cities that "need help." It's a roster of places that have been governed, mostly for decades, by liberal Democrats. The moderator's question was oh-so-trendy because President Trump had just tweeted out his message that Baltimore is a Hell-hole, and that its congressman—for the last 23 years!—Elijah Cummings (who happens to be black), is partly to blame.

During a tour of Baltimore last year, the city's mayor, Catherine Pugh (no white supremacist she), described the situation there in language rather more graphic and startling than anything Trump has ever said: "What the hell? We should just take all this sh*t down. . . . Whoa, you can smell the rats. . . . Whew, Jesus . . . oh, my God, you can smell the dead animals."

When a couple of years ago Trump described some African countries as Hell-holes (the transcript's a bit fuzzy) he was gang-banged by the usual posturing hypocrites, not one of whom was known for vacationing in said Hell-holes, nor probably in Baltimore either. Oh, my God, you can smell the hypocrisy.

But debater Gillibrand wasn't about to take on the situation in Baltimore. She pivoted to the Democrats' post-Russia-collusion campaign hope: white supremacy.

So in answer to the question, what would you "do for Baltimore and other cities that need help?" she replied, "I can talk to those white women in the suburbs that voted for Trump and explain to them what white privilege actually is."

Come again? Is she hearing impaired? No, she's just doing what comes naturally: playing the race card.

"When their son is walking down the street . . ."—whoa! Whose son, exactly? *Their* son? Gillibrand's talking to a bunch of white women ("those white women in the suburbs"): How can a plurality of white women have "a" son? One son between them? Between *all* of them? Or just some of them? Even the pointy-headed professors at the Harvard-Yale-Princeton-Stanford Center for the Study of Bizarre and Quite-Unbelievable Sexual Antics and Practices haven't produced a male baby from a group of women, not of any color.

Gillibrand means, "When *their sons* are walking down the street . . ." Is that too technical for a girl from upstate New York to master (snowflake alert: use of word "master" may channel unpleasant feelings of male dominance)? Probably not, and if she can't manage a sentence as simple as that one, how would she ever manage the nuclear codes?

"When their son is walking down the street with a bag of M&Ms in his pocket, wearing a hoodie, his whiteness is what protects him" from being shot, said Gillibrand.

How to play the race card! Gillibrand's half right, but wholly wrong. It's their boys' white skin color that may protect them, but it has nothing to do with privilege. It has to do with the odds, odds that almost everyone knows: it's more likely that a non-white boy in a hoodie is a "problem" than a white boy in a hoodie.

One person who knows that is Jesse Jackson. That's why he said, famously: "There is nothing more painful to me . . . than to walk down the street and hear footsteps and start thinking about robbery, then look around and see somebody white and feel relieved."

Why did Jackson feel relieved, Sen. Gillibrand?

Jackson knew the numbers as does almost everyone else. According to a study by the Vera Institute of Justice, black people are 3.6 times more likely to be incarcerated than white people, down from 6 times in 1996. According to the FBI Uniform Crime Reports, in the year 2008, black youths, who make up 16 percent of the youth population, accounted for 52 percent of juvenile violent crime arrests. This means that, however unfair it may be to assume that a black male is criminally inclined, it is not entirely irrational.

As interesting, or perhaps more interesting, black adults in the United States consistently express *more* concern about crime than white adults. Does Sen. Gillibrand have any clue why? Could it be that most black crime is committed on black people, for whom crime prevention is therefore exceedingly important?

Black boys tend to be a problem, but it really isn't entirely their fault. Most of them grow up in broken "families": the black illegitimacy rate is 77 percent. That's the real problem, in part a legacy of the sexual sixties. Would Gillibrand go to war against the sexual sixties? Not bloody likely.

Illegitimacy's a problem Sen. Gillibrand and her fellow contestant don't dare discuss. They'd rather play the race card and blame all ills on whites, and white supremacy, and white supremacists, and Donald Trump. And you. And me.

Oh, my God, you can smell the hypocrisy.

David Brooks, Change, and White Tie and Tails
September 4, 2019

David Brooks got his big chance in journalism from the same man I did, William F. Buckley Jr., the founder of the Conservative Movement and the most important intellectual of the second half of the twentieth century. Brooks writes regularly for the *New York Times*, the same newspaper that this week (scandal alert) was importuned by the Left into changing a headline because it seemed too favorable to President Trump. Brooks hasn't written about that yet.

But last week he wrote a column titled "Listen to Marianne Williamson." For those of you who can't tell the players without a scorecard, Williamson is one of a plethora of candidates for the Democratic Party's nomination for president. Her chances of success are only slightly better than yours. But it is fair to say that the chances are overwhelming that you'd be a better president than she would be, a judgment based on Buckley's theory that we'd be better governed by the first two thousand names in the Boston telephone directory than by the two thousand faculty members of Harvard University.

Brooks, along with Ross Douthat and Bret Stephens, is probably billed by the *Times* as one of its house conservatives, a comparative description that might even fit an unplugged electric typewriter given the *Times*'s other columnists—Paul Krugman, Thomas Friedman, Charles Blow, Roger Cohen, Frank Bruni, and more. Still, Brooks is interesting to read, unlike the others.

But Brooks, like candidate Williamson, is afflicted with anti-Trumpism: "We just have to get away from all the evils that Donald Trump personifies." And, "Every day," says Brooks, "he will stage a little drama that is meant to redefine who we are, what values we lift up, and who we hate."

Brooks means that to be a description of evil. But is it really?

Trump is an unlikely president. He ran against the zeitgeist. No one, including Trump himself, expected him to win. What he ran against was the corrosive liberalism that has been ascendant in American politics since about the time of, perhaps not Franklin Roosevelt, but certainly of Lyndon Johnson. Or perhaps it was against the progressivism of President Woodrow Wilson's time. But "liberalism"—the old liberalism that had some good points—has morphed into something unrecognizable. It has changed so quickly that even the positions of Barack Obama (on immigration, for example) are no longer acceptable to modern Democrats, certainly not to the candidates vying for their party's nomination.

President Wilson was a eugenicist. Today, abortion, eugenics' heir, is the *ne plus ultra* litmus test of acceptability for Democrats. We have become a nation of abortionists—though it is fair to ask, "Whadda ya mean 'we,' kimosabe?" Donald Trump wants to redefine who we are, and why the Hell not—Hell being capitalized because it's a place, and a place where many abortionists are likely to go.

Donald Trump wants to redefine who we are and what values we lift up? A lot of people will say, "Right on!"

Trump seems to believe in the concept of "nation." Strangely, the concept of "nationhood" has become opprobrious to Democrats (or so they tell us). They say it really means "white" nationhood and is racist to the core. But does anyone really believe what Democrats say? Or believe that Democrats believe what they say?

Democrats say they are for open borders, which really means no borders at all. And many of them—most?—also support allowing illegal aliens to vote. What is *that* all about? Why do Democrats want to allow people who are not American citizens and who are here illegally to vote, a treasured right of the American people?

Is it cynical or realistic to answer by saying that Democrats just want power: and if they allow millions of illegal, non-English-speaking uneducated immigrants to vote, they will have a better chance of seizing power?

Donald Trump is willing to stage a little drama to make the point that America belongs to Americans, not to illegal Mexican immigrants.

It isn't fair to say Trump is willing to "stage a little drama that is meant to redefine who we hate." "Hate" is too strong a word. But then again, maybe we should hate people who want to flout our laws and change our customs, or if not them at least their enablers.

Brooks says Democrats need to remind Americans of the values we still share, which he says are pretty basic and can be simply expressed. One of those values, according to Brooks, is unity.

"Unity: We're one people. Our leader represents all the people. He doesn't go around attacking whole cities and regions." Of course, it's the Democrats, and especially those Democrats who aspire to be our leader, who have been calling whole groups of Americans white nationalists. But Brooks is probably referring to Trump, who recently said Baltimore is a Hell-hole. Well—it is!* The city has been governed by Democrats forever, and the disease ailing it is not likely to be cured until it's diagnosed.

Another value Brooks wants us to remember is opportunity: "We want all children to have an open field and a fair chance in the great race of life."

Please. A noble sentiment, but hardly one Democrats give a fig for. One of THE GREAT NATIONAL SCANDALS in this country is the state of primary education. Education is run by and for the teachers' unions, of which the Democratic Party is a wholly owned subsidiary. Democrats don't give a fig for giving children a fair chance in the great race of life. Is there a single sentient being who doesn't know that? Where is Brooks when we need him?

Teachers' unions and the Democrats who support them (99.999 percent) haven't yet been suitably attacked by Trump. Maybe he's

___

* See what Baltimore's own mayor said about it: https://www.instagram.com/p/BnohVfMl_HO/?utm_source=ig_embed

waiting for the second term. If Trump won't stage a little drama in order to reform education, who will? Marianne Williamson? Puh-lease.

Trump is an agent of change, not a white tie and tails tony status quo diplomat. The cushy pols who run this country don't want change, but Brooks and Williamson should. With a little bit of luck, in 2020 Americans will vote to give the change agent another term. Then, perhaps four years from now, we can circle back for the opinions of David Brooks and Marianne Williamson.

More Hypocrisy at the *New York Times*
September 6, 2019

Global warming has nothing on the pollution of the ubiquitous charges of racism rising to the skies from the left-wing fever swamps. Everything now is racism. How dull.

An example of the never-ending focus on race is a recent op-ed in the *New York Times* entitled "Race in the Pediatric E.R." (Next week: "Racism in Public Toilets.") The author, Jessica Horan-Block, is described as a supervising attorney at the Bronx Defenders.

Her opening paragraph tells you where the story is going: "When a child experiences a mild head injury and a parent seeks medical attention, what happens next in New York City seems to depend on the ZIP code and the color of the parent's skin."

Predictably, the white mother and father in the story were met with compassion and sympathy at the hospital. The black mother, obviously, was met with "suspicion, interrogation and accusations of child abuse, even after explaining to the hospital staff her 9-month-old daughter's accidental head bump with her brother." It was determined that the child had suffered two minor skull fractures with a small underlying bleed.

What happened then seems inexcusable: the baby, who was still nursing, was not allowed to go home with her mother; and subsequently, the mother was accused, without any evidence of wrongdoing (we have only Ms. Horan-Block's word for this, but for the story's sake we have no reason to doubt it), of child abuse by intentionally causing the child's skull fractures.

The story, heart-rending of course, suggests egregious error on the part of hospital personnel. But what is the larger message? What is the *general* point we are supposed to take from the particular facts? Probably—especially given the story's title and the publication that ran it—that evil racism is everywhere, even in your local hospital. Is that fair?

Probably not. In 2014, a report in JAMA (the *Journal of the American Medical Association*) titled "The Prevalence of Confirmed Maltreatment Among American Children, 2004–2011" found that black children had the highest risks of maltreatment, at 20.9 percent, followed by Native American children at 14.5 percent, Hispanic children at 13.0 percent, white children at 10.7 percent, and Asian/Pacific Islander children at 3.8 percent. In other words, the risk of black children being maltreated was found to be almost twice that of white children.

The Annie E. Casey Kids Count Data Center has different numbers: it found that the rate of children confirmed by child protective services as victims of maltreatment in the United States in 2017 was: Hispanic, 23 percent; black, 18 percent; white, 5 percent; and Asian, 1 percent. In that study, black children were more than three times as likely to be maltreated as white children.

Horan-Block writes: "New York City must grapple with how and why it has permitted a system to hurt children by believing some parents but not others." But we know why: the numbers have told us.

If you're a hospital worker, you may not have read those studies, but you probably know their gist, which is likely common knowledge in the hospital's corridors and cafeteria.

When a black baby comes in with a head wound, what are you to do? You know nothing about the circumstances other than what is told to you by the parents, about whom you also know nothing *except their race*. What is your responsibility? Or perhaps the question that should be asked is, to whom are you responsible? The mother or the child?

In her op-ed, Horan-Block is pulling a fast one: she knows, she says (and we are compelled to believe her), the cause of the skull fractures. But the hospital staff didn't know the facts she describes to us. She should have spent some time telling the story from the staff's perspective: this child is black and black children are abused more frequently than white children. It would also be interesting for us, and presumably Horan-Block too, to know how many children with injuries consistent with parental abuse had been seen by those staff members that day, or that week, or that month—and how many were confirmed to have been caused by parental abuse.

Of course, that complicates the story: but *that* is the real story, and the real dilemma. Are some hospital staff members racists? Almost certainly—original sin not yet having been abolished—but the persistence of original sin is not usually the stuff of *Times* op-eds.

But for those hospital staff members who are not racists, the question is how to balance the rights of *this* parent with the welfare of *this* child? The question for the rest of us is, are we going to sacrifice the welfare of children in order to avoid being called racists by the PC-racism police?

Of course, instead of asking the tough questions, it's easier just to bang the racial injustice drum, which it would seem is what Ms. Horan-Block has done. How dull of her.

Another Day, Another Shooting. Boring!
September 18, 2019

Another day. Another shooting. So what? Pass the sugar, please.

You didn't read about it? Probably not. That's because it happened in Chicago.

You don't read about Chicago shootings for two reasons: One, because they're like automobile accidents: they happen all the time. The other reason is that the Chicago shooting death toll is embarrassing to the liberal establishment, which runs Chicago today and has since the memory of man runneth back not to the contrary. Tougher policing in Chicago might help, but if you're a liberal you can't go there. So people in Chicago—well, in parts of Chicago, but not the parts *you* are likely to frequent—die every day, sacrificed to the liberal zeitgeist which sees cops as bad guys.

But, every now and then, we have a "mass shooting," and a holy war cry goes up for . . . GUN CONTROL!

Last year 561 people were shot and killed in Chicago. So far this year, 330. According to *Time*, the death toll from mass shootings in 2018 was 80; so far in 2019, the number is 57.

Two points need to be made about the numbers: first, they vary slightly depending on the source. But second, the number of mass shooting deaths is *way below* the shooting deaths in Chicago.

So here's the question: Why are liberals so much more concerned about mass shootings than they are about Chicago shootings? The answer is because they don't actually care about the shootings: what they want is power—the power to take guns away from law-abiding people.

The liberals demand one or more of several "solutions" to the mass shooting problem. One is to outlaw "assault weapons." "Assault weapons" is a category invented by liberals. It has no particular meaning. One aspect of "assault weapons" is that they hold multiple bullets (as do, of course, most handguns, which they don't classify as "assault weapons"). Former Vice President (and current contender for the Democratic nomination for president) Joe Biden has said *no weapon* should be able to hold more than one round. He may really believe that (a Biden truth), or he may simply have plagiarized the position from someone else.

A problem for liberals is that a ban on "assault weapons" has been tried (1994–2004). It failed. Even the *Washington Post* has said the results were, at best, inconclusive.

Another liberal chestnut is stringent background checks. The problem with that is that people who can't buy guns legally will simply get them illegally. (The *Washington Post* estimates that there are more than 393 million civilian-owned firearms in the United States.) And many of the mass shooters have in fact gotten their guns legally. Liberals really just want to harass ordinary people who want to own guns—and they want a list of gun owners, the better to confiscate their guns some day.

A third is a national "red flag" law. But fifteen states already have red flag laws, and there's no indication that a national red flag law would work any better than the state laws have. In theory, states could seek restraining orders against people who are considered an imminent risk to commit gun violence. Hmm. How much power would that give the police in San Francisco to harass members of the National Rifle Association, which San Francisco has just declared a domestic terror organization? And what happens if Smith doesn't like his neighbor Jones: he can sic the police on him under a red flag law, and then what happens to Jones's Second Amendment rights?

That's three strikes. The liberals are out.

But here's an idea for limiting mass shootings that liberals haven't considered yet: restrict news coverage of them. There is some evidence (and it seems plausible) that the media attention given to mass shooters makes them role models for impressionable individuals who then commit mass shootings of their own. Many media outlets routinely omit the names of sexual victims. If the media don't stop covering mass shootings voluntarily, perhaps they should be *urged*, by legislation, not to cover them.

"Oooh," you say, "What about their First Amendment rights?"

Oooh, okay. Then what about the Second Amendment rights of gun owners and prospective gun owners? Nothing in the Constitution indicates that First Amendment rights are less susceptible to restriction than Second Amendment rights.

Of course, the media would howl—that alone makes suggesting the restriction worthwhile. A congressman who doubles as a constitutional scholar should propose the idea.

Meanwhile, mass shootings will continue, and we will have to get used to the existence of evil and original sin, which progressive liberals, clinging to their Darwin and Nietzsche, still think can be bred out. (In the old days, they pushed eugenics as the solution.)

Mass shootings may be here to stay. But that's no reason not to have better policing of the streets of Chicago.

Laws, Guns, and Freedom
October 30, 2019

In the end it's not laws that keep people free. It's the people.

Benjamin Franklin said famously that the Constitutional Convention had delivered to the people a republic "if you can keep it," not "if the laws will keep it for you."

What we in the US are seeing now, and have ever since Donald Trump was elected, is an attempt by Democrats, primarily (but with no objections from Never-Trump Republicans), and encouraged by a totally discredited left-wing press, to manipulate the laws to nullify the election and remove Trump from office. We've seen this movie before.

In Britain also, we are seeing all the proper people doing everything in their power to nullify Brexit, called for by a popular vote.

And we also saw people in Europe run over by their "betters" in the lead-up to the European Union. The French people voted not to join—obviously the wrong decision, and so obviously the wrong decision that the French rulers decided to vote again. That is, the *rulers* decided that *they* would vote again, and get it right. So they repaired to—the symbolism is pungent (pungent with the smell of blood)—they repaired to Versailles where *they* voted to join the EU.

To visit Versailles is to understand regicide.

In Ireland too, the people voted by 54.3 percent not to join the EU (Barack Obama got 52.9 percent of American votes). Having gotten it wrong (a "triumph of ignorance"), they were compelled by their betters to vote again. The second vote was in favor of joining. Why wasn't there a third vote, or a fourth, or a fifth vote? The answer is, because the rulers decided that on the second vote the people had gotten it right by endorsing the rulers' position.

All those actions were *perfectly* legal.

In the US, the current crisis has been provoked by a "whistleblower" law, a law that gives any disgruntled government official the power to throw monkey wrenches into the workings of government. A yet-unknown individual, but one rumored to be a partisan Democrat, operating solely on hearsay (as we understand it at this point, the whistleblower hadn't heard the conversation, and hadn't read the transcript), claimed that President Trump had said something wrong in a telephone conversation with the president of a foreign country (Ukraine). Yet now the nation is convulsed; impeachment is in the air; the nation's needs will be ignored; no legislation will be passed for the next year or more; the whistleblower's charge will be examined; and the House may even vote to impeach the president. Of course, the Senate will not vote to convict, so the whole thing is a grande charade. All *perfectly* legal.

It should remind us of the Watergate movie, where a president who had won a landslide victory only months before—60.7 percent of the popular vote and forty-nine states—was toppled by left-wing Democrats and their media allies getting even for Nixon's having nailed Alger Hiss, the Left's darling who (uh, oh) turned out to be a Soviet spy. Note that the Watergate putsch was *perfectly* legal.

At the same time all this is happening, left-wing pols and some Republican dupes (no, Virginia, not *all* Republicans are dupes) are calling for gun control. Energy exploration and production expert Hunter Biden's father, Joe Biden, wants a ban on all military-style weapons as well as a ban on high-capacity (i.e., more than *one* round!) magazines; and also more "red flag" laws. Red flag laws, currently on the books in fifteen states, allow police, family members, and others (e.g., cranky neighbors) who fear (or say they fear) that a gun owner has become dangerous, to file a seizure warrant for that person's weapons, reversing the burden of proof: the gun owner is presumed dangerous and has to prove he is not—making a travesty of both the Sixth and Second Amendments.

As of now, there is no national gun registry, but Democrats dream of creating one so officials can confiscate the firearms of dangerous people. Like you.

Not a good idea in a country where people aspire to be free.

The history of Venezuelan gun control is instructive. In 2012 the Venezuelan National Assembly enacted the "Control of Arms, Munitions and Disarmament Law," with the explicit aim to "disarm all citizens." There were only a few objections, from some pro-democracy opposition figures. After the law took effect, there was a months-long amnesty program that encouraged Venezuelans to trade in their arms for electrical goods. Only 37 (!) guns were surrendered voluntarily. Thousands were confiscated by force. In 2014 Chavez's successor, Nicolás Maduro, is said to have spent more than $47 million enforcing the gun ban. Now, as we have seen, the disarmed populace has no chance of defeating the Maduro thugs.

And it was all *perfectly* legal.

As it could be here.

Laws written on paper aren't enough to keep a people free. Freedom has to be written in their hearts as well.

Colleges Are Suffering from a Sexual Assault Epidemic—And Elites Want Us to Send More Kids

November 1, 2019

Why do the American people push college education on the young—and want to spend more money doing that? According to the *Washington Post*, a large number of students at "prestigious colleges" become perpetrators or victims of nonconsensual sexual violence (including rape). Is that just the result of alcohol (that's bad enough), or is it a cultural deficit that needs serious attention?

On the same day we learned that Democrats in the House of Representatives were offering a plan to make college more afford-able, we also learned from the *Washington Post* that at thirty-three prestigious colleges one-fourth of undergraduates tell of nonconsensual acts. Alas, the nonconsensual acts the students are complaining about are not the left-wing indoctrination carried out against them by most college teachers.

The survey apparently documents the "disturbing prevalence" of sexual violence at prestigious public and private colleges. Here's a great line from the *Post* piece, and perhaps right from the survey: "25.9 percent of female undergraduates had experienced nonconsensual contact through physical force or because they were unable to give consent."

Hmm. "Unable to give consent." Why? Were they all Roman Catholics who spoke only Latin?

Or were they, perhaps . . . drunk? And if so, whose fault was that? Please don't say Donald Trump's.

And wouldn't it be interesting to know other facts about both the victims and the perpetrators? Such facts as: Did they grow up in two-parent households? Do they go to church? And if so, which church? And where did they come from? New York City? Or fly-over land? In other words, what is their culture?

If you were told that one-quarter of airplanes crashed, you'd never fly again. If one-quarter of girls/women at colleges are sexually assaulted (some of which assaults are genuine rape) why would you send your daughters to college? Or at least, why would you send them to the "prestigious" colleges represented in this survey?

But now Democrats in the House of Representatives want to make attending these major prestigious cesspools even easier. Basically, what the Democrats want to do—when you strip away the wrapping paper and ribbon—is throw more money at the colleges. The Republicans won't go along, of course—although you can never be entirely sure of the "of course."

We all know that college tuition has vastly outpaced inflation while the quality of education has gone down. The advertisement should be: "Remember, you pay more, but you get less!"

A sensible education bill would require colleges to reduce their tuition to the level it was at, say, ten years ago. Most other organizations have been able to harness modern technology and do more with less. Why not colleges?

It is generally agreed that the effect of the massive government student loan program has been to allow colleges to increase the number of administrators and diversity programs—and pay employees more while delivering less education to students. It's the students who have borne the burden, some not paying off their loans until their own children are about to go to college themselves. What a rip-off! If Congress has any role, it is to make the institutions behave. Shutting off the money spigot is the beginning of wisdom.

And Congress could also condition any taxpayer funding for colleges on the reduction of sexual assaults to the levels they are in the surrounding communities—though picking the baseline community statistic might require some, uh, adjustment. A college student may be safer on the University of Chicago campus than in south side Chicago, but that may not be good enough.

Meanwhile, Attorney General William Barr gave a speech at Notre Dame which has the Left apoplectic. He talked about a "campaign to destroy the traditional moral order" waged by "militant secularists." Yes, and . . . ? What's the Left's complaint? Do they deny Barr's claim?

Ask yourself this: What remains of the traditional moral order (the traditional culture) when a quarter of college undergraduates at the nation's prestigious colleges are sexually assaulted?

You shouldn't have to be a theocrat to disapprove of Bill Clinton and Harvey Weinstein—but it probably would help. "People"—well, all the smart glitterati, anyway—knew for years about militant secular culture vandals Clinton and Weinstein, but kept mum. Now they profess to be "shocked" to find out that Clinton and Weinstein were behaving like . . . Clinton and Weinstein.

Barr has done a terrific public service—for which he will be roundly condemned by twice the number of usual suspects.

On the basis of his Notre Dame speech, Barr could even run for president. But then, of course, he'd have to stop investigating Joe Biden.

Controversy's Name Is the Department of State's Commission on Unalienable Rights

November 5, 2019

"Motorcyclist Who Identifies As Bicyclist Sets Cycling World Record." Funny. And you may be relieved—or perhaps disappointed—to discover it's a spoof. But you can't tell at first, can you? It sounds too much like "Transgender Cyclist Wins Masters Track Cycling World Championship." That one's real. Some people think transgendered people have a "right" to pretend they are of the opposite sex, with all benefits, rights, privileges, and emoluments pertaining thereto. It's a human right, isn't it? Perhaps even an unalienable right.

December 10, coming soon to an activist near you, is Universal Declaration of Human Rights Day. It commemorates the day in 1948 that the United Nations General Assembly adopted the Universal Declaration of Human Rights. The Trump administration has been giving some thought to that declaration.

Last July, Secretary of State Pompeo created in the Department of State a Commission on Unalienable Rights—and not a moment too soon.

The concept of human rights is in need of some clarification. The commission's purpose is, as stated by the Department of State, to "provide the Secretary of State advice and recommendations concerning international human rights matters. The Commission will provide fresh thinking about human rights discourse where such discourse has departed from our nation's founding principles of natural law and natural rights." Great unhappiness in some quarters ensued: the terms "natural law" and "natural rights" make some people nervous.

Part of the problem is rights explosion: as Pompeo stated before the first commission meeting, "One research group has found that between the United Nations and the Council of Europe, there are a combined 64 human rights-related agreements, encompassing 1,377 provisions." Even as "provisions" they can create problems when they are perceived by the world community as not being sufficiently protected.

Practically before Secretary Pompeo's words announcing the commission had faded away, people began to object to the formation of the commission. Katherine M. Marino, an assistant professor of history at the University of California, Los Angeles, said, "Pompeo's commission will actually threaten sexual equality, LGBTQ rights and reproductive health globally."

Marino also criticized the selection of Harvard Law School Professor Mary Ann Glendon as the chairman of the commission, for saying, "It is not the case that whatever a particular nation state decides to call a woman's 'right' is necessarily a universal human right."

Marino continued: "Differentiating between 'unalienable rights' and 'ad hoc rights' does the same thing as Glendon's contrast between human rights and women's rights: They both narrow the meaning of human rights to the natural law and rights of the US political tradition. This undermines the international feminist movement and other movements for social, economic and racial justice that have driven the development of universal human rights over the 20th century."

The polite response is probably, "Not everyone will agree."

Jayne Huckerby, Sarah Knuckey, and Meg Satterthwaite, writing on www.justsecurity.org, said: "Civil and human rights advocates raised immediate alarm when news of the Commission was first reported, fearing that its focus on 'natural law' was code for anti-LGBTQI, anti-choice, and anti-women's rights agenda(s)" and noting that "Glendon has long opposed abortion and marriage equality." Notice the not-so-sly insertion of the term "marriage equality" to normalize same-sex "marriage," opposed as recently as November

2008 by the noted right-wing extremist bigot Barack Obama, who said at that time: "I believe marriage is between a man and a woman. I am not in favor of gay marriage."

Human Rights First, a left-wing organization, put out a statement "in partnership with nearly 180 human rights, faith-based, civil liberties, professional, academic, and social justice organizations, as well as 250 former senior government officials [i.e., "the swamp"], foreign policy experts, scholars, and religious leaders" calling on Secretary Pompeo to disband the commission. (It's good to have all their names listed in one place.)

Their gripe is that "the Commission's chair and members are overwhelmingly clergy or scholars known for extreme positions opposing LGBTQI and reproductive rights, and some have taken public stances in support of indefensible human rights violations. The Commission's chair has stated that marriage equality undercuts the welfare of children. A Commission member has similarly stated that 'the unavoidable message' of same-sex marriage 'is a profoundly false and damaging one.'"

To which one might comment, politely, "People disagree; elections have consequences."

The Center for Reproductive Rights put out a statement saying: "Contrary to its asserted purpose, there is no need to redefine or develop foundational principles on human rights. There is a clear and unequivocal consensus by U.N. human rights treaty bodies and independent experts that reproductive rights are human rights, grounded in the right to life [savor that!], health, equality, non-discrimination and freedom from cruel, inhumane and degrading treatment, among other rights." What would we do without independent experts?

And do those experts include the folks in Venezuela, the country which, on October 17, was elected by the UN General Assembly to the Human Rights Council, the body responsible for "promoting and protecting all human rights around the globe"?

The commission's two public meetings so far, under the expert guidance of Professor Glendon, have been addressed by Professors Michael McConnell, Wilfred McClay, Cass Sunstein, and Orlando Patterson. Their papers or summaries of them will eventually be available online at the commission's website. They discussed (compared and contrasted) natural rights (they can be alienated);

unalienable rights (they cannot be); human rights (how are they different?); the Bill of Rights; Franklin D. Roosevelt's 1941 Four Freedoms; the United Nations Declaration of Human Rights and other formulations; and the historic and grand pronouncements of the Founding Fathers (hypocrisy, given the existence of slavery, or the seed for American exceptionalism?).

As is apparent from the comments of those who wish the commission had not been formed, they think relying on America's Founding Fathers to inform us about rights is too limited—too limited to normalize their own special proclivities.

A careful reading of the UN Declaration on Human Rights might be instructive for some of them. For example, Article 16 says, "Men and women . . . have the right to marry and to found a family." The implication is obvious: a family is founded by a man and a woman. Could Pompeo's opponents possibly claim with a straight face that the people who wrote those sentences had homosexual marriages in mind?

Abraham Lincoln is said to have asked a man, "If you call a sheep's tail a leg, how many legs does the sheep have?" When the man answered "five," Lincoln replied, "Calling a tail a leg doesn't make it one." And calling a man a "wife"?

Professor McClay said in his remarks that we should be careful not to create too many rights, and shouldn't extend them to . . . trees and bushes—a light remark that provoked a questioner representing an LGBTetc organization to ask (after McClay had left to catch a plane) if the speakers at subsequent public meetings could be challenged.

McClay was presumably teaching, softly, that creating a right in one person may, or will, create an obligation in an "opposite" party. A's right to eat at B's lunch counter, however just that may be, nevertheless deprives B of his right to determine who sits at his property. A homosexual's right to have any baker he selects bake him a cake of his designing may deprive a baker of his right not to bake that cake or even associate with that person, for whatever reason he may have. A "formerly male" tennis player's right to play in a women's tournament will deprive women of their right to an equal playing court.

To the surprise of absolutely no one, the UN continually puts out a lot of *Mad* magazine-type releases, e.g., "UN urges global move to meat and dairy-free diet." And the "Office has worked with judicial authorities and institutions to address gender stereotypes"—stereotypes as in "male and female created He them"? And of course the UN is pro-abortion.

Of the current forty-seven members of the UN's Human Rights Commission, three (Eritrea, Somalia, and Sudan) have Freedom House's worst aggregate score for political rights and civil liberties. And we want to rely on the United Nations to lecture us on human rights?

Secretary Pompeo's commission should provide a better guide—a guide steeped in the American tradition, a tradition that is the world's best hope, and the "last best hope on earth."

And a lesson for motorcyclists who identify as bicyclists.

Generalissimo Francisco Franco Is Still Dead. Or Is He?

November 9, 2019

This just in: Generalissimo Francisco Franco is still dead, according to people who spoke to us on condition of anonymity because they were not authorized to comment. Reports of the general's death may not have been exaggerated after all, but the general is not at rest yet (or at least his mortal remains are not), and it's not clear the Spanish people can rest yet either. Franco's remains have been moved from an underground basilica that he built after he won the country's civil war in 1975 to a family crypt near Madrid. Luckily for some Spaniards, Franco's remains are not being moved to Chicago, a move that might have enabled him to remain active in politics.

The cost of the transfer is estimated to be $70,000; enough to give each person in Spain living below the poverty level $145.71, which would buy them thirty-seven and a half Starbucks latte grandes (excluding tips). The leader of the opposition party said not one cent should be spent on moving Franco's remains, an amount that would not even buy a used Starbucks napkin. "I'm more worried about living dictators than dead ones," he said, which would likely have brought warmth to Franco's heart if it were still beating, which, as we say, reliable sources insist is not the case.

During Spain's civil war, the two factions were aided by, on one side, the fascist countries of Germany and Italy, and on the other by the Soviet Union. If you don't know your history—or Spain's—which side would you have been on? The answer, probably, is "the wrong side." Another answer is, it depends who writes the history: Fox News or CNN. One thing is clear: that period's history wasn't written by General Franco. He, after all, was a dictator.

Just what the rap is against dictators like Franco is not clear. Presumably they decide in their own wisdom to do things the people don't like. That may not be very democratic, but it really is quite European, making the case against Franco somewhat confused.

When the Irish voted against joining the European Union they were told—faith, 'tis the truth—to vote again (and presumably again, and again, and again if necessary) until they got it right, which they did on the next vote.

When the French voted against joining the EU, their betters didn't bother to instruct them to vote a second time (couldn't risk it): they themselves, in a symbolic beheading of the people, simply repaired to Versailles with champagne and caviar to vote the proper way, in favor of joining the EU.

More recently the British voted to leave the European Union but have been stymied by the political class which likes wining and dining in Strasbourg (home of *fois gras*). If the pro-Brexit pols had a little more Franco in them, the Brits would have been out months ago. But we digress.

Or do we?

The impeachment charade being played out in this country would have Franco marveling at the Democrats' chutzpah. If the Democrats can eject a legitimately elected president *of the United States*, a small-time dic like Franco should have been able to do a lot more in his country.

One of the raps against Franco was that he controlled the press. He believed—where have we heard this before?—that truth is what the people believe. *Plus ça change.* Now there is, at least in theory, a free press in Spain, although Spain lacks freedom-of-information legislation and sunshine laws—laws that even democratic governments chafe under. Says the *Columbia Journalism Review*, "It is very difficult to do serious government reporting without the benefit of hard facts." Whoa, Nellie!

And difficult for the people to know what the facts are if the press doesn't report them, eh, *Columbia Journalism Review?* Watch mainstream television and read mainstream papers in this country and you see bias in action as perhaps never before, at least never before in our lifetimes. Some "news" outlets now report that a majority of Americans support impeachment. And why shouldn't they, given what they read and hear all day long? And why should Europeans be different?

Dictators operate in secret, and so do Democrats, or at least the Democrats currently bent on impeaching President Trump. Franco lives! At least in spirit.

But we can now confirm: Generalissimo Francisco Franco is still dead!

Rest in peace, general. We still may be able to learn something from your time.

Big Tech On Trial
November 10, 2019

November 10 marks the hundredth anniversary of *Abrams v. United States*, a notable Supreme Court case involving free speech and Oliver Wendell Holmes.

Russian immigrants in New York who had distributed anti-war leaflets during World War I were charged with violating the Espionage Act of 1917. In a 7–2 opinion, the Supreme Court, sustaining the immigrants' conviction, held that the law did not violate their freedom of speech.

Holmes, who had upheld criminal convictions in free speech cases only months earlier, changed his mind in *Abrams*, and famously dissented: "The best test of truth is the power of the thought to get itself accepted in the competition of the market."

Immediately before "the best test of truth" Holmes wrote that men "may come to believe even more than they believe the very foundations of their own conduct that the ultimate good desired is better reached by free trade in ideas."

Holmes's "free trade in ideas" quote is likely to be trotted out by the Google-Facebook-Twitter-Amazon juggernet to justify their being left alone by government antitrust forces. The question for these forces, and the public, is whether there is really the competition in the market that Holmes was (and we are) relying on.

Is there any real competition to Google, Facebook, Twitter, or Amazon? Especially in the political campaign realm where they wield tremendously consequential power? Selling ideas is not the same as selling socks.

CEO Jack Dorsey has said Twitter will ban all political ads starting November 22. The "all" may sound catholic until you realize Twitter was one of Trump's most successful campaign strategies, and was likely to be again. Not for nothing is Trump called the Twitterer-in-Chief. Banning political ads is like limiting campaign expenditures: it benefits primarily incumbents and the media, which—as everyone except ABC, CBS, CNN, NBC, MSNBC, the *New York Times*, the *Washington Post*, and all their (need we say "left-wing"?) enthusiasts and lobbyists will concede—is primarily liberal.

And what counts as political? Suppose someone in the district of a candidate running against a serious gun controller writes a piece reporting that the 2018 death toll from mass shootings was . . . *only* eighty. Wow. Do media moguls and other gun controllers want voters to know that? Or do they want the public to think the "mass shooting" death toll is much higher?

Mark Zuckerberg says Facebook will not censure political ads, much to the consternation of its employees. Question: How much sub-rosa censuring in the free trade of ideas can those employees do without Zuckerberg's knowing?

Google owns YouTube. Dennis Prager testified before Congress that YouTube has at various times restricted about one hundred of Prager University's videos, including "Why Don't Feminists Fight for Muslim Women?" (by Somali-American women's rights activist Ayaan Hirsi Ali); "Are the Police Racist?"; and "Why Is Modern Art So Bad?"

We should digress for a moment to ask, why *is* modern art so bad?

Does Google believe in Holmes's free trade in ideas? Yes, *of course* it does—just not in dangerously subversive ideas, like the ones the government objected to in *Abrams*.

And is it likely that Amazon, owned by Jeff Bezos (the owner of stridently left-wing the *Washington Post*), would traffic in "dangerously subversive ideas"? Something like 50 percent of all books in the US are sold by Amazon. If any company is a marketplace of ideas, certainly Amazon is.

Amazon is said to have banned books by the "alt-right," which may sound innocuous and hardly a traducing of the free trade in ideas. But it's a good bet the term can ooze over to include books written by conservatives that Amazon doesn't like. All kinds of things could happen: books just wouldn't get listed . . . you know how sloppy employees can be. And how would anyone ever be able to tell?

In current antitrust law, a small degree of market power (which is not the same as monopoly power) is very common and understood not to warrant antitrust intervention. A dry cleaner in a good location may be able to charge slightly more than one in a different location, and no one will object. But even a trivial skewering of the marketplace for ideas by one of the juggernet information companies could make the difference between "President Trump" and "President Clinton." Trump won Wisconsin by 0.77 percent of the vote.

It's time to revisit antitrust. The original antitrust thinking of 1890 was reinterpreted in the 1970s–80s by what is sometimes called the "once-revolutionary Chicago School of Antitrust." But the world has changed again since then. People who believe in competition, especially in the marketplace of ideas, shouldn't let the juggernet information companies stop the clock at Chicago time. Like Holmes, we should be willing to change our minds.

Today Is Bill Buckley's Birthday: Tease a Liberal
November 24, 2019

William F. Buckley Jr. was born ninety-four years ago today (Nov. 24). He started the Conservative Movement. The Conservative Movement elected Ronald Reagan. Ronald Reagan won the Cold War, freeing millions from tyrannical slavery. And Ronald Reagan won an economic war at home, and then abroad, teaching the nations free-market principles, which lifted billions of people out of poverty.

God moves in mysterious ways, and reminds us, by having given us Bill Buckley, that each individual, made in His image, can move mountains.

Bill (I knew him well: I was executive editor of *National Review* and subsequently chairman of its board of directors; and skied and sailed with him for forty years) burst onto the American scene, like the Fourth of July, with his first book, *God and Man at Yale*, published in 1951 when he was only twenty-six. Bill wasted no time: the polemics began on the dedication page:

For God
For Country
and for Yale
. . . in that order

Bill kept his priorities straight for his whole career—writing 56 books, 400 hundred articles and book reviews, 2,000 speeches, and 4,000 columns, more or less, along with founding his magazine, *National Review*; and Young Americans for Freedom; and the New York Conservative Party; and The Philadelphia Society; and his television program, *Firing Line*; and The Fund for American Studies. With toil and labor he worked night and day. He was doing God's work, with his own right hand—but unlike God, he didn't seem to rest.

It's not a stretch to say that Bill forewarned, in *God and Man at Yale* (sixty-eight years ago!), the end of colleges and universities, and education, as we knew them. With a few exceptions, Hillsdale being one, college education has completely collapsed. It's mostly a package of woke, snowflakery nonsense today—with a $60,000-debt attached. In a day not too far away now, and right here in the land Bill loved, young people will stop going to colleges with their safe spaces, stop wasting two or four years of their lives, and engage in better pursuits—for themselves surely, and perhaps in service to their country and their fellow countrymen as recommended in Bill's book *Gratitude.*

Bill's best book was probably *Up From Liberalism*, which is a romp through the Liberals' giant sandbox, sand kicked exuberantly into their eyes—but only to scrub away their blindness. The book ends with a list of conservative proclivities and a paean to localism, which we might call federalism. "And then let us see whether we are better off than we would be living by decisions made between nine and five in Washington office rooms, where the oligarchs of the Affluent Society sit, allocating complaints and solutions to communities represented by pins on a map." That's still true enough to have been written yesterday.

Life with Bill Buckley was also a hoot. I remember a dinner with Mayor Bloomberg. It must have been the mayor's first encounter with Bill's wife, Pat, a formidable force he no doubt remembers—and if he doesn't, he's certainly not fit to be president. The mayor was droning on about the dangers of secondhand smoke. Pat was all over him, mercilessly—and having a whale of a good time. The mayor sought to buttress his case by quoting from a study from the Johns Hopkins School of Public Health, then recently renamed, as Pat, er, forcefully told the mayor (Pat's voice rising, the mayor's stature shrinking), the Johns Hopkins *Bloomberg* School of Public Health. Did he expect them to produce (voice rising higher) a result he didn't like?

She cut off his arguments at every turn. Louder and louder. Bill, trying vainly to keep "order" (the mayor was their guest) was saying, "Ah, Ducky, I think what the mayor was trying to say . . ." "Bill," came the response even more forcefully, "I can hear what he's saying." "Ah, er, Pat, the point . . ." "BIIILLL, WHY ARE YOU SUPPORTING HIS RIDICULOUS POSITION?"

Why indeed?

Pat was right. The danger of secondhand smoke was always overrated, and still is, by the trendy medical community and others still—always—allocating solutions to communities represented by pins on a map.

At the end of *Up From Liberalism*, Bill wrote: "I mean to live my life an obedient man, but obedient to God, subservient to the wisdom of my ancestors, never to the authority of truths arrived at yesterday at the voting booth. That is a program of sorts, is it not? It is certainly program enough to keep conservatives busy, and Liberals at bay. And the nation free."

Yes. But the forces of evil itself, not just of the affluent society facisti, are . . . everywhere. Even so, we can be of good cheer. As Bill said in 1959 at the end of his speech in Madison Square garden at a rally opposing the visit of Nikita Khrushchev (the First Secretary of the Communist Party of the Soviet Union) to the United States: "In the end, we will bury them."

And so we did. God does perform wonders. One of those was, ninety-four years ago, giving us Bill Buckley.

Fascism Lives!
December 3, 2019

British Fascist Oswald Mosley has been dead for nineteen years, but his spirit must be spinning for joy in its tight little grave at the report published recently by The British Academy, which calls for businesses to "place purpose at the heart of the corporation" instead of profit. The BA busybodies' goal is to have corporations do good for the "wider community" instead of maximizing shareholder wealth. Puh-lese—or *per favore,* as they said in Mussolini's Italy.

However much they dress it up, the proposal is just black-tie fascism: pro-experts, anti-people. It's anti-people because it says that the people (think the "little people" in Imelda Marcos's memorable phrase) don't know how to spend their own wealth—the dividends they get from holding shares in corporations—as well as the experts do. They seem to want *an economy no longer aimed at individual profit, but one concerned with collective interest.*

Colin Mayer, the professor who wrote the report, claims that the corporation has failed to deliver benefits to the wider community. "It is only over the last half century that corporate purpose has come to be equated solely with profit" the report claims. Exactly how to define the "wider community" may be up for grabs, but it's undeniable that over the last half century or so billions of people have been lifted out of poverty. If that isn't the "wider community" what is? The faculty club at Cambridge University?

Who or what do the authors of this paper think did the heavy lifting of those billions out of poverty: British foreign aid? Lord Peter Bauer described foreign aid as poor people in rich countries giving aid to rich people in poor countries. Foreign aid is the kind of nonsense only bureaucrats and university professors—and those on their payrolls—could believe in.

Now the same kind of people who push foreign aid are hoping to divert corporate energies into similar nonsense: having the state—"*l'état*:" see, Louis XIV—direct corporate wealth to their favorite programs and pastimes. As they see it, "The object of the regime in the economic field is to ensure higher social justice for the whole of the people."

"Profit is a product of the corporate purpose. It is not the corporate purpose. In some, but by no means all, cases, corporate purposes should include public purposes that relate to the firm's wider contribution to public interests and societal goals." Himmler/Goring may not have said, "When I hear the word 'culture' I reach for my gun," but when you hear the words "public interests" and "societal goals" you should head to the nearest ballot box and take your plebeian friends with you.

Try this one on for size: "Corporate ownership is currently equated with shareholders. Instead it should be associated with defining and implementing corporate purpose. The rights and responsibilities associated with corporate purpose should replace property right views of ownership. Different types of owners are suited to different types of corporate purposes and activities. This points to the need for diversity in corporate ownership."

A true cynic would assume the authors of the report planned to sell (or perhaps had already sold) the market short before issuing the report. The mind reels trying to think of other ways to do as much damage to the market, and to the wealth of millions of hard-working British workers and savers: (1) uncontrollable bubonic plague; (2) a hydrogen bomb exploding in Oxford; or (3) a direct hit by an asteroid.

None of this is to imply that corporations behave perfectly. Corporate managers—in place because of the managerial revolution that James Burnham wrote about in 1941—too often manipulate corporate practices to benefit their own compensation packages. Better governance *is* needed in the board room. In Sweden the top five shareholders are part of the nominating committee for directors. Those top five are likely to care about corporate profits rather than directors' salaries. They can dissuade the managers from finagling with buy-backs and other stratagems that do no good for the corporation, or do actual harm, but line the top managers' pockets with gold. That kind of "reform" is not what the authors of this report have in mind.

We are told that "the report is primarily diagnostic in identifying the nature and source of the problems rather than prescriptive in proposing detailed policy recommendations. These will be the focus of phase two of the research programme, which will start in 2019." OMG! Do I hear 3019? Anyone? Anyone?

As Mussolini said years ago, the Italian economy was "no longer an economy aiming at individual profit, but an economy concerned with collective interest." And "The object of the regime in the economic field is to ensure higher social justice for the whole of the people."

After reading far too many pages of fascist gobbledygook, one realizes that the most dispiriting sentence appeared on the *very first page*: "This report from the British Academy sets out a new framework for business in the 21st century, drawing on the *finest minds in the UK* and beyond" (my italics). If it was really the finest minds in the UK that produced this document, Britain's only hope now is rampant, plebiscitary democracy. And one-way tickets to Davos for all of the report's authors. And their children. And grandchildren.

Antitrust and the Candlestick Makers
January 11, 2020

As ye sow, so shall ye reap. If you allow high school students to learn American history from *A People's History of the United States* by communist Howard Zinn (now, fortunately, deceased) or from *The American Pageant* by Kennedy, Bailey & Cohen, you should not be surprised if the students—and any books they write—are left leaning as well.

Certainly *Goliath* by Matt Stoller is a left-leaning account of American business and antitrust, even if its author did not study American history from Howard Zinn. It's a fair bet that whatever Stoller read when he was young was a clone of Zinn's book.

Goliath is subtitled "The 100-Year War between Monopoly Power and Democracy." The first several chapters describe the horrors of business in America's Gilded Age, but we are made suspicious as early as the *preface*, where Stoller castigates the Sackler family whose company made the opioid drug OxyContin. "And the Sackler family name, as of 2019, graced facilities at Harvard and Yale," Stoller writes. Oh, really! In academic aeries that's called an "outhouse smear." Or something like that. The president of Harvard wrote last May, "Dr. Arthur Sackler [the man who donated funds to Harvard] died before the drug was developed. His family sold their interest in the company before the drug was developed."

Details, details, my good man. Sackler, Epstein, Hitler—none of those damn Jews is any good.

After that, you have to take everything Stoller writes with a grain of . . . OxyContin.

And then there is this problem (and we're still in the *preface*!): Stoller writes, "In the meantime [i.e., since the mid-1970s], old problems have returned. Wage stagnation and economic inequality is [sic] back with a vengeance. . . ." Stoller is pulling a fast one here because he is looking only at dollars, not at what those dollars can buy. Fact (one of many given to us by Phil Gramm and John Early writing in the *Wall Street Journal*): "Cars last 81.3 percent longer and are 72.7 percent safer" than in 1972.

Details, details, my good man. And don't forget this detail: unemployment figures for blacks, Hispanics, and women are the lowest in decades. And everyone, *everyone*, has a cell phone. Some have two. Or *three*.

We are told, "The barons of industry were unapologetic, almost gleeful" and "there was endless corruption, corporate pay-offs to politicians, newspapers, and academic experts, city bosses, everyone." Yup. Don't doubt it. And they called the wild west the "Wild West" for a reason.

We are told that J. P. Morgan "was finally able to seize control of the railroads after the panic of 1893, a financial crisis caused in part by railroad overbuilding."

Yup, but why were the railroads overbuilt? Because politicians got their grubby hands on them and were fleecing the public. But the Great Northern Railroad, under James J. Hill, received no federal subsidies and was so successful that it was the only transcontinental railroad not to lose money during the Panic of 1893. Does Stoller know that?

Stoller's heroes are the trust busters, the originals and their disciples. But there is no *analysis* of antitrust. Readers who want that analysis can find it in Robert Bork's *The Antitrust Paradox*, a singularly influential book, one that changed the course of antitrust, and not in the direction that Matt Stoller likes.

Stoller rails against the A&Ps of yesterday and the Walmarts of today, which were successful because ordinary people like shopping at them. If you're a young mother of three, do you really want to have to drag the children and the dog out of the car to shop, seriatim, at the butcher, the baker, and the candlestick maker?

Chapter nine, "The Free Market Study Project," is must reading for all think-tank presidents and fundraisers. It's an account of how a group of conservatives changed the course of economics. As told by Stoller, it's a screenplay for a Bond film. Friedrich Hayek, author of *The Road to Serfdom* and founder of the Mont Pèlerin Society, was the first intellectual guru of the movement. He was joined by three others at the University of Chicago: Frank Knight, Jacob Viner, and Henry Simons. But then they recruited the real genius, the third economist of the group (*scary music*): Aaron Director (Dr. No). Director recruited his brother-in-law, Milton Friedman (Francisco Scaramanga), and George Stigler (Colonel Moon). They are important, but the real villain is (*scarier music*) Robert Bork (Odd-job).

Bork's views and writings on antitrust were dispositive and have informed all of antitrust thinking since the book's publication in 1978. You can get your very own hard copy of *The Antitrust Paradox* from AbeBooks for only $480!

The chapter shows the power of ideas, properly packaged and disseminated. And how ironic it is that in a book hostile to the ideas he promoted, Aaron Director receives his due.

Stoller lectures about the evil of predatory pricing—the practice of a merchant lowering his prices below his cost to attract customers in order to put his competitors out of business. For the most part, predatory pricing works in theory but not in practice. The merchant who lowers his price, and therefore takes a loss, must then raise his price above the competitive price after his competitor has gone out of business. But when he raises his price, he is likely to attract a new competitor, which means he won't be able to recoup the loss he incurred by the previous lowering of his price. When I was chairman of the Federal Trade Commission I put out an APB for a predatory pricing case—with an award attached: lunch with the chairman! No predatory pricing case was ever found. (Maybe the prize should have been a guarantee of life *without* ever having to have lunch with the chairman. . . .)

Recently, however, there was a case that looked as if it involved predatory pricing, but although Stoller mentions it, he doesn't analyze it nor does he tell us that the Federal Trade Commission examined it and decided not to take any action. Diapers.com, a subsidiary of Quidsi, was selling diapers and baby care products online. Amazon expressed an interest in acquiring Quidsi, which the firm rejected. Shortly afterwards, Amazon started selling diapers for up to 30 percent less. Quidsi was unable to compete, and sold out to Amazon—whereupon Amazon raised its prices. Nevertheless, the FTC took no action. Why? Stoller doesn't say—or even guess.

Stoller goes after Amazon, Google, and Facebook, but only because they're big. For him big *is* bad, but he can't quite explain why. Maybe he doesn't shop, as do the millions of moms who can now (without leaving home) order goods from the shoe store, the baker, and the frozen food maker.

It's too bad Stoller didn't write more pointedly about the conflict at the heart of the dispute between old antitrust theory and new (Chicago school) antitrust theory. New antitrust cares about consumers. Old antitrust, whatever its origins, seemed to care more about workers and producers. Today, after a few decades of the giant sucking sound Ross Perot warned about, many have become skeptical of Chicago school antitrust and have become more solicitous of workers, so many of whom were unemployed before Donald Trump took office.

This issue can be raised by this question: Which is more important: marginally lower prices for underwear or more jobs for American workers? Stoller might have raised that question—and then answered it. He didn't.

Nor does Stoller discuss what may be a valid reason for being suspicious of Amazon, Google, Facebook, and Twitter: their tremendous power over *information*, a special concern of Americans reflected in the First Amendment. Information is different from underwear: just a dab of book censorship or search-results skewering might swing an election (Trump won Michigan by 0.3 percent). That is something we should take seriously. Where's Stoller when we need him?

Goliath is not an uninteresting book and is worth skimming, if you have time. But you can read, and skim, only so many books in a year—or a lifetime. Should this be one of them? Probably not, unless antitrust is your subject.

Introductions and Speeches

Introduction of Mark Steyn
Pacific Research Institute for Public Policy
Annual Dinner
Ritz Hotel

November 10, 2018

Ladies and Gentlemen:

Mark Steyn is not an individual. Mark Steyn is an industry, a conglomerate, a multi-faceted educational and entertainment force.

He is an international bestselling author, a Top Five jazz recording artist, and a leading Canadian human rights activist.

Mark Steyn's human rights campaign to restore free speech to Canada led to the repeal by Parliament of the notorious "Section 13" hate-speech law, a battle he recounts in his book *Lights Out: Islam, Free Speech and the Twilight of the West.*

With fans around the world, Mark Steyn has appeared on stages across the planet from Toronto's Roy Thomson Hall to the Sydney Conservatorium of Music. His 2016 nationwide tour of Australia was sold out, coast to coast. He has spoken in the Canadian Parliament, the Danish Parliament, and the Australian Parliament, where he was introduced by the foreign minister, Julie Bishop.

Mark is a category 5 hurricane force in the journalistic world.

First, you go to SteynOnLine.com. There you can sign up to be a member of the Mark Steyn Club, where you can read Steyn's Sunday Poem. You don't want to miss Mark's reading of "Jenny Kiss'd Me"— though you do have to become a member to watch him.

For those of you who work for a living and just don't have time for the news, you can click on to "Mark's Week in Review" and catch up on the inanities that plagued us during the week. And you can watch him regularly on Tucker Carlson's show

For the more serious-minded of you, there is Steyn's Song of the

Week, where Mark critiques popular songs—how they were written, how they rhyme, what they mean, why you should love them.

And you won't want to miss Mark's very own vocal CDs: among them, *Feline Groovy, American Songbook Singalong,* and *Broadway Double-bill.*

It all began years ago, with Mark's first show, *In the Dark with Mark.*

And now, decades later, I understand that the combined annual revenue of Mark Steyn enterprises—and Google, is $110 billion.

As you can see, Mark is quite famous, but he is also very accessible. If you'd had the time last September you could have joined the very first ever Mark Steyn Club Cruise—Steyn at Sea—along the St. Lawrence and the Eastern Seaboard at the height of the fall foliage. You might even have been on his show, which he broadcast from the ship.

I wasn't able to make that cruise myself, though I did have the pleasure of being on a cruise with Mark several years ago. I forget what boat we were on. I forget who else was on board. And I forget where we went, and why.

But I will never forget being with Mark in the ship's Karaoke bar watching him sing "Hey, Big Spender." Wow! What a sight.

Ladies and Gentlemen—all you big spenders who've come out to this year's Pacific Research Institute's gala:

Here now is a man of distinction, good lookin', and so refined: the incomparable Mark Steyn.

Introduction of Tucker Carlson
Pacific Research Institute for Public Policy's
40th Anniversary Dinner
Ritz Hotel

March 23, 2019

Several years ago, as Adam and Eve were leaving the Garden of Eden, Adam is reported to have said—reported by Woodward and Bernstein of course—Adam is reported to have said, "My dear, we live in a time of change."

Well, we too are living in a time of change, of political change. The Democratic Party is not your grandfather's . . . chauffeur's party. The Democratic Party is on the verge of changing into a genuine socialist party, driven largely, it seems, by younger members who are too young to remember, and have not taken the time to study, the chaos and misery spread by socialism in the twentieth century.

The Republican Party is also changing, and that has made many Republicans uncomfortable. Donald Trump is a terrifying maverick to some Republicans and a breath of fresh air to others.

One of his changes is how America should treat foreign trade. There is a myth, widely believed, at least by Republicans, that Americans are, always have been, and should remain, committed to "free trade"—whatever that is. But of course that isn't true. The eighteenth and nineteenth century managers of US policy could hardly be described as free traders.

Free trade, in fact, may not have existed anywhere since David Ricardo made the case in 1817 for comparative advantage, illustrated by his example of British cloth merchants trading with Portuguese wine makers.

What we have today, and what we have had almost since the beginning of the Republic, is managed trade. NAFTA, the North American Free Trade Agreement, was a thousand pages long. It is simply incorrect to describe trade governed by a thousand pages of rules and regulations as "free."

In the complex world we live in today, and will always live in from now on, trade will be managed. The political question then becomes, For *whose benefit* should it be managed? Trade, as well as market capitalism, and even democracy, are only tools, not goals. And therefore we must always ask, What is it we seek to build with those tools?

In a monologue on his eponymous television show on January 2 of this year, our speaker tonight gave his answer to that question. Trade, and perhaps all policies, including most especially immigration (which can be viewed as trade in people) should be managed in a way that puts America, and most especially American families, first.

Our speaker knows families—he has one himself: four children, and a wife he fell in love with in the *tenth* grade. For all of his working life he has been a journalist, writing and appearing on television. He is also, as many of you may know, a founder of *The Daily Caller*. It is fair to say that he has had, like my friend and mentor Bill Buckley, several decades of practice ticking people off.

Thomas Edsall, one person he ticked off recently, writing in the *New York Times* about our speaker's January 2 monologue, said this: "One of Tucker Carlson's own primary concerns is immigration— and, as a likely subtext, race." You gotta love that: ". . . as a *likely* subtext, race." That guy Edsall sure knows how to shovel the muck.

If patriotism is the *last* refuge of a scoundrel, the next to the last stop on the line is charging your opponents with racism. And that is the stop where most of the prominent Democrats seem to be getting off these days. There's a big terminal at that stop, big enough I think to hold the Democratic National Convention in, in 2020.

Ladies and Gentlemen: It is a singular pleasure for me to introduce to you the host of the most interesting and informative—and amusing—serious commentary program on television today, and a friend of mine: Tucker Carlson.

Index

ABC News 222, 251
AbeBooks 259
abortion 10–12, 22, 69–72, 108, 140, 156, 158, 184–85, 209, 233, 245–46, 248
Abrams v. United States 250–51
absentee voting 29
Ackerman McQueen 226
Adams, Charles Francis 148
Adams, Henry 147–48
affirmative action 34, 161, 202
Afghanistan 51, 220
Agricultural Adjustment Act 64
Airumian, Marusya 131, 133
Alexander the Great 147
Ali Baba Group Holding, Ltd. 203
Alito, Samuel 168
Alter, Jonathan 65
Altuzarra, Joseph 44
Amazon (Amazon.com) 94, 105, 165–67, 251–52, 260
American Action News *viii*
The American Conservative viii
American Council of Trustees and Alumni (ACTA) 34
American Greatness magazine *viii*
American Manufacturing Council 99
The American Pageant (textbook) 145–46, 148–50, 163–65, 170–71, 257
The American Spectator viii
Andrews, Christopher 13
Angelou, Maya 93
Anglican communion 5–8, 86, 143
Annie E. Casey Foundation 236
antitrust (see also "monopolies") 251–52, 257, 259–61
A&P grocery stores 259
Applebaum, Anne 62–64
Apple Inc. 182
Argentina 174
Arias, Oscar 93
Arpaio, Joe 44
Arum, Richard 198–99
Australia 95, 263
authoritarianism 17, 20–23, 40–42

Bacon, Kenneth H. 93
Baidu, Inc. 203
Bailey, Thomas A. 145, 148, 257
Barrett, Amy Coney 126
Barr, William 243
Barrymore, Drew 24–27

Barrymore, Jaid 26
Battle of the Morannon (*The Lord of the Rings*) 32
Battle of Tours 156
Bauer, Lord Peter 255
Baylor University 101
Benghazi 38
Ben-Ner, Avner 120
Benson, Lloyd 187
Bernstein, Carl 265
Bettelheim, Bruno 93
Bezos, Jeff 105, 166–67, 252
Biden, Hunter 203, 241
Biden, Joe 193, 202–3, 205, 238, 241, 244
Bill of Rights 247
birther movement 116–17
Bishop, Julie 263
Bismarck, Otto von 47
Black, Conrad 74
Black Lives Matter 97–98, 151
Blackstone Group 182
Bloomberg, Michael 22, 91, 254
Blow, Charles M. 65, 162, 178–79, 191, 228–29, 233
Blumenthal, Richard 156
Booker, Cory 187, 189
Boot, Max 189–91
Bork, Robert 108, 129, 158, 168, 259
Brazil 210, 212
Brennan, John 123–24
Brewer, Wiliam A., III 226
Brexit 240, 249
Bridges, Linda *viii*
Broaddrick, Juanita 38
Bronx Defenders 235
Brooks, David 44, 232–35
Bruni, Frank 43, 233
Buckley, James L. 152, 207
Buckley, Patricia Taylor 254
Buckley, William F., Jr. *vii–viii*, *xv*, 14, 36–37, 47–48, 93, 138–39, 164, 189–91, 199, 207, 210, 232, 252–55, 266
Bullitt, William 145
bureaucracy 38, 53, 60, 84, 107, 140, 185, 255
Bureau of Labor Statistics 121
Burke, Arleigh 100
Burke, Bill *xvii*, 109, 110, 111
Burkina Faso *xvii*, 118
Burnham, James 40, 99, 184, 256
Burnham, Jim 40

Burnham's Second Law 184
Burundi 119, 122
Burwell v. Hobby Lobby Stores, Inc. 69
Bush, George H. W. 48
Bush, George W. 48, 72
Buttigieg, Pete 214, 221–22
BuzzFeed 180–81

Cambridge University 13, 255
campaign finance reform 4, 22, 251
Canada 24, 42, 95, 142, 174, 210, 212, 263
Caplan, Bryan 198–99
Capone, Al 173
Lord Caradon (Hugh Mackintosh Foot,
    Baron Caradon) 93
Carey, Lord George (Archbishop) 143
Carlson, Tucker 166, 229, 263, 265–66
Carrier Corporation 75
Carter, Ash 2, 127
Cassidy, John 65
Cass, Oren 175
Catholicism 6, 22, 32, 85–87, 90, 94,
    109–10, 126, 130, 139–140, 157, 179,
    185, 212, 242
CBS News 28–29, 112, 251
Center for Reproductive Rights 246
Central African Republic 119, 122, 140
Central Intelligence Agency (CIA) 123–24
Chappaquiddick 128, 130, 158
Cheng, Lee 35
Chiang Kai-shek (Jiang Jieshi) 146
China 11, 13, 33, 41–42, 48, 76–78, 146,
    172–74, 182, 196–97, 202–5
Chinagate 38
chlamydia 11
Christianity 27, 46, 70, 86–87, 92, 106,
    126, 140, 143, 156, 174, 186, 194, 212
Christmas *xvii*, 43, 46–47, 109, 111, 140,
    217
Churchill, Winston 47, 145–46
*Citizens United v. Federal Elections
    Commission* 168
civil rights 20, 28–32, 107, 130, 139, 150,
    160–62, 169, 190–91, 229
Civil Rights Commission 31
Clarke, Jason 128
class conflict 14
climate change 10, 17, 22, 72, 182, 191
Clinton, Bill 2–3, 8, 10, 12, 23, 38, 50, 52,
    63, 96, 106–7, 109, 115, 166, 243, 252
Clinton Foundation 50–51, 88, 107
Clinton, Hillary *xv*, 1–4, 10–12, 15, 22–24,
    37–44, 50–52, 59, 61, 63, 65–66, 71, 78,
    88, 96, 103, 106–7, 109, 112–15, 124,
    136, 141, 144, 174, 216–17
cloning 12

CNN 98, 205, 218, 249, 251
Code of Federal Regulations 46
Codevilla, Angelo 10, 144
Cohen, Adam 38, 66
Cohen, Lizabeth 145, 148, 257
Cohen, Michael 180
Cohen, Richard 38
Cohen, Roger 233
Cold War 42, 74, 141, 165, 190, 196–97,
    204, 223, 252
college admissions quotas 34
Collins, Gail 90–92
Columbia Journalism Review 250
Columbia University 222
Columbine High School 131–32
Comey, James 2, 74, 78–79, 112–13, 125,
    216
Common Core curriculum 10
communism *xv, xvi,* 41–42, 66, 74–76, 88,
    138, 145, 163, 190, 204, 217, 255, 257
Competitive Enterprise Institute 22
Condé Nast 44
Confusio, Imabita *xvi*, 73
congenital adrenal hyperplasia (CAH)
    12–13
Conquest, Robert 41
Conservative Political Action Conference
    39
Consumer Finance Protection Bureau
    (CFPB) 53–55
contraceptives 22, 90–91
Cook, Tim 182
Coolidge, Calvin 61, 67
Cooper, Charles 227
Cooper & Kirk 227
Cordray, Richard 54
Corfman, Leigh 105, 106
Cornell University 28
corporate income tax 49, 55, 57, 166
Council of Fashion Designers of America
    43
Covert, Bryce 69, 70
Cox, Christopher W. 226
Cranmer, Thomas (Archbishop) 86
Crews, Wayne 22
Crick, Francis 92
Cruz, Ted 9, 23
Cuba 33
Cummings, Elijah 230
Cuomo, Andrew 166
Cuomo, Chris 205
Curry, Bishop Michael 6

Daily Caller *viii*, 266
Darwin, Charles 147, 239
Day, Dorothy 87

D-Day 125, 142, 144, 205–9, 211
de Blasio, Bill 166, 201
Declaration of Independence 210
Dedijer, Stevan 93
deep state 144, 151–52, 216
defense 2, 49, 55–56, 127, 139, 157, 196, 203, 205
Defense of Marriage Act 12
Deferred Action for Childhood Arrivals (DACA) 116–18
Delrahim, Makan 81
DeMint, Jim 48
Democratic Republic of Congo 119
Denmark 263
Department of Education 10, 56, 102, 125
Department of Health and Human Services 69, 220
Department of Justice 22, 28, 32, 50, 81, 88–89, 106–7, 130, 150
Department of State 63, 107, 172
Department of the Interior 159
Department of the Treasury 49
deregulation 81–82, 115, 121, 127, 140
détente 48
Development, Relief, and Education for Alien Minors (DREAM) Act 117
DeVos, Betsy 103
Diagnostic and Statistical Manual of Mental Disorders (DSM) 12
Diapers.com 260
Dionne, E.J. 21, 23
Director, Aaron 259
Dodd-Frank Wall Street Reform and Consumer Protection Act 49, 53, 58, 176
Dorsey, Jack 251
Douthat, Ross 232
Dowd, Maureen 214
Dow Jones Industrial Average 174
DREAMers (Development, Relief, and Education for Alien Minors Act) 117
drugs 160, 258
Dukakis, Michael 187
Duke University 72
Dunaway, Faye 87

Early, John 258
EB-5 visas 76–78
Edsall, Thomas 266
Education and Research Institute (ERI) 146, 148, 150, 165, 171
Edwards, John 93
Egan, Timothy 22, 43
Egypt 146

Eisenhower, Dwight D. 149–50, 161, 190, 206
Eliot, Charles W. 19–20
Eliot, T. S. 88, 215
El Salvador 140
Emanuel, Rahm 52
Emergency Banking Act 220
Endangered Species Act 48
Entertainment Weekly 24
Environmental Protection Agency (EPA) 10, 48, 58
Episcopal church 5–8, 85–87
Epstein, Jeffrey 258
equal protection 108, 119
Equatorial Guinea 23
Eritrea 248
Espionage Act of 1917 250
ethanol regulations 9, 58–59
European Union (EU) 240, 249
Evans, M. Stanton 48
executive orders 1, 4, 66
Exxon 62–63
Ezekiel 3:16–19 i

Facebook 200, 251, 260
Fact magazine 21
Farrar, John 129
fascism 44, 46, 74–75, 249, 255, 257
Federal Bureau of Investigations (FBI) 1–2, 50, 74, 78, 89, 112–13, 116, 124–25, 151–52, 215–16, 219, 231
Federal Communications Commission (FCC) 54
Federal Deposit Insurance Corporation 65
The Federalist viii
Federal Register 22
Federal Reserve 53
Federal Trade Commission (FTC) 54, 83, 135, 260
FedEx 63
Feingold, Russ 4
Feinstein, Dianne 126, 139, 179
feminism 93, 251
Filegate 38
Fiorina, Carly 158–60
Firing Line 47, 253
First Amendment 15, 22, 33, 38, 59, 239, 260
First Things viii
Fitzgerald, F. Scott 183
Flanagan, Caitlin 35
Flanders and Swann (British comedy duo) 25
floating currencies 49
Florida State University 101

Flynn, Michael T. 78–79
Ford, Christine Blasey 153–57
Foreign Intelligence Surveillance Act (FISA) 124–25
Foreign Policy magazine 93
Founding Fathers 31, 139–40, 179, 247
Four Freedoms 247
Fourteenth Amendment 21
Fox News *viii*, 1, 218, 229, 249
France 44, 57, 142, 205, 208, 211–12, 223–24, 249
Franco, Francisco 248–50
Franklin, Benjamin 239
Fraser Institute 42
Frazier, Kenneth 99
Freedman's Bureau 169
Freedom House 248
The Freeman magazine 164
free trade 49–50, 61, 140, 173, 250–52, 265
Friedman, Milton 167, 183, 259
Friedman, Thomas 233
Friedman, Vanessa 43–44
Friends of the National World War II Memorial 144
Fund for American Studies 253
Fund, John 107
Fusion GPS 216

Gaddis, John Lewis 74
Gallup 15, 122, 188
The Gambia 122
Gargan, Joe 129
Gavin, James M. 93
gay rights (see also "homosexuality") 6–8, 13, 18, 27, 32–33, 46, 73, 85, 87, 92–93, 108, 122, 126–27, 141, 162, 188–89, 194–95, 245–47
gender issues 12, 18–19, 31, 38, 72–73, 92–94, 120, 126, 186–87, 191, 248
General Electric 164
Genesis 19:28 163
Gergen, David 79
Germany 14, 42–43, 57, 142, 146, 196–97, 204, 211, 217, 249
Gillibrand, Kirsten 112, 114–15, 230–32
Ginsburg, Ruth Bader 14
Giuliani, Rudy 205
Glasnost 164
Glass-Steagall Act 64
Glendon, Mary Ann 245–46
Goldblatt, Laura 98
gold standard 49
Goldwater, Barry 21, 23, 32, 139, 190–91
Google LLC 25, 67–68, 104, 183, 251, 260, 264
Gorbachev, Mikhail 163–65

Gore, Al 49, 136
Goring, Hermann Wilhelm 256
Gorsuch, Neil 61, 75
Gramm, Phil 258
Grant, Ulysses S. 147–48
Grassley, Chuck 77–78, 168
Great Recession 140
Great Restoration 5
Great Society 20, 48
Greece 208
Green, Al 79
green cards 117
Green, Mark 127
Green, Tom 24
Grenada 165
Gross Domestic Product (GDP) 45, 49, 58, 76–77, 141, 174, 176, 196–97, 213
Group of Five (G5) 197
Group of Seven (G7) 62, 196
Guinea-Bissau 119
gun control 10, 42, 133, 140, 170, 227–28, 238, 241
guns *xvii*, 17–18, 79, 131, 133, 139–40, 173–74, 225, 228–29, 237–39, 241, 251, 256

Haiti 119, 121, 140
Hamilton, Alexander 50
Harkness, Stephen 109
Harris, Kamala 179, 185
Harvard Crimson newspaper 34
Harvard Lampoon 174
Harvard Law School 17, 19, 198, 245
Harvard University *xv*, 17, 19–21, 33–36, 67, 71, 92, 94, 122, 160, 174, 198, 231–32, 245, 258
Hayek, Friedrich 164, 259
Hayward, Susan 87
health insurance 22, 90, 92, 140
Health Savings Accounts 11
Hellman, Lillian 23
Hensarling, Jeb 53
The Heritage Foundation 48
Hill, James J. 258
Hillsdale College 253
Hilton Hotels 86
Himmler, Heinrich 256
Hirono, Mazie 179, 185
Hiroshima 207
Hirsi Ali, Ayaan 251
Hiss, Alger 48, 175, 240
Hitler, Adolf 14, 40–42, 44, 75, 258
Hobbes, Thomas 80
Hobby Lobby 69
Hoffa, Jimmy 10
Holder, Eric 107

Hollywood 74, 104, 109, 161, 164, 170
Holmes, Oliver Wendell 250–52
The Holocaust 44
Home Owners Loan Corp 65
homosexuality (see also "gay rights") 7, 13, 19, 127, 186–88, 194, 246
Hoover, Herbert 66
Hoover, J. Edgar 74
Hopkins, Harry 64, 66
Horan-Block, Jessica 235–37
Hoyer, Steny 121–22
Huawei Technologies 174, 197
Huckerby, Jayne 245
Huffington Post 65
Hull, Cordell 172
Human Events 164
human rights 244–48, 263
Human Rights First 246
Humphrey, William E. 135
Huntington, Samuel P. 212

IBM 183
Icahn, Carl 58–59
ID card 21
identity politics 19–20, 38, 86, 93–94, 122, 161, 182, 223
illegitimacy 20, 30, 160–61, 202, 215, 232
immigration *xvi*, 21, 39, 66, 78, 95–96, 117–19, 122, 137, 159–60, 192, 211–12, 224–25, 228–29, 233–34, 250, 266
Immigration Act of 1882 96
impeachment 5, 9, 39, 44, 79, 80, 114–16, 180–81, 213, 218, 240, 249, 250
Independent Regulatory Agency *xvi*, 52
Ingraham, Laura 229
InStyle magazine 24–25
insurance 22, 84–85, 90–92, 140
Internal Revenue Service (IRS) 42, 49
iPhones 42
Iran 64, 145–46, 174
Iraq 51, 142, 190
Ireland 223, 240, 249
Islam 30, 251
Israel 178
Italy 76, 122, 196, 208, 249, 255, 257

Jackson, Barbara Ward 93
Jackson, Jesse 231
James, Letitia 226
Japan 99, 142, 146, 153, 170, 172, 205, 207
Jarrell, Randall 31
Jefferson, Thomas 210
Jeong, Sarah 178
Jesus of Nazareth 47
Jim Crow laws 210
Jimenez, John 67–69

John Birch Society 189
Johns Hopkins University 254
Johnson, Andrew 169–70
Johnson, Hank 178
Johnson, Lyndon B. 42, 48, 61, 121, 233
Johnson, Samuel 45
Jones, Paula 38
judicial vacancies 60
"juggernet" 251–52
Julius Cæsar 147
justsecurity.org 245

Kansas-Nebraska Act 4
Katherine, Duchess of Kent 87
Kavanagh, Riley 94
Kavanaugh, Brett 153, 155–58, 168
Kealey, Terence 56
Kennedy, Anthony 13
Kennedy, David M. 145, 148, 257
Kennedy, Edward "Ted" 108, 128–29, 131, 158
Kennedy, John F. 43, 63, 130, 166, 187
Kennedy, Randall L. 93
Kennedy, Robert F. 128
Kerry, John 63, 73, 93
Khrushchev, Nikita 41, 255
Kimmel, Husband E. 172
King, Colbert 21
King, Martin Luther, Jr. 139, 149–51
King, Steve 177–79
Kipling, Rudyard 208
Kirk, Russell 139
Kislyak, Sergey 79
Kissinger, Henry 48
kleptomania 12–13
Knight, Frank 259
Knights of Columbus 179, 185, 187
Knox, Ronald 85
Knuckey, Sarah 245
Kopechne, Mary Jo 128–31
Kopelman, Will 25–26
Kramer, Amit 120
Kremlin 74, 83, 145
Krugman, Paul 43, 233
Ku Klux Klan (KKK) 97–98, 121
Kurta, Anthony 127
Kushner, Jared 76–78

Lambert, Ray 206–7
LaPierre, Wayne 226–27
Lattimore, Owen 74
Lawrence v. Texas 108
Lazarus, Emma *xvi*, 94–96
Lee, Brianna 131–32
Lee, Robert E. 221
Lenin, Vladimir 41, 163

Le Pen, Marine 44–45
Lerner, Lois 42
Levin, Mark 166–67
Lewinsky, Monica 115, 166
Liberia 119
Libya 38
Lieberman, Joe 152
Lighthizer, Robert 173
Lincoln, Abraham 133, 169, 191, 247
Look, Christopher, Jr. 129
Lord of the Flies xvii, 131, 133
lottery system (for immigration) 117–18
Louis XIV 256
Lovins, Amory 93
Lowell, A. Lawrence 19–21
Luce, Clare Boothe 47, 49, 87

Macías, Francisco (Macías) Nguema 23
Macron, Emmanuel 207
Mad magazine 247
MAGA 43, 50
Magna Carta 208
Malawi 122
Manafort, Paul 217, 219
Manchester, William 93
Mann, Bruce H. 17–18
Manning, Teresa 69
Mao Tse Tung 41, 209
Mar-a-Lago 59, 128, 174
Marcos, Imelda 255
Marie Claire magazine 24, 26
Marine Mammal Protection Act 48
Marino, Katherine M. 245
Markham, Paul 129
Marshall, Burke 130
Marxism 14, 18, 41, 141
Marx, Karl 41
Massachusetts Institute of Technology
    (MIT) 56
Mattis, James 127
Mayer, Colin 255
Mayer, Jean 93
McCain-Feingold Act 4
McCain, John 4, 40
McCarthy, Mary 23
McClay, Wilfred 246–47
McConnell, Mitch 61, 133, 246
McCullough, David 93
McGovern, Jim 121–22
McKinsey & Co. 158–59
McNamara, Robert 130
Media Alert News viii
Medicaid 49
Medicare 49
Menendez, Bob 107
Meng Wanzhou 174

mental health 229
Merck Group 99
Me Too (#metoo) 156
Mexican border wall 4, 39, 66, 117, 137,
    191–92
Mexico 4, 30, 69, 78, 140, 210, 212, 222,
    224, 234
Meyer, Nicole 76, 77, 78
Microsoft 68
The Middle East 7, 38, 80
Milbank, Dana 81–83
millennials 71, 188
Milton Academy xvi, 92–94
Minow, Martha 17–18
Mitchell, John 2
Moffet, Carolyn 23
monopolies (see also "antitrust") 257
Mont Pèlerin Society 259
Moore, Nathan 97, 98
Moore, Roy 104–7
Morgan, J. P. 258
Morrow, Frederic 150
Mosley, Oswald 255
Mother Jones 73
MSNBC 65, 218, 251
Mueller, Robert 87–89, 112, 114–16, 123,
    125, 133, 135, 140, 151–53, 176–77,
    180–81, 203, 215–19
multiculturalism 14, 96, 179
Murphy, Vivek H. 93
Murray, Charles 15, 40, 162, 183
Museveni, Yoweri 122
Musk, Elon 182
Mussolini, Benito 75–76, 255, 257

NAACP 150
Nader, Ralph 34, 93
Nagasaki 207
National Association of Manufacturers
    48
National Industrial Recovery Act 65
National Labor Relations Board 61
*National Labor Relations Board v. Noel
    Canning* 61
National Oceanic and Atmospheric
    Administration 48
National Public Radio (NPR) 214
National Review viii, 24, 36, 40, 48, 74,
    139, 164, 166, 184, 190, 253
National Rifle Association (NRA) 225–27,
    238
National Security Agency (NSA) 124
Nation magazine 65, 69, 73
natural gas 49, 196
naturalization 96
navy xvi, 51, 99, 100–101, 171–72, 190

Nazism 40, 42, 97–98, 211, 217, 221
NBC 251
Neal, Patricia 87
neo-nazis 97–98
Network for Teaching Entrepreneurship (NFTE) 68
Never Trumpers 97, 144, 216, 239
"The New Colossus" 94
The New Criterion 24
New Deal 47–50, 168, 182–83, 190
The New Republic 93
Newsmax viii
New Yorker 65
New York Times 22–23, 29, 31, 43, 58, 60, 65, 69, 74–76, 90, 97–98, 149, 157, 162, 165–66, 175, 177–79, 184, 191, 196, 200, 202, 209, 214–15, 217, 222, 228–29, 232, 235, 251, 266
New York Times Company v. Sullivan 157
Nietzsche, Friedrich 239
Niger 119, 122
Nishimura, Bryan H. 51, 52
Nixon, Richard 2–3, 48, 128, 134, 161, 175, 177, 240
Nobel Prize 82
Noise Control Act 48
Nord Stream 2 196, 197
North American Free Trade Agreement (NAFTA) 49, 176, 265
Northam, Ralph 184–85
North Atlantic Treaty Organization (NATO) 115, 196
North Korea 62, 64, 114–15
North, Oliver 226
Notre Dame University 243–44

Obama, Barack 1–2, 4, 14–15, 22, 29–30, 33, 35, 42, 44–46, 48–49, 52, 54, 58, 61, 65, 67, 73, 84, 102–3, 107, 113, 116–17, 123, 125, 127, 139, 168, 175–76, 192, 233, 240, 246
Obamacare (Affordable Care Act) 5, 11, 49, 66, 69, 79, 84–85, 90, 115, 168, 214, 228
Obergefell v. Hodges 108
Obiang, Teodorin (Obiang) Nguema Mbasogoea 23
obstruction of justice 180
Ocasio-Cortez, Alexandria ("AOC") 163, 165–67, 181–83, 213–15, 225
Occupational Safety and Health Administration (OSHA) 48
Omar, Ilhan 213, 219
One Belt, One Road 196–197
opioids 175, 183
Oppenheimer, J. Robert 93

Organization for Economic Co-operation and Development (OECD) 57
O'Rourke, Beto 222
Orwell, George 191
Oxford University 13, 256
OxyContin 258

Pacific Research Institute 263–65
Page, Lisa 112
Palin, Sarah 45
Paris Climate Accord 176
Patterson, Orlando 246
Saint Paul 186
Paul, Rand 191–92
payroll tax 49
Pearl Harbor 142, 170–72, 205
Pelosi, Nancy 214
Pence, Mike 44, 79, 115
penny plan 49
People 24–26
perestroika 164–65
Perez, Tom 69
Perón, Eva 40
Perot, Ross 260
Persia 145
Petraeus, David 51
Peyronnin, Joe 65
PHH Mortgage 53
The Philadelphia Society 36–37, 253
The Philippines 170
Pichai, Sundar 183
Pike, Bishop James 7
pipelines 49
Planned Parenthood 10, 49, 69, 71–72, 138
Plessy vs. Ferguson 157
Plyler v. Doe 116, 117, 119
Pocan, Mark 79
Poland 145, 146
police *xvii*, 10, 21, 129, 140, 178, 191–92, 237–38, 241
Pompeo, Mike 244–46, 248
Pope Francis 27
Popsugar 26
pornography 161
Portman, Rob 144
Portsmouth Abbey 94
Portugal 212, 265
Post, Emily 134
poverty 15, 45, 48, 70, 82, 119, 202, 248, 252, 255
Powell, Adam Clayton 150
Powers, Kirsten 87
Prager, Dennis 251
Prager University 251
Prelogar, Elizabeth 88

Pressley, Ayanna 213
Pribus, Reince 22
Princeton University 71, 231
progressivism 17, 20–23, 31–33, 38, 42, 45–46, 50, 52, 55, 58, 61, 71, 76, 79–80, 103–4, 121, 146–47, 152, 211–12, 215, 233, 239
Pro Publica 226
Pugh, Catherine 230
Putin, Vladimir 144, 218
Pythagoras 92

Quarles, James L., III 88
Quayle, Dan 187
Quidsi 260

racism xvii, 23, 28, 30, 98, 119–23, 150, 159–60, 184, 189, 191, 209, 213–15, 228, 233, 235–37, 266
Racketeer Influenced and Corrupt Organizations Act (RICO) 22
Raffarin, Jean-Pierre 45
Rampell, Catherine 23
Rao, Neomi 187
rape (see also "sexual violence") 102–4, 242
Reagan, Ronald 1, 10, 23, 48, 49, 55, 59, 61, 82–83, 99, 138, 161, 163–65, 190, 206, 227–28, 252
regulations 4, 10, 38, 46–49, 52–55, 58–59, 61, 66, 69, 82, 123, 135, 176, 192, 265
Reif, L. Rafael 56–57
Reischauer, Edwin O. 93
Renaults, Louis 107
research grants 55–57
Rhee, Jeannie 88
Rhodes, Cecil 209
Rhodes Scholars 209, 221–23
Ricardo, David 265
Richard III 39
Richard, Ivor 93
Richardson, J.O. ("Joe") 171–72
Rich, Marc 38
Ricochet viii
Ridley, Matt 56–57
Roberts, John 168
Rockefeller, John D. 109
Roe v. Wade 108, 185
Roksa, Josipa 198–99
Rollins College 72
Rometty, Ginni 183
Romney, Mitt 5, 105–6
Roosevelt, Franklin D. 42, 47–48, 54, 61, 64–66, 74, 121, 125, 135, 143–46, 163, 168–73, 183, 208–10, 220, 233, 247
Roosevelt, Theodore 60, 62

Rosenstein, Rod 89, 152
Royall, Isaac (Sr. and Jr.) 17–20
Rubio, Marco 23
Russell, Susan 7
Russia 42, 63–64, 74, 76–77, 79, 87, 95, 106–7, 112–14, 123–25, 145–46, 151–53, 173, 176–77, 180–81, 196–97, 204, 215–19, 230, 250

Sackler, Arthur 258
Safe Drinking Water Act 48
Salvian 186
sanctuary cities 137
Sanders, Bernie 33, 40–42, 69, 113, 126, 182
Sarbanes-Oxley Act of 2002 49
Satterthwaite, Meg 245
Saucier, Kristian 51–52
Scalia, Antonin xv, 14–16, 157
Schlafly, Phyllis 127
school choice 49
Schumer, Chuck 78, 123
Schwarzman, Stephen 182
Schweizer, Peter 203
science 11–13, 15, 17, 57, 71
Scrooge, Ebenezer (Dickens character) 24, 27
Second Amendment 38, 133, 225, 238–39, 241
Sessions, Jeff 50, 51, 104, 106–7, 112–13, 117
sexual violence (see also "rape") 242
Shelley, Percy Bysshe 31
Shriver, Sargent 130
Silberman, Laurence H. 152
Silverglate, Harvey 46
Simons, Henry 259
Simpson, O.J. 39
Sitwell, Edith 87
Sixth Amendment 241
Small Business Administration 67
Smith, Adam 14, 57, 164
Smith, Stephen 130
Snyder, Jimmy "the Greek" 134
socialism 23, 38, 40–42, 59, 82–85, 163, 169, 191, 193, 200, 225, 265
social justice 72, 246, 256–57
Social Security 8, 49, 141, 190
Soedjatmoko 93
Somalia 213, 248, 251
Sorensen, Theodore 129
Soros, George 58, 59
Soviet Union (USSR) 33, 64, 74, 126, 145–46, 163–65, 240, 249, 255
Spain 212, 248
Stalin, Joseph 41–42, 144–46, 209

Stanford University 231
Starr, Ken 115
The Statue of Liberty *xvi*, 94–96
Steele, Christopher 124, 180, 216
Stephens, Bret 209, 232
Steyn, Mark 263, 264
Stigler, George 82, 259
Stimson, Henry L. 172
Stoller, Matt 257–61
Stone, Roger 217, 219
Strategic Defense Initiative (SDI, "Star Wars") 165
Strzok, Peter 112
St. Sebastian's School *xvii*, 109–11
student loans *xviii*, 198
Stuyvesant High School 200–202
Sudan 248
Sunstein, Cass 246
Supreme Court 13–16, 28, 32, 38, 43, 54–55, 61, 65–66, 69, 71, 75, 80, 108, 116, 119, 121, 125, 133–35, 150, 153–54, 155–58, 168–70, 176, 188, 192, 228, 250
Suzman, Helen 93
Swarthmore College 72
Sweden 256
Switzerland 5, 223–25, 257
Syria 62

tariffs 75, 174, 204
Taub, Amanda 21
taxation 10, 34, 49, 55, 57, 66, 78, 90, 115, 119, 121, 127, 137, 166, 181–82
Tax Foundation 55
Taylor, Stuart 34
Tencent Holdings Ltd. 203
Tennessee Valley Authority 65
terrorism 96, 154, 238
Tesla 182
textbooks 145–48
Thailand 63
Thatcher, Margaret 42
ThinkProgress 69
Thomas, Clarence 158, 168
Thomas, Jeremy 24
Tillerson, Rex 62–64
Time 237
Tlaib, Rashida 213
Together Cville 98
Toklas, Alice B. 87
Tonchi, Stefano 43
Townhall viii
trade wars 196
Trading with the Enemy Act 220
transgender movement 18–19, 22, 27, 30–31, 38, 72–73, 122, 125–27, 141, 186–87, 244

Travelgate 38
TrueAmericanHistory.us 148
Truman, Harry 37, 74–75, 207
Trump, Donald J. *viii*, *xvi*, 1–5, 8–11, 14, 16, 21–24, 27, 30, 33, 36–40, 43–47, 49–55, 57–62, 64–66, 69, 71–81, 83, 85, 88–90, 95–99, 101, 103–6, 108, 112–27, 133–38, 140–42, 144, 146, 149, 151–53, 158, 160, 162–63, 166, 168–70, 173–77, 179–82, 189, 191–93, 196, 198, 204–7, 213–19, 221–23, 228–35, 239–40, 242, 244, 250–52, 260–61, 265
Trump, Ivanka 59, 90
Truth-in-Securities Act 64
Twentieth Amendment 64
Twitter 123, 251, 260

Uber 67–68
UCLA 245
Uganda 122
Ukraine 62–64, 240
unemployment 37, 45, 58, 70, 121, 123, 127, 149, 160, 162, 175–76, 183, 189, 215, 229, 258, 260
United Kingdom 5, 71, 80, 139, 142–43, 170, 185, 212, 249, 255–57, 265
United Methodist Church 194
United Nations (UN) 244–45, 247–48
University of California, Los Angeles 245
University of Chicago 243, 259
University of Edinburgh 12
University of Minnesota 101–2, 120
University of Tennessee 101
University of Texas at Austin 63
University of Virginia 98
Unz, Ron 34
Uranium One 107, 113
USS *Alexandria* 51
USS *FitzGerald* 99
USS *John S. McCain* 99–100
Us Weekly 24, 26

Van Dyk, Ted 160
Vanity Fair 93
Venezuela 196, 246
Vera Institute of Justice 231
Vietnam 156, 175, 215
Viner, Jacob 259
Vineyard Gazette 130–31
Voegeli, William 190
Vogue 43–44
von Drehle, David 193–95
von Furstenberg, Diane 43
Von Spakovsky, Hans A. 107
voter ID 28–29, 219
voting hours 29

Voting Rights Act 28
Vought, Russell 126
Vox 21

Wagner, Richard 211
Wallace, George 10
Wallace, Henry A. 74–76
Wallace, Henry Scott 74–76
Wall Street Journal 35, 56, 160, 229, 258
Walmart 259
Walter Payton College Prep 132
Walton, Sidney 206–7
Walz, Tim 121–22
Warhol, Andy 176
Warren, Elizabeth 121–22, 198
The Washington Examiner viii
Washington, George 41, 147, 210
The Washington Post 21–23, 35, 38, 62, 74,
  81, 104–7, 130, 132, 155–58, 160, 189,
  193–96, 222, 227, 238, 242, 251–52
The Washington Times viii
Watergate 48, 52, 74, 128, 240
Waters, Maxine 79, 115
Watson, James 92
Watt, James 159
wealth tax 10
Webster, William H. 152
Weinstein, Harvey *xvii*, 101–2, 104–5,
  107, 109, 141, 244
Weissmann, Andrew 88, 217
Welby, Archbishop Justin 6–8
welfare 15, 23, 65, 95–96, 101, 141, 153,
  166, 211–12, 223, 237, 246
Western Civilization 14, 21, 32, 38, 96,
  108–10, 120, 126–27, 139, 156–57, 170,
  180, 184, 187, 202, 208, 215, 217
The Western Journal viii
West, Togo D., Jr. 93
Wheeler, Tom 54
whistleblowers 240
Whitehouse, Sheldon 22
white supremacy 97–98, 121, 178, 230,
  232
Widdecombe, Ann 87
Wilberforce, William 139
Wilde, Oscar 42, 168
Willey, Kathleen 38
Will, George 39–40, 139
Williamson, Marianne 232–33, 235
Wilson, Woodrow 30, 42, 61, 121, 150,
  233
Winfrey, Oprah 45
Wintour, Anna 44
witch hunts 151, 153, 216
W magazine 43
Wollman Skating Rink 83

women's rights 245, 251
Woodward, Bob 265
World Bank 77
World War I 93, 250
World War II 142–44, 153, 182, 205–6
Wyzanski, Charles E., Jr. 93

Xi Jinping 173–75, 196

Yale University 19, 71, 132, 139, 224, 231,
  253, 258
Yarmuth, John 79
Yemen 63
Yoest, Charmaine 69
Young Americans for Freedom 253
YouTube 251

Zinn, Howard 257
Zuckerberg, Mark 251

About the Author

DANIEL OLIVER grew up in New York City. He went to a respectable college and a respectable law school and served in a very respectable army. After graduating from law school, he practiced law with famed novelist Louis S. Auchincloss. In 1970 he served as director of research for James L. Buckley's successful campaign for the U.S. Senate from New York. Then he was invited by William F. Buckley Jr., the progenitor of the Conservative Movement, to join the staff of *National Review* magazine as executive editor. While living in New York City, he ran for the New York State Assembly three times, the first time from West Harlem.

In 1981 he moved to Washington to serve in the Reagan administration, first as general counsel of the Department of Education, then as general counsel of the Department of Agriculture, and then as chairman of the Federal Trade Commission. All three appointments required confirmation by the U.S. Senate.

After serving in the Reagan administration, Mr. Oliver spent a year and a half living in Paris with his wife and two of their five children, writing about European affairs. Subsequently, he returned to Washington.

In 2005, when his wife was confirmed as the U.S. Ambassador to the United Nations Educational, Scientific, and Cultural Organization and moved to Paris, Mr. Oliver started writing columns regularly. His columns have appeared in most conservative publications.

Mr. Oliver has served on the boards of several public policy institutions, including Pacific Research Institute for Public Policy, of which he is a former chairman, and Education and Research Institute, of which he is the current chairman. He also served as president of the Philadelphia Society (1991–92). He has a doctorate in political science (*honoris causa*) from Universidad Francisco Marroquin in Guatemala.

Mr. Oliver and his wife, Louise V. Oliver, live in Washington, DC. They have five children and thirteen grandchildren.

www.ingramcontent.com/pod-product-compliance
Lightning Source LLC
Chambersburg PA
CBHW020243290326
41930CB00038B/200